A Long
Bright
Future

A Long Bright Future

AN ACTION PLAN FOR A LIFETIME OF HAPPINESS, HEALTH, AND FINANCIAL SECURITY

Laura L. Carstensen

BROADWAY BOOKS

NEW YORK

BROADWAY

This book is not intended to take the place of medical advice from a trained medical professional. Readers are advised to consult a physician or other qualified health professional regarding treatment of their medical problems. Neither the publisher nor the author takes any responsibility for any possible consequences from any treatment, action, or application of medicine, herb, or preparation to any person reading or following the information in this book.

Published in the United States by Broadway Books, an imprint of The Crown Publishing Group, a division of Random House, Inc., New York.
www.crownpublishing.com

BROADWAY BOOKS and the Broadway Books colophon are trademarks of Random House, Inc.

Library of Congress Cataloging-in-Publication Data

Carstensen, Laura L.
A long bright future : an action plan for a lifetime of happiness, health, and financial security / by Laura L. Carstensen
p. cm.
Includes bibliographical references.
1. Longevity. 2. Aging. I. Title.
RA776.75.C37 2009
613.2—dc22
2008053383

ISBN 978-0-7679-3012-3

PRINTED IN THE UNITED STATES OF AMERICA

Book design by Chris Welch

1 3 5 7 9 10 8 6 4 2

First Edition

This book is dedicated to my parents, Pam and Edwin Carstensen, for their unfailing love and support and for engendering in all five of their children the freedom to ask, What if?

and

to Richard Rainwater for his vision and support that created the Stanford Center on Longevity

CONTENTS

ACKNOWLEDGMENTS

In many ways, this book is a product of the culture that is Stanford University. The university's long-standing dedication to public good and its close ties to Silicon Valley create a culture rife with the spirit of possibility. I cannot imagine a better home for the Stanford Center on Longevity. The Center is built around the brainpower represented among its affiliated faculty and students and is staffed by extraordinary people who come to the Center with expertise in politics, business, demography, and entrepreneurship, along with a commitment to build a world that supports long life. My perspective on longevity is the product of living and working in this very special place.

While I alone take full responsibility for any mistakes made in this book, much credit for what is right goes to my Stanford colleagues. I am grateful to Professors Tom Rando, Alan Garber, Victor Fuchs, Tom Andriacchi, John Shoven, Mary Goldstein, Dan Kessler, and each and every one of my colleagues in the Psychology Department. Professors Lee Ross and Jeanne Tsai repeatedly challenged my thinking in ways that only one's dearest friends are able to do. So many conversations with colleagues at other universities across the country and around the globe also affected my thinking, corrected my misunderstandings, and offered me new insights. Scores of those conversations occurred in the home of the late Margret and Paul Baltes, both distinguished pioneering gerontologists and life-span psychologists, and some version of those conversations continue today with Professors Ulman Lindenberger, director of the Max Planck Institute for Human Development in Berlin; and Ursula Staudinger, academic dean and vice president at the Jacobs University Bremen; and in many other contexts across Europe. Other turning points came from conversations with Dan Blazer, Duke University; Fredda Blanchard-Fields, Georgia Tech University; and Susan Charles, University of California. Duncan Moore, professor of optical engineering, has been a partner and friend of the Center since its inception. I learn from my colleagues in the MacArthur Foundation Network on Aging Societies, inspired by and guided by Jack Rowe, every time I see them. I thank Richard Suzman, director of the Behavioral and Social Research Program at the National Institute on Aging, for forcing a sustained and productive dialogue across disparate fields of study, which is the only way that we will solve practical challenges of aging societies. I am also thankful for the support and hospitality of the American Academy in Berlin and the Guggenheim Foundation.

Since the Stanford Center on Longevity was founded, the walls that surrounded my academic life began to fall. Who could have imagined that Jane Hickie, after working for decades with former governor of Texas Ann Richards, would have decided to join the Center? I will always be indebted to Jane, not only for seeing the big picture and envisioning alternatives, but for her uncanny understanding of the steps necessary to traverse from one world to another. The Center brought to Stanford Adele Hayutin, whose grasp of global demographics and its implications for us all are unmatched, as is her ability to craft images that convey what even a thousand words cannot.

My students inspire me daily. Especially those graduate students, post-doctoral fellows, and undergraduates who have worked in my laboratory. Candice Lowdermilk and Charlotte Lai kept my lab on track during the writing of this book. Greg Samanez-Larkin, Cara Rice, Helene Fung, and Hal Ersner-Hershfield made numerous contributions. The entering Stanford freshmen I taught with my graduate student Ninna Notthoff in 2008 joined me in thinking outside of the box. And I thank my assistant, Jill Chinen. I honestly think that my productivity would be halved easily were it not for her. She, Lauren Smith, and Tracy Dow anticipate and solve problems—many times before I see them.

I thank my friends who are writers: Randy Bean, Doug Foster, and Susan Krieger; their tutelage over the years has been a great gift. My thanks also go to Joan Hamilton for her assistance drafting a prospectus that initially caught the attention of my agent, Esther Newberg, and my editor, Phyllis Grann, both of whom have been wonderfully responsive and helpful every step of the way. I am especially grateful to Kara Platoni, who was my writing partner throughout this project. Her talents, intelligence, persistent questioning, and gift with words were instrumental in crafting this book.

Just as this book reflects the many resources at Stanford, it reflects the love, support, intelligence, and basic good sense of my family. I know first-hand the value of families that span generations. My grandmother Opal Carstensen showed me at a young age that friendship really can penetrate generations and my great-aunt Mabel extended that same special friendship to me at pivotal times once I was grown. We should all hope to have my great-aunt Nell's wit and good sense at 100—or at any other age.

It would be impossible to overstate my father's intellectual contributions to this book. I often tell my colleagues that I have an unfair advantage, a distinguished scientist for a father who will read anything I send him and return it with comments pretty much always within twenty-four hours. He seemingly knows everything and his critical thinking and clarity have shaped many of my ideas about longevity. He is a person I can only aspire to emulate.

When my siblings and I were children, my mother and father taught us to take our work very seriously and ourselves not so much. My parents raised Richard, Allen, Dee, Tina, and me with a good deal of laughter and one admonition: do the very best we could at whatever profession we chose. A naturalist, a craftsman, a musician, and an educator, my siblings are among the most interesting people I know. My son, David Pagano, and his wife, Jennifer, influenced this book directly and indirectly in countless ways, and with my remarkable grandchildren, Evan and Jane, carry on a tradition of love and dedication to family.

My husband, Ian Gotlib, who is also my colleague, was most personally affected by my writing of this book. Anyone who has ever lived with someone writing a book knows that it can be difficult. Through it all, Ian never once complained. Not only that, he read every word of the manuscript, some parts countless times, and listened to my ideas and each time made them better. Thank you, Ian, for living your life with me.

A Long
Bright
Future

❋

Introduction

You could grow old in a bookstore searching for a good book about aging.

Really, there seem to be only three kinds of them out there, and believe me, I've looked. There are those that prophesy economic doom as the baby boomer generation reaches retirement, there are those that urge you to look forward, through rose-tinted glasses, to a time of wisdom and "saging," and there are those that try to convince you that with proper diet and exercise, you don't have to grow old at all.

This isn't one of those books. Instead, it's an approach to a uniquely twenty-first-century question: what are we going to do with supersized lives? The twentieth century made us a fabulous gift with no strings attached: a third part of life, another thirty years on average. That's what we need to begin talking about now.

Here's the situation: While there's no way to reverse the aging process, it's true that, on the whole, life is getting longer. For most of human history, life expectancy was about twenty years—just barely long enough to ensure the survival of the species. Sure, a few people in every epoch hung in there long enough to be considered "old," but they were the outliers, not the norm. Over time, that norm slowly crept upward, hitting the mid-thirties in the nineteenth century. Then—in the blink of an eye, in evolutionary terms—the average lifetime increased dramatically. By the end of the twentieth century, life expectancy was seventy-seven years. Today it is seventy-eight.

What's wild is that seventy-eight is just an average. There are many among us today who are breezing past eighty and ninety, and into the triple digits. Today there are about 50,000 centenarians in the United States, roughly three times the number there were just ten years ago. According to the U.S. Census Bureau, that number will likely exceed 1 million by 2050 . . . and that's a conservative estimate. Nervous folks who direct pension plans are considering the possibility that a far larger number will reach one hundred. One prominent demographer has suggested that *one-half* of the baby girls born in 2000 will live for a century.

Children who are now in grade school will grow up in a society in which very old age is commonplace. We have reached a point in human history when most babies—not just a lucky few—will grow up in families in which four and five generations will be alive at the same time. The population pyramid, that classic demographer's illustration showing an enormous baseline of births slowly being winnowed to a tiny peak representing those who survive to old age, will become an archaic image of the past. The ramifications of such a radically altered society are just beginning to dawn on us. Everything will change: education, work, financial markets.

Think of old age as new. If you don't yet know how to navigate your way through the new old age, join the club. And while you're at it, stop kicking yourself for not intuitively having it pegged—the fact is, humans are wired to live in the present, not plan for the future. Our evolutionary survival hinged on our adroitness in dealing with the problems of the here and now, not our ability to stockpile resources and make plans for some vague, distant future we might never enjoy. If anything, biology tells us to eat, drink, and be merry, for tomorrow we die. Let's put it this way: nature abhors a 401(k).

When we do try to override our biological bent toward *now* with thoughts of *later,* we often find ourselves at loose ends. When we plan, it's usually for the beginning of life, not the end. Consider all of the planning that goes into molding a child's existence: Parents micromanage everything from what their child experiences in the womb (think prenatal vitamins and Mozart played at belly height) to steering them, eighteen years later, toward the right college. Once we are old enough to be out on our own, we pour endless hours into daydreaming and chatting with our mentors and friends about how to structure our own young futures: choosing a career, finding the right mate, and starting families of our own.

Many of us have hazy fantasies about retirement day, but when was the last time you caught yourself daydreaming about what you're going to be doing twenty years *after* you've been handed your gold watch? Instead, we tend to view the years after sixty-five as "leftovers," as the sum of whatever hand luck and genetics has dealt us. Some people find the prospect of planning for their older years—with its intimations of loss, decay, and death—so profoundly unpleasant that they put off thinking about it at all.

People often talk about aging as if it sneaks up on them by surprise—they catch a glimpse of themselves in a mirror and realize that an old person is staring back.

And it's not just us. Institutions like Social Security and Medicare, launched in the 1930s and 1960s, respectively, were designed for people who collected benefits for only a few years before dying. These institutions are not ready for generations that live—indeed, thrive—into their eighties. As a society, we have little concept of what it would be like to be a happy, healthy one-hundred-year-old. Nobody told us what to do with a retirement that could conceivably last forty years. Humans depend profoundly on culture for their well-being, and because these extra years were added to life so suddenly, our culture has not caught up.

But now the baby boomers, always the cultural envelope pushers, are at it again. Seventy-seven million people in the United States are just beginning to enter this third stage of life. In the next twenty years, instead of one in ten Americans being over age sixty-five, that number will be one in four. So far, to the extent that we've collectively imagined the results of this massive demographic shift, we've anticipated it with fear, particularly when biting our nails over the effects that an enormous wave of retirees will have on the nation's already overburdened social programs. We assume that having to provide support for a growing segment of the population made up of diseased and cognitively impaired old people will threaten all that we know.

Indeed, the media has a long history of reflecting our collective anxiety about growing older: I like to call this the Misery Myth. We hear that age robs us of looks, health, work, friends, money, and love. We see older people portrayed as cranky, frail, or demented. We hear horror stories about zombified elderly people packed into substandard nursing homes. When we do hear about successful aging, it's almost always wrapped up in a glossier story about how to stay young, how to *avoid* old age. Even those who mean to advocate for older people often end up describing their situations in the most dire language possible, as a way of ensuring our continued sympathy and support. There's almost a taboo against saying that older people are doing well—it's as if you don't care about them enough to admit that their lives are really awful.

A case in point: A few years ago, I was a guest on the *Today* show, presenting some findings from my research team suggesting that older people experience fewer negative emotions than younger people do in day-to-day life. When I arrived at the studio, the producer warned me that Matt Lauer, who was to interview me, was skeptical about these findings. Throughout the interview, he made his doubts clear. He was incredulous when I said that the majority of older people are not lonely or depressed. To me, the oddest part was that his interview with me was sandwiched between a report on the death, at age eighty-four, of legendary publisher Katharine Graham and an interview with Jack Welch, former CEO of General Electric and arguably the most successful businessman in United States history. After the cameras turned away—and Lauer persisted in telling me that I couldn't be right—I pointed out to him that Katharine Graham and Jack Welch were technically "old people." He looked at me as if I'd just insulted two of his favorite friends.

But the fact is, research shows over and over that most older people are happier than the twentysomethings who are assumed to be in the prime of life. People over the age of sixty-five are the most mentally stable and optimistic adults. They have the lowest rates of depression. Most older people are relatively happy, they're active, and they live quite successfully on their own, not in nursing homes. Older people focus more on positive images and messages in everyday life than younger people, they resolve interpersonal problems more effectively, and they regulate their emotions better than any other age group. Their social spheres may have contracted and their interest in brand-new adventures lessened, but they put a high priority on emotionally satisfying experiences. On the whole they are not seeking to widen their social circles, yet they treasure the time they spend with people they love. Some researchers dub this the "paradox of aging," that a group that is collectively losing its physical stamina, youthful attractiveness, and opportunities for economic growth is, somehow, happier.

Admittedly, there are problems associated with aging as we know it—an overly romanticized picture of aging in America does as much harm as an overly negative one. Age-related diseases lower the quality of life for hundreds of thousands of older people and their families, and Social Security and Medicare are facing real financial trouble. Yet the ballooning of life expectancy is occurring just as science and technology are on the cusp of solving many of the practical problems of aging. Imagine this: What if we could not only have lots of added years, but spend them being physically fit, mentally sharp, functionally independent, and financially secure? At that point, we no longer have a story about old age. We have a story about long life.

This story is ours to write. Life stages are social constructions, not absolute realities. The economic institutions and cultural scripts that guide us through life—that tell us when to get an education, when to marry and have children, and when to retire—were designed for lives roughly half as long as the ones most people live today. We have the opportunity to rethink life's stages in profoundly novel ways.

What does it mean to live for nearly a century? What is old age for? Where should the extra years go? In a popular joke, an old man sighs, "No one told me all the extra years come at the end." Well, they don't have to. We could insert them anywhere.

It won't be solely up to genetics or good luck. A significant part of how well older people fare is determined by education, intellectual engagement, social networking, and planning—all things we can control as we envision our futures. We become what our environment encourages us to be. That was the first lesson I learned about what it's like to be old, and I learned it at the age of twenty-one.

At that time in my life, I was a single mother—married at seventeen, my husband and I had separated within a few months of the birth of my son. One night, when I was riding home from a concert in a friend's VW van, the driver drunkenly piloted us off the road, rolling the van down an embankment. I sustained about twenty fractures. My femur was severed and my lung was punctured. I had lots of internal bleeding and I was temporarily blinded due to the swelling in my head. For weeks, it wasn't clear whether I would live or die.

After the worst of it, I spent nearly four months in an orthopedic ward lying flat on my back, with one leg strapped in the air. The hospital nurses gave me a job: I was to talk to the three old women who shared the room with me, to make sure they didn't get too delusional and disoriented from living in the perpetual hospital gloom.

In many ways, all four of us were old. I couldn't get around any better than they could. Everything hurt. We were isolated from the rest of the world. My roommates and I got used to having nurses do everything for us, like unwrapping the packets from our food trays before we would eat. Then one day the nurse put my tray down and rushed off to help another patient. I remember getting angry because I was hungry and wanted to eat my lunch but she hadn't unwrapped anything on the tray. Then I realized, *I could do it.* I will never forget that insight about the importance of the social world. If I had become passive and dependent in a matter of months at age twenty-one, what happens to people when the social world tells you for years that you are not expected to contribute, that other people will care for you, that you should sit back and take what is offered?

That was not only the beginning of my interest in aging, but the start of my career in psychology. My professor father, recognizing my intense boredom during those bedridden days, volunteered to attend college psychology classes and tape-record the lectures for me. When I was well enough, I continued at the University of Rochester, first in a wheelchair, and then with a cane—almost as though I was aging backward. At age fifty-five, I am clearly in better physical shape than I was at twenty-one.

My experience in the hospital led me in some very basic way to separate the *problems* of aging from aging itself. When you are young and impaired, the expectation is that you should fix the problem. When you are old and impaired, people say you should accept it. There is a joke about a ninety-four-year-old man who goes to his doctor to complain about a persistent pain in his right leg. His physician says, "What do you expect? That leg is ninety-four years old!" The old man replies, "Yes, doc, but the left leg is ninety-four years old, too, and it is just fine." Stuck in bed, treated like someone four times my age, I started thinking about aging, about how much is biological and how much is the social world telling you what you're supposed to do. Don't misunderstand me: aging is very much a biological process. But the environments in which we age play a critical role in steering the course.

Today, I am a professor of psychology at Stanford University and I am founding director of the Stanford Center on Longevity, where our goal is to harness the benefit of those extra thirty years to improve the quality of life for everyone, from early childhood to old age. At this point in my life, I've been privileged to know many hundreds of older people, some as participants in my research, some as clients in therapy, and others as friends and relatives. These relationships have prevented me from holding on to stereotypes of old people, both the negative images of crotchety cranks and positive views about the kindly, wise living saint. Broad stereotypes of old people, whether idealized or negative, simply don't hold. I have repeatedly witnessed the tragedy of Alzheimer's disease as well as the physical frailty that often accompanies aging. But I have also had many friends who are anything but frail or dull.

Friends like Grace Lowell, a dancer, teacher, and music therapist trained in a Jungian tradition, have consistently challenged me to ask what old age is for. Grace, who died just shy of age ninety-eight, considered herself a pioneer striving to explore a stage in life she never expected to experience. After retiring from the stage, Grace had turned to teaching and was among the first in the nation to offer ballet classes to two-year-olds. Heading her own dance school well into her nineties, Grace maintained that aging had made her a better teacher. With less physical strength, she couldn't chase the little ones around, so she found ways to outwit her pupils by connecting with their minds. For this dancer, as for Jung, the really interesting stages of development occur after the physicality of youth has passed, after we transcend our bodies and can get to the more substantial parts of life.

Of course, I also can't help but include the many older university colleagues I see on a daily basis, brilliant leaders whom no one thinks of as "old." John Gardner—a social reformer and public servant often described as the quintessential American hero—returned to Stanford as a consulting professor at the age of seventy-seven, and remained there until his death in 2002. My good friend Mark Freedman, founder and CEO of Civic Ventures, likes to point out that Gardner's greatest achievements, from crafting Lyndon Johnson's Great Society agenda, including the creation of Medicare, to founding the Corporation for Public Broadcasting, were accomplished after he had reached nominal retirement age. I recall a conversation I had with Gardner one afternoon: He told me that when his mother was one hundred years old, she had told him she found "this business of aging" to be "upsetting." Gardner had reassured her that she was exceptionally healthy and able for a person her age. She'd replied, "Oh, it's not me I'm worried about, it's you and your brother."

But I have also seen another side of aging, which presents the opportunity for things to go wrong. For people without access to health care and education, or who are lacking avenues for career advancement, aging is a starkly different process. I have been associated with the Over 60s Health Center in Berkeley, California, for more than twenty years. Established by the Gray Panthers, Over 60s was the first community-based medical clinic to serve the elderly poor in the nation. It was through my association with Over 60s that I met Lillian Rabinowitz, an activist who fought her entire life for health care reform. Lillian never took her eye off the suffering of older people without means. I will always remember the day we first met and began discussing what social scientists were saying about the later years in life. The conversation drifted to the work of Erik Erikson, who wrote about making peace with life in the later years. Lillian remarked, "Don't you think this is a lot of crap? Life is hard when you're old." We were friends from there on out. Lillian would agree that aging per se isn't the problem, but she never let me forget that there *are* problems.

Aging is a complex subject, and I don't mean to oversimplify it in this book. I am not going to lay down a bunch of rules, or urge you to adopt a certain diet, and you're not going to have to buy an update every year as the shifting winds of pop science advise you to take this vitamin or do that brain exercise to ward off the physical effects of aging. Instead, this book will give you the tools to understand what aging is and what you can realistically expect old age to be like in the twenty-first century, and describe how our culture can adapt as the boomer generation sets off on the biggest demographic adventure in history.

As a boomer myself, I believe that we never did live up to

our generation's advance billing. In the 1960s and '70s, we were chanting in the streets, saying that the world was not living up to our moral standards, that we were going to change the world and make it better. We said we'd never trust anyone over thirty. We proclaimed that our generation would start a social revolution. Then we got distracted. We started to raise families and pursue careers.

Now we're the older people we said we'd never trust, but we still have the chance to pull off a social revolution. We are the first generation in memory that could leave our children's generation worse off than our own, but there's still time for us to radically alter that course. Our next challenge is to make old age not only acceptable but inviting—to make sure that our lives in this unexpected overtime will be a contribution, not a burden, either to ourselves or to those who come after us. We can craft an old age that will be intellectually stimulating, socially rewarding, productive, and fun. The greatest gift we could give future generations is to say, "Here's the way *you'll* want to be old." Even better, we can ensure that today's nursery schoolers are the first generation to live in a society that prepares them to live long and healthy lives, lives that we will orchestrate.

I truly believe that we can do it. We've got the smarts and we've got the numbers. Think of it as the Boomers' Last Revolt.

Let's start planning!

1

Five Myths About Aging You Can't Afford to Believe

If we're going to develop a clear-eyed view of our futures, as a prelude to making old age better and longer-lasting, we're going to have to get rid of as many myths about aging as we can—and there are plenty. In fact, there is a very good chance that much of what you think you know about aging is wrong.

The entire aging process is fraught with unappealing stereotypes and discouraging myths, probably because few of us see aging up close until we're fully immersed in it ourselves. American society is so age segregated that the few older people we do know are usually our grandparents or elder relatives—a small and decidedly unrepresentative sample whose very status as close family often blurs the nuances of their personalities and their lives. We often appreciate just the roles they fill, not the people they are.

After all, how many of us have subtle and complex understandings of the older people in our families until we're older ourselves? I certainly didn't ask a lot of questions of my older relatives when I was young. I loved them, but didn't really try to get to know them as individuals. For their part, older relatives may not spend much time disclosing the details of their personal lives to the younger generation; a family's focus is usually on the young ones. Until my aunt Mabel was in her nineties, I assumed she had been single all of her life. In fact, she had had a short and turbulent marriage when she was young woman. Until I was middle-aged, I didn't know her sister had been found dead in a hotel room, and I still don't know the circumstances that surrounded her death. I didn't know that my grandfather was the person in his small Nebraska town to whom everyone turned whenever they needed any sort of appliance or radio repaired. The man apparently had an instinct for electricity. Maybe it is no coincidence that his son, my father, grew up to study electromagnetic fields. But I didn't make these connections until I was aging myself.

In the absence of personal knowledge, we may expect all older people to be cut from the same cloth as the few we happen to know. I suspect that this is why aging stereotypes tend to run to one-dimensional polar opposites, either based on happy times at holidays with beloved older family members, or on negative interactions with people who seem extremely irritable or sick. Worse, when we imagine what we'll be like ourselves when we're older, we tend to extrapolate from our limited family experiences, and that's not always a pretty picture—it depends on whether your particular aunt Betty baked cookies or had dementia. Time after time, I've given talks about aging and people in the audience tell me either that they believe a particular finding because their grandmothers are *just like that,* or they refuse to believe it, because their grandmothers aren't like that *at all.*

Few of us see the scope, the range, or the complexities of older lives. For purely selfish reasons, this is problematic because it makes it hard to know where we're headed ourselves, and to consider the vast range of possibilities ahead. The truth of it is that older people's life paths are anything but binary; there's a good deal of shading between saintly granny and sour grump. Their lives are also anything but bland. In fact, in terms of personality and life experience, older people are the most diverse part of the population. My dad likes to say that all babies are alike—as infants, they have little opportunity to differentiate. But with every decade of life, every twist in the life path makes people more individual, less likely to have been shaped by the exact same set of experiences as anyone else. Consequently, as a person grows older, chronological age tells us less and less about what they will be like. It makes no sense to embark on discussions about aging societies by reducing older populations to their lowest common denominators.

As a practical matter for people who want to plan happy, healthy long lives for themselves, or for a society that wants to engineer them for everyone, these myths don't just seed doubts, they are impediments to change. They create worries that cloud the imagination and blunt hope, even if they never pan out. They create social stresses and divisions between generations that don't really need to exist. They promote anachronistic expectations about old age that, as a species and a society, we have simply outgrown, and that are out of step with the way real people live today. Much of the time, they paint such a grim picture of the future that we dread thinking about it, never mind planning for it!

Let's start by getting rid of five of the worst myths:

- The "Misery Myth" that older people are sad and lonely
- The "DNA Is Destiny Myth" that your whole fate is foretold in your genes
- The "Work Hard, Retire Harder Myth" that we should rush to exit the workforce
- The "Scarcity Myth" that older people are a drain on the world's resources
- The "We Age Alone Myth" that how we fare in old age is entirely an individual matter, and not a function of society

Myth #1: Older People Are Miserable

The biggest myth on the menu is that older people are inevitably unhappy, lonely, and dejected. If you've been dreading the passage of time because you worry that your happiest days are behind you, take heart. I've spent the last thirty years investigating the psychology of aging, and my research consistently shows that, in terms of emotion, the best years come late in life.

With the exception of dementia-related diseases, which by definition have organic roots, mental health generally improves with age. Older people as a group suffer less from depression, anxiety, and substance abuse than their younger counterparts. In everyday life, they experience fewer negative emotions than people in their twenties and thirties—the people we stereotypically think of as the most happy—yet just as many positive ones. Moreover, older people manage negative emotions better than younger people do. When negative feelings arise, they don't linger the way they do in the young. Many people, even social scientists, are shocked by these findings. They challenge our implicit understanding of happiness, which is that it flows from the esoteric qualities of youth: health, beauty, power. But if these naturally recede with age, why are older people so content?

This has been dubbed the paradox of aging, but I maintain there is more logic than paradox. The answer lies in something we might commonly call life perspective; a more technical term that I and my colleagues have introduced is "socioemotional selectivity." I'll discuss our theory about this concept in greater depth in chapter 4, but the crux of this idea is that human beings are unique in their ability to measure the passage of time against a sort of internal "life span clock," keeping track of where they are in the life cycle. When we are young, time seems expansive, and we focus on acquiring knowledge, seeking novel experiences, and enmeshing ourselves in a large network of friends and colleagues. As we age, we sense the clock winding down and our attention shifts to savoring the time that is left, focusing instead on depth of experience, closeness, a smaller set of goals, and a highly selected group of loved ones.

This change in perspective seems to bring with it a new way of evaluating what is worth one's time, attention, worry, or wrath. For many, this translates into a greater tendency to let go of life's negatives, and to focus on the positives. My mother managed to nail this perspective with a single sentence in an e-mail she sent me last week: "Still having terrible winter weather, but isn't that full moon beautiful?"

For most older people, simple pleasures expand in importance. Sticky interpersonal situations don't seem worth the trouble. Good times are cherished, and there is greater recognition that bad times will pass. People are more likely to forgive when time horizons are limited. Even the very experience of emotion changes with age; feelings grow richer and more complex.

Indeed, social circles shrink over the years, but it's not an indicator of loneliness. Usually this shedding of connections is felt as a beneficial change, as people distill their social roster to their most valued friends, weeding out the coworkers and casual acquaintances who took up so much time and effort before. Older people report being more satisfied with their social relationships than younger people do, particularly prizing their relationships with their children and other younger relatives.

Marriages deepen, too, starting around the time that the last of the couple's children leaves the nest; in fact, many couples reach honeymoon levels of satisfaction when the kids move out. One of my favorite findings about long-term marriages is that even unhappily married couples report that, after many years together, they are happier than they used to be. It's actually the relatively early years of marriage, particularly the points at which the kids are either toddlers or adolescents, that take the biggest toll on marital contentment.

Mind you, it's not that young and middle-aged married couples don't enjoy parenting or love their children—they do. Rather, children tend to produce tensions between mothers and fathers. Young parents suddenly have less time for enjoyable activities with each other and find themselves in frequent conflicts over how to care for the baby. Even in homes where the parents strive to be egalitarian, a more gendered division of labor arises. Fathers may feel left out of the close bond that forms almost instantly between mother and child, and feel pressured to work increasingly hard outside of the home to provide for the new family. Stay-at-home mothers often feel burdened and left out of the world.

Once the children are grown and launched from the home, couples reconnect. I try not to smile when the college students I teach at Stanford express concern about how their parents are doing now that they're gone. I find it endearing that they worry about how their parents will ever manage without them, but I gently reassure them that "empty nest syndrome" is atypical. I can put it less gently here: children make parents very happy . . . when they're living somewhere else.

In addition, the predictability and emotional support of a decades-long relationship offers its own comforts. Older couples report that they argue less, either because they've resolved their most troubling differences or learned to work around them. Grandparenting, which combines many of the joys of being around children without responsibility for their constant care, is an additional source of satisfaction.

If you're wondering which age group is actually the least happy, it's the twentysomethings. Despite being flush with youthful vigor and opportunity, they are the most depressed and stressed out of any age group. Part of this stems from their own perspective on where they are in the human life cycle—as young adults, with oceans of time in front of them, they are constantly faced with decisions to make about their futures, from who they will be to what they will do. Worse, they're acutely sensitive to what everyone else thinks about them and their choices.

You might think that such an open field of choices is a gift, but it is more commonly stressful, frequently overwhelming. People feel worse when the future seems diffuse, and better once they have made a choice or set a goal and started to work toward it. "How can I make this marriage work?" is, in some ways, a more graspable question than "Will I ever find the perfect mate?"

Older people have reassurances that the twentysomethings do not; they've already made their major life choices, and they worry less about what others think of them. It's not that they're hardened, it's that they're more selective about whose opinions matter, handpicking only a few to esteem, rather than fretting about how they are perceived by everyone they encounter.

This is not to say that old age is an epoch of unrelenting warmth and good cheer; it has its share of hardships and disappointments. It's just that by the time people get there, they're more attuned to the sweetness of life than to its bitterness.

Myth #2: DNA Is Destiny

Many people believe that aging is like Russian roulette: something will eventually get you, so you might as well live dangerously—drink, smoke, eat frosting straight from the can. In theory, this wouldn't be a terrible modus operandi if everyone was guaranteed a painless, instantaneous death: One minute you're living the high life, the next you're gone in a blaze of glory. Live fast, die young, right? It would certainly solve the Social Security problem.

But in reality, there are worse fates—with more lingering suffering—than death. One of the paradoxes of American longevity, at least of the way it's experienced now, is that medical science has become powerful enough to rescue people from the brink of death but remains largely impotent when it comes to erasing the effects of the lifetime of bad habits that brought them there. Once you've hovered near death's door, even the "saved" rarely return to a fully healthy state. I often wonder what would

happen if people considered the idea that they might not die because of their risky health habits, but instead suffer for a very long
time. My aunt Mabel, for example, had emphysema. I was surprised because I'd never known her to smoke. "How much?" I
asked when she told me, at age ninety-two, that she'd been a
smoker. "Pack a day, after I quit," she quipped. Yet, even though
she really had stopped smoking more than three decades earlier,
she was still being punished for it with every breath.

People tend to write off death as a consequence of dangerous
behavior, because at least then suffering ends. Yet from a quality-
of-life standpoint, the key factor isn't really *when* you die—the
point at which you finally touch down on the other side of existence. It's how long you spend on final approach, circling the
eternal airport. Considered this way, the most deleterious effect
of extreme obesity caused by a poor diet and a sedentary lifestyle
may not be sudden death from a heart attack, but rather decades
of fatigue, breathing difficulties, and disability from conditions
like diabetes and arthritis. Dangerous behaviors like drunk driving certainly can be lethal, but they can also lead to paralysis or
chronic pain. Even lesser side effects of unhealthy habits add up
when you realize they could be bothering you well into your
eighties or nineties. Imagine half a century of smoker's cough.

Yet trying to acquire habits that promote long life can seem
like a lot of work for a very uncertain reward. After all, people interested in boosting their longevity have been bombarded with
an often contradictory list of directives to follow. We've been told
to avoid fats . . . except for omega-3 fats. We're supposed to drink
red wine . . . but not too much red wine. For a while we were
supposed to take vitamin E capsules . . . but now maybe not. On

top of that there are the seemingly endless exhortations about good habits to adopt: try yoga, meditate, exercise your brain, switch to whole grains, eat foods rich in antioxidants. These are all fine ideas, and you can tell pretty quickly how these measures impact your well-being today. But how do you know if they're adding years to your life?

Well, don't overthink it. Research tells us that a very small number of factors make a big difference in longevity, and they're all pretty commonsense. A Harvard University study that's been running since the 1930s, tracking the lifelong health of both Harvard graduates and people born in inner-city Boston, shows that longevity hinges largely on seven lifestyle choices, which, if made by age fifty, serve as excellent predictors of well-being after age seventy. They are not smoking, not abusing alcohol, getting regular exercise, maintaining one's weight, and having a stable marriage, an education, and good coping mechanisms for dealing with life's troubles. But if you're over fifty and are now trying to play catch-up, it's not too late, says Dr. George Vaillant, the study's director. "There were several men in the study who, unlike Elizabeth Taylor, had perfectly abysmal marital records up to fifty with one divorce after another but got remarried late in life and lived happily ever after," he says with a chuckle. "In terms of obesity, it's never too late to get slim." As for people who give up drinking after fifty, he says that as long as you've avoided irreversible liver disease or brain injury, "After five years your life is pretty much as good as new."

Although the Harvard study found that some factors outside of individual control, like the social class you are born into, have great bearing on how fit you are when you arrive at old age, interestingly, even these effects wear away after age seventy, at which point longevity is more heavily determined by health habits. Indeed, another recent study showed that after age seventy, a mere four factors—exercising, not smoking, consuming alcohol only moderately, and following a Mediterranean diet heavy on fruits, vegetables, and healthy fats like olive oil—reduce by a whopping 60 percent one's chances of dying from any cause over a ten-year period.

This flies in the face of one of the great temptations of the genomic age, which is to believe that the fate of our health, including the hour of our death, is locked into our DNA at conception. It's true that for a small handful of qualities, genes tell pretty much the whole story. Genes determine eye color, for example, and sex. Some diseases, like Huntington's disease, are fully determined by genes. And it's true that family history can indicate your risk for serious medical problems such as heart disease, diabetes, and certain forms of cancer, all of which could shorten your life.

But a predisposition is not the same as a prediction. Twin studies have made it abundantly clear that even two people with the same birthday and parents—and in the case of identical twins, the exact same DNA—can have different health and aging trajectories. A recent study conducted at King's College London showed that when one twin exercised regularly and the other did not, their bodies aged remarkably differently on the cellular level. This difference was measured by comparing the length of the twins' telomeres, the protective caps on the ends of each cell's chromosomes, which are considered reliable biomarkers of aging. Telomeres wear away with time, leaving the cells more vulnerable to genetic damage, which can precipitate diseases like cancer. Yet the twins who exercised had longer telomeres than their sedentary siblings—in some cases, the difference was equivalent to about nine years of aging.

What about risk of disease? Let's take a genetically linked condition, Alzheimer's disease, which is the most common form of dementia. Twin registries in Norway have kept careful records on twins for several decades, and these records allow researchers to closely track health outcomes in pairs of people whose genetic makeup is identical. In 79 percent of cases tracked, if one twin developed Alzheimer's, the other did as well, showing the strong role heredity plays in developing the disease. You might worry that this means that if anyone in your family tree has Alzheimer's, you're automatically doomed. But remember that identical twins, who completely share each other's DNA, have a genetic relationship that's much closer than other family ties. You share only half of your DNA with each parent, and a quarter with each grandparent. Siblings have about half their DNA in common, and cousins about one-eighth. Then, remember that despite having identical genes, in 21 percent of those cases, the second twin did *not* develop Alzheimer's. That's because another factor is at play: environment.

Genes don't express in a vacuum. Their expression takes cues from the body's environment, which can include not only one's physical surroundings, but diet, stress, chemical exposure, and behavior. Even with the same DNA, no two people's bodies experience the same wear and tear over a lifetime. A random gene mutation, an exposure to a virus or toxin, or a traumatic injury that causes inflammation can all trigger in one family member an outcome that remains just a latent possibility in another.

Behaviorally, too, environments modify the expression of genes. A classic textbook example is phenylketonuria. Phenylketonuria—also known as PKU—is a genetic disorder that blocks the body's ability to utilize phenylalanine, an amino acid naturally occurring in protein-rich foods like breast milk, eggs, and many kinds of meat, but also commonly found in artificial sweeteners and diet sodas. Untreated, PKU can lead to seizures and severe mental retardation. However, once it is detected, symptoms can be eliminated by following a special diet. Today screening for PKU occurs before newborns are discharged from hospitals, so full-blown cases can be avoided.

Or, consider the contradiction posed by type 2 diabetes, which has a very strong genetic link. A child has about a fifty-fifty chance of inheriting type 2 diabetes if both of his parents have it, and a one-in-seven to one-in-thirteen chance of getting it if only one parent does. However, according to the American Diabetes Association, although genetic risk for type 2 diabetes is seen in people throughout the world, the disease itself flourishes only in places where people follow a Western lifestyle, getting little exercise and eating too much fat and not enough fiber. It's a strong case for the power of environment over gene expression, made stronger by the fact that even pre-diabetic people, who are on the cusp of developing the full-blown disease, can seemingly turn back time with a few behavioral changes. In one study, pre-diabetic people who exercised for thirty minutes daily and lost 5 to 10 percent of their body weight were 58 percent less likely to actually get diabetes than those who did not.

Genes respond to environment, and this is good news, even for people who have a high risk of a certain malady, because you do have control over many kinds of environmental inputs. Some of this is pretty commonsense: you could be heavily programmed genetically for alcoholism—say, both of your parents were alcoholics, and so were your grandparents—but if you never touch a drop, you will not become one yourself. Yet some of the really exciting science in genetics these days is making the less obvious connections between behavior and health clear, too. Intelligence, physical fitness, resilience—protective qualities that help determine how well one ages—are all influenced by genes, but they may also be strongly influenced by behavior and by one's physical and social environment. Having smart parents is a nice genetic advantage; getting a first-rate education is even better.

One of the most extraordinary developments of the last decade has been the advent of businesses that will provide you with a transcript of your entire genetic makeup to show if you are carrying genes that code for certain diseases. But people who take advantage of these services should be leery of accepting a printout as their fate. At best, genetic screening can only suggest a likelihood of developing certain disorders, not prove that you absolutely will get them. Genetics may deal you certain cards, but you choose how to play them. Some people will find out that they are at risk for heart disease, throw up their hands, and go buy a burger. Others will devote themselves to ab crunches and tofu.

One last thing: Human beings do not have a single gene that controls age itself, or that programs when you'll die. There's no "off" button hidden in your DNA that is going to activate for everyone in your family at the same age. In fact, the Harvard lifelong health study, which tracks the death dates of participants' parents and grandparents, indicates that except in extreme cases—when an inherited illness causes family members to die before age sixty—ancestral longevity isn't a very important predictor of individual longevity.

Nevertheless, there is an extraordinary tendency, almost a superstition, to believe that we'll die at the same age and from the same causes that our parents or grandparents did. If your relatives died young, that prospect can be enormously stressful and provoke a sort of defeatist attitude about your own chances. Or, if your family has a history of living to a ripe old age, it can provoke a similarly problematic sense of immunity, what economists call "moral hazard." Either one can lead to the kind of "live fast, die young" behavior that, if it doesn't kill you outright, is going to make old age a drag once you get there. Fatalism won't do you any favors. It's human to want to believe in a destiny, but it's smarter to believe in the one you make for yourself.

Myth #3: Work Hard, Retire Harder

Here's a true paradox for you: although Americans and Europeans are living longer and in better health than ever before, they are retiring *earlier* than their predecessors retired in the 1960s, '70s, and '80s. You've got it—added years of life have translated directly into more years of leisure. On a kneejerk level, this sounds fantastic. Wasn't the twentieth century the era of the labor-saving device, and of getting more for less? Shouldn't we all knock off as early as we can and hit the beach?

Not really. In fact, not only is the prospect of millions of people attempting forty-year retirements bad for the economy, but there is no reason to believe that it's good for anyone—not the retirees, and certainly not the relatively small number of younger workers left supporting an enormous population of pensioners.

Nearly always, discussions about retirement age immediately turn to the debate about Social Security, entitlements, and the need to keep promises made. Some people argue that after workers have spent decades paying into the system, they should be allowed to retire and collect benefits from it as soon as they can. Others say that if millions of people do this, it will bankrupt the system, annihilating financial support for future generations. (In my mind's eye, I can already see the "Save Social Security" signs on the picket lines.) Here are two truths: (1) Social Security isn't going to go belly up and (2) we need to work longer. We'll return to discussing social insurance programs in chapter 5, but for now let's accept what most economists have concluded about Social Security: the system needs some work, but with a few changes it is certainly sustainable in the near future. With somewhat bigger but not insurmountable changes, it can flourish in the long term, too. The real problem with focusing retirement discussions too closely on Social Security is that the conversation quickly devolves into one about budgets. Instead, I want to focus on life.

Consider the life cycle of the American worker: People get an education early and enter the workforce around the time they find a mate. They start families, then reach the peak of their careers while raising young children and often simultaneously supporting older relatives. During this middle part of life, people work very long hours, often holding two, sometimes three jobs at once. Then sixty-five comes and—bingo—retirement. We're expected to transition overnight from a life of near-constant work to one of near-total leisure. In the American model of retirement, we play golf every single day, or embark on epic retirement adventures, like building a dream house or sailing the world.

It made sense to stop work completely at sixty-five in an era when people were expected to live—and draw benefits from the retirement system—only for another decade or so. But now that people are more commonly living into their eighties, nineties, or beyond, that could mean spending two or three decades on the golf course. That's a lot of greens fees, especially considering that tomorrow's retirees may have fewer financial resources on which to draw for their support. The company pension has given way to the 401(k) and the Individual Retirement Account (IRA), both plans in which workers have to voluntarily enroll, and in which they invest their own money. Yet only six in ten American workers are saving for retirement, and nearly half of them have squirreled away less than $25,000. To make up the shortfall, some current retirees are returning to work. Others are trying to get by on less.

So how's this life cycle model working? Badly. Not only do we have older people who can't afford to retire, but we have younger workers practically killing themselves to save enough for a multidecade retirement. That's on top of the other stresses that occur in middle age as one raises a family, cares for aging relatives, and tries to succeed at a career. How does one set aside enough for several decades without work while also saving for the kids' college tuitions and paying down a mortgage and credit card debt? As we see ourselves failing, the stress mounts. Younger parents are the most stressed age group in the workforce; they often feel that they must relegate family needs to second place in order to keep up with the demands of their jobs. The greatest irony is that although most Americans will live longer than ever before, in their day-to-day lives they feel that they do not have enough time.

The worst of it is that we're all racing to the finish line because that's when we think we'll finally get a chance to put our feet up and enjoy ourselves. But we end up missing out on some of the most important parts of life that occur along the way. Because families and careers are pursued simultaneously, the middle of life is packed so full that parents sometimes miss their children's first steps, first words, school performances, and other milestones. Contrary to popular opinion, adult children genuinely want to assist their parents when they need help—they care enormously. They spend money and try to visit. But there is only so much they can do given all of the demands on their time.

There is something very wrong with this picture: Time after retirement is the only stage in life that has been elongated. The problem isn't you, it's the model, which was built for short lives, not long ones. It makes no sense to cram all of the work into the beginning, and all of the relaxation into the end. Making enough money in forty years to support ourselves for another forty is a tall order, no matter what state Social Security may be in by the time you reach retirement age. Keep in mind that Social Security is not a savings program—it's a social insurance program to make sure you won't be left completely broke. If you expect to live as well after retirement as before, you're going to have to save a lot of money without relying on the government or your employer to do it for you . . . and the typical American retirement savings of $25,000 isn't going to even come close.

Psychologically speaking, it's fascinating that people are so astonishingly bad at financial planning. We're not entirely stupid. We haven't completely lost our ability to add numbers. I think the problem is that for most Americans, the task is so overwhelming, and seems so utterly unachievable, that we give up altogether. Hearing that we're not alone—that the entire country is in debt—perpetuates our magical thinking. If no one else is saving, that makes it more acceptable to dream instead of putting money aside. Some people think that maybe they will inherit a nest egg from their parents, often having no idea what sort of fortunes their parents have accrued. On average, that's a very bad idea, since the typical inheritance in the United States is only a few thousand dollars. Others—and you know who you are—just hope to win the lottery. I expect that people would save more if they had more time to build up their accounts and a shorter period of retirement to save for, because this would be a race they might be able to win. It's one reason why we need to work longer.

We have an opportunity to redesign our work lives so that work is less demanding and more satisfying throughout life. If we plan to work more years later in life, we can reduce the strain in the middle years. Raising retirement age alone isn't enough. If that were the only change, it would be devastating for people who work grueling jobs, or those who have waited years to explore interests outside of work. But we also have to recognize that the majority of Americans enjoy their professions and say they would not mind continuing to work until age seventy, seventy-five, or beyond, assuming that they are in good health. For the most part, they are: 88 percent of those in the sixty-five to seventy-four age range are healthy enough for work. Sixty percent of people over age eighty-five—that is, the majority—do not have health problems that would preclude work either. Indeed, older workers report being the most satisfied with their jobs.

We need a menu of options, and that could include part-time work, volunteer work, or adopting an entirely new second career. We need incentives like phased retirements, flexible work schedules, job retraining, and the ability to work from home. The beauty of a longer but more moderately paced career cycle would be that we could have more leisure throughout life, more time with our children while they are young, and remain engaged in our communities as we age, giving back some of the expertise we've accumulated throughout our time in the workforce.

Sure, this may not sound like your grandparents' retirement. But we should recognize our old age will be different from our parents' and grandparents'—in fact, it's not going to be like anything American society has ever seen before. I suggest that we embrace that difference. Retirement is a human invention. If some of the original concepts have gone stale, there's no reason we can't reinvent them. With a little creativity, we could craft work lives that are more satisfying and far less conflicted than the ones we have today. Rather than hold on tightly to the way things are, or just nibble around the edges of change, let's redesign work. For once, time is on our side.

Myth #4: Older People Drain Our Resources

The specter of scarcity looms over all sorts of debates about how aging will affect our allocation of resources—everything from money to health care to jobs, even to physical space on the earth. The scarcity myth goes like this: If people hang around for an extra two or three decades, there simply won't be enough of anything to go around. Instead of contributing to society, older people will hog resources needed by everyone else. Their continued presence will cause global overpopulation and the accelerated depletion of the natural environment. There will be less open space, less clean air and water, less food. This is arguably the most dangerous of the myths because it sets the stage for intergenerational competition, when there is truly no reason for it to exist.

Let's start with overpopulation. It's true that the earth cannot sustain unchecked population growth. Back in 1798, the English political economist Thomas Malthus was already warning that "the power of population is indefinitely greater than the power in the Earth to produce subsistence for man." He was, of course, right. During the twentieth century, the population of the world increased from about 1.6 billion to over 6 billion people. The only way we stayed ahead of the game is that technological advances allowed us to increase production. Technology, however, inevitably extracts its own toll on the earth, so we cannot count on technology to save us forever.

However, longevity isn't what's feeding population growth. On the contrary, the regions of the world with the longest-lived people are the very same regions where population has already stabilized and, in the next ten years, is expected to decline. In the half century between 1955 and 2005, the fertility rate in the industrialized world dropped from 2.8 to 1.6 births per woman, well below the 2.1 births per woman needed to replace the current population. (The worldwide average dropped from 5 births to 2.7 per woman in the same time period.) By 2030, more than half of all countries are projected to have fertility fall below the replacement rate.

Why is this happening? It's because the same factors that lead to increased life expectancy—education, income, good health care, sanitation, and nutrition—lead to decreased fertility. When infant mortality is low due to a high quality of life, parents do not fear that their children will die, and they naturally limit the size of their families. The larger global transition from rural agrarian societies to urban industrialized ones has prompted other family planning changes, such as the decreased need for child labor. So while it's true that greater longevity is prompting a boom in the older segment of the population—indeed, the global population of older people is expected to triple by 2050, when 1.5 billion people will be over age sixty-five—in the industrialized world it's being accompanied by a simultaneous decline in births. The result, in these countries, isn't a population that's larger, it's one that's grayer.

Far less attention is being paid to regions of the world where life expectancy is low. In these same places, fertility is high. The population on the African continent is expected to double in the next forty-five years. In fact, virtually all of the global population growth in the twenty-first century will occur in Africa, parts of Asia, and the Middle East. In these regions of the world, the Malthusian prophecy has a chance to be realized. In areas that lack the infrastructure to ensure safe drinking water and the sophisticated agricultural technologies to increase food production, larger populations pose a serious threat, most directly to the people living in these regions but also to world stability. When basic needs go lacking, people die prematurely. Political fires are fueled. Moreover, when population aging occurs very rapidly in a region, as it is expected to do in Africa, and countries are unprepared economically, young people cannot find work, and civil unrest ensues.

The ramifications of differential aging around the globe are only beginning to dawn on a few informed demographers and political scientists, but the futures of regional populations are linked. The bottom line: population growth is an issue, but Grandpa living longer is not the problem. The true issue is that the gift of increased longevity is unevenly distributed around the globe. In some parts of the world where the youth population is booming, those children may never have the chance to grow old.

The overall graying of the globe would in fact be a good thing. The ideal world population is a relatively small one in which everyone born lives a long, healthy existence. Yet proponents of the scarcity myth believe that the aging of populations will inevitably give rise to intergenerational strife, as the number of retirees in industrialized nations gradually outstrips the number of young workers. It's true that in many developed countries, including Italy, Germany, Japan, and Russia, the labor force is currently shrinking as the population ages. (In the United States, on the other hand, the workforce is actually growing due to immigration.) In many parts of the world, older people will be withdrawing funds from public pension plans faster than the younger workers can pay into them.

This shift is often portrayed as a competition, as though resources we perceive as scarce—Social Security benefits, access to

health care—are the prizes in a zero-sum game being played between generations; in order for one group to get what it needs,
the other group must get nothing. I recall driving to work one
day while listening on the radio to a debate about health care ra-
tioning. One side said that we should treat older people's problems as aggressively as younger people's problems because it
would be unfair not to do so. The other side said that we can't afford to provide expensive care to people who will die soon any-
way. Can you imagine a similar public debate based on race or
sex? Yet we have these discussions freely about age. The issues
have been framed as though there are essentially two options under debate: either treat older people as a special category, unde-
serving of full access to life, or let entire societies go broke.

Some believe that the financial resources and voting clout of
the baby boomers will threaten education and other services designed for younger people. In his 2007 novel *Boomsday*, satirist
Christopher Buckley envisions widespread attacks on gated retirement communities and golf courses by angry young people
because the senior citizens' lobby keeps convincing Congress to
grant older people more benefits that will bankrupt the next
generation. Buckley dubs the baby boomers "the most self-
indulgent, self-centered population cohort in human history,
with the possible exception of the twelve Caesars."

I laughed all the way through *Boomsday* and bought copies for
my friends. It's hysterical. But it's satire. There is no evidence for
intergenerational warfare here in the United States. We could
probably start it if we set our minds to it, but surveys of college
students indicate that they think the government should do more,
not less, for older citizens, who, after all, are their grandparents.

And people don't suddenly become self-obsessed when they grow old. On the contrary, aging is associated with deepening concerns about one's younger family members and the earth. Yet we do have a brief window in which we should change the culture from one that draws dividing lines between generations (as if people are born either young or old) to one that thoughtfully addresses long life, a shift that will improve quality of life for all, reinforce a sense of continuity among individuals, and illuminate the connections between generations.

Weirdly, the scarcity myth actually hinges on two totally opposite nightmare scenarios. The first, of course, is that unproductive older citizens will take up space while consuming resources better used by everyone else. The flip side is that the senior class might instead turn out to be *too* productive. In this scenario, people living extra-long lives would refuse to retire and soak up so much room in the job pool that younger workers couldn't get ahead. I don't believe this worry is going to pan out. If boomers retire later, it will ease the stress on the Social Security system, as well as give individuals more time to shore up their personal retirement savings. It will also boost the welfare of the entire society. Harvard economist David Wise estimates that American gross domestic product could actually get a 7 or 8 percent boost by the year 2030 if members of the boomer generation work five extra years. When you look across countries, those in which older people work have the lowest unemployment rates among the young.

We need older people in the workforce. In a number of fields, the United States will actually face a skilled labor deficit as the boomer generation retires. The U.S. Bureau of Labor Statistics is currently projecting that the boomers will leave behind 33.4

million job openings as they retire over the next decade. (Overall economic growth, by contrast, is expected to produce only 17.4 million jobs.) Some of the most affected fields will include teaching, management, library science and administrative positions. The nonprofit world is expecting a crisis-level shortage of leaders. In addition, the needs of an aging boomer generation are expected to generate 4 million new jobs in health care and social assistance.

The aging of the workforce will be a truly massive demographic shift, and it's difficult to predict exactly how it's going to affect the economy, which is undoubtedly feeding these fears of shortages and scarcities. In the absence of definitive answers, there is one thing we can do for sure. We can stop sending older people the ultimate mixed message: we can't afford to take care of you, but we can't afford to let you have a job so you can take care of yourself. We should be worried about an old, sick population that doesn't work. We should celebrate an old, healthy population that does.

Myth #5: We Age Alone

We are not in this aging thing alone, although it can certainly feel like that some days. Time catches up with the best of us, as well as the prettiest, the strongest, and the most successful. The next time you glance enviously at a beautiful young model, know that she's aging just like you are.

Some of us think we can outsmart the process. We develop little tricks. Lights with dimmers. Clothing that forgives. Neuropeptide parties. A hairstylist I once frequented told me that when he desperately wanted to look the way he did as a young man, he would lie flat on his back, hang his head over the side of the bed, and look in the mirror, thereby making gravity his friend.

So let me be as clear as I can possibly be: There is nothing known to humankind—no crème, no diet, no exercise regimen—that can pause or rewind aging. In a noble effort to thwart the swindling of snake-oil salesmen, in 2002 a group of fifty-one distinguished scientists published an essay in *Scientific American* clearly stating that there are no legitimate anti-aging potions or products on the market anywhere in the world. My friend Jay Olshansky, a biodemographer at the University of Illinois, likes to put it this way: "Longevity salesmen have been around for thousands of years—in fact, I consider them as being the second oldest profession. They are trying to sell a commodity that they do not own and which they cannot either measure or control. When there is a practitioner of 'anti-aging medicine' in the vicinity, guard your wallet."

When I chat about this with my friends, I am pleased to be able to cite such a distinguished source. My friends are nonplussed. "What about seaweed?" they ask. Hope springs eternal.

And so we spend more money on wrinkle cream, because even though we realize intellectually that aging is a normal part of life, even though we know, rationally, that this life path has been trod by millions before us and no one has escaped it, at some crazy, subconscious level we think that if we are dedicated enough, imaginative enough, we might be the first to cheat time.

Let's stop.

Aging is inevitable. *How* you age is not. You will very likely spend about three decades of your life as an old person. Deal with it. Death is the only alternative. If you can put behind you the fantasy of eternal youth, you can begin to plan seriously for what comes next. You can begin to think hard about the type of old person you want to be. Cool and hip? Relaxed, aloof, and serious? Will you be the gentle mediator or the sharp-tongued old person who tells it like it is? Will you help younger people develop their careers or show them by example how to be renowned at age ninety? Will you be the best grandparent any child ever had? Will you be the designer who develops a very fashionable clothing line for women over seventy? Will you become a steward of the environment, or protect your neighborhood? There are so many ways we can reconceptualize long lives, and we'll talk about them more in chapter 3.

Those who turn sixty-five in the next twenty to thirty years will have an advantage no previous generation in human history has ever had: strength in numbers. This is both a great opportunity and a great responsibility. We have a duty to age as well as we can, and—precisely because we're *not* in this aging thing alone— we need to make sure that as many of us as is humanly possible age as well as they can too.

Let me put this bluntly: At the dawn of the twenty-first century, we are beginning to see two old ages emerging. One is for the healthy and affluent, and one is for the poor and disabled. Those who are educated and financially secure have been aging in remarkably good health, and have the kind of assets that will allow them to thoroughly enjoy their retirement years, traveling, reading, attending performances of internationally acclaimed dance troupes and the ballet recitals of their grandchildren. Those who have not had many social advantages and who have little education are far more likely to be sick, disabled, and having a harder time getting through the days. They are more likely to need to rely on their family for assistance with basic needs, families that will likely have fewer resources themselves.

Being poor not only reduces quality of life, it extracts the ultimate toll: it takes years from people's lives. It's always been that way, and one can make the case that advances that reach the affluent eventually benefit the less affluent as well. But trickle-down models shouldn't assuage too much collective guilt. The difference in life expectancy between the most and least affluent Americans nearly doubled in the last twenty years, from 2.8 years in the early 1980s to 4.5 years at the turn of the century. To pit extreme demographic variances against each other, affluent white women now live, on average, fourteen years longer than poor black men in America. There is a real danger that some of the benefits of the collective progress that has led to long life may once again slip back into being the sole province of the wealthy.

The vitality of truly advanced societies is rooted in motivated, healthy, and well-educated populations. Societies thrive when everyone in the group does. In order to stand a chance of making continued improvements to the global standard of living, we have to build a world that gives everyone a fair shot at aging well.

2

What Is Aging?

The story of how we, as a society, somehow launched ourselves into an era of very long life doesn't begin with a discussion about older people. It begins with a story about babies.

The first big step you took toward living to age one hundred was surviving your first year of life—and that's not as self-evident as it may seem at first. Life expectancy, or the average length of life in a population, had been short for most of human history because of childhood deaths. The historical average in premodern times—roughly twenty years—reflected both the high incidence of infant mortality and women's risk of dying in childbirth.

Though life expectancy inched upward over the millennia, childhood death was common even at the dawn of the twentieth century. In 1900, one in eight babies born in the United States died before the age of one. Roughly 25 percent died before they were five years old. Parents viewed babies as little angels, sent by God to visit, but not necessarily to stay.

Then, in one century, infant mortality decreased by 90 percent in the United States. Maternal mortality dropped by 99 percent. What a dramatic difference saving the lives of society's very youngest members had on overall longevity: between 1900 and 2000, twenty-eight years were added to the average life expectancy. About ten of those years came from saving the lives of children under the age of five, and seven of those ten years had already been gained by midcentury. To be clear, that didn't mean every member of society magically gained an extra twenty-eight years, regardless of age or health. It meant that as more children survived to maturity, society as a whole became longer-lived. By 1960, 70 percent of infants born could be expected to live to age sixty-five. At our current point in history, infant mortality is so low in developed nations that it can't be reduced much further. What happened?

Don't succumb to the temptation to assign all the credit to medical advances that reduced infant mortality, or give evolution a nod for enhancing the hardiness of the species. Crediting medicine alone doesn't do justice to a much more complicated story, and biological evolution had nothing to do with the addition of nearly thirty extra years of life expectancy in one century. Evolution doesn't work that way. Culture does.

Life expectancy changed because people changed the way they lived. Culture moves faster than evolution; it is the crucible in which medicine, technology, and social practices are forged, and all of these shape not only how we live, but for how long. Before we could become a long-lived species, human culture had to go through a massive collective social shift that prioritized all of the elements that we know foster long life. And that started not with how long we lived, but where.

Throughout most of human evolutionary history, people lived in small groups or villages. In small groups, communicable diseases can run their course and die out as the immunity of the collective increases. Once hunting and gathering was abandoned in favor of agriculture about five thousand years ago, people began to live in larger groups, eventually cities and towns. Population density increased dramatically, as urban life brought people together and yoked their destinies. City living had its advantages. It protected residents from starvation and exposure to the elements. It fostered intellectual life. Discoveries could be shared, and written records could be passed from one generation to another, resulting in an accumulation of knowledge that spanned multiple generations. Innovation took off, and science was born.

But there was a downside, too. Proximity allowed diseases, like smallpox, to infect entire communities. Domestic animals served as a reservoir for the storage and mutation of infectious organisms. Shared waterways frequently became contaminated with typhoid and cholera, infecting the masses. Absent organized sewage disposal, human waste made its way into soil and drinking water. Agriculture helped stabilize the food supply, but diets became less diverse, more dependent on a few high-carbohydrate crops, like rice and potatoes, and less on the more nutritionally balanced diet of nuts, berries, and proteins that fed our hunter-gatherer ancestors.

Malnourished populations are especially susceptible to contagious diseases, and early societies faced them with little means of defense. The bubonic plague (or Black Death) of 1348 wiped out nearly one-third of the European population within five years. For the next two hundred years, smaller epidemics of plague appeared in more circumscribed regions of the world, taking a severe toll on human life. Without understanding the reasons for these scourges, people struggled to make sense of the punishments they took. Although initially many viewed the plague as evidence of God's scorn, people sometimes turned the blame on each other, attributing the plague to poisoned wells or trouble brought by ethnic minorities, compounding already unimaginable loss with even more horror.

Even in relatively modern times, diseases spread easily among densely packed populations. In the late 1800s, pneumonia and the flu were the leading causes of death. The 1918 influenza pandemic combined the deadly power of germs with the turmoil of World War I, as armies of infected people were shipped around the globe. The virus is believed to have spread worldwide from a military base in the United States as contagious soldiers departed to fight in Europe; it ultimately killed more than 50 million people worldwide, more than the war itself. For a time, it depressed the average American life expectancy by twelve years.

But if plagues and epidemics can be said to have a bright side, it's that they provide an impetus for the kinds of collective changes that safeguard community health. The earliest and largest increases in life expectancy were due to basic improvements that prevented germs from spreading in the first place: better waste disposal and the purification of food and water supplies. By the middle of the twentieth century, look how far American households had come in defending themselves against contamination: Electricity had become a part of nearly every household, allowing food to be refrigerated and homes to be heated. Garbage collection and clean tap water had become a given. Pasteurization had eliminated a major channel of foodborne disease, and food and medicine now came with the Food and Drug Administration's stamp of approval.

As public health improved, not only did more babies survive infancy, but their entire childhood was healthier. Besides the quarter of all infants who died before the age of five a century ago, hundreds of thousands more were infected with contagious diseases like polio and scarlet fever, leaving them with lifelong disabilities and increased susceptibility to subsequent illnesses. The special nutritional needs of infants were unknown; in many cases, nutritional deficiencies were thought to be contagious diseases. Chronic malnutrition was commonplace. In the early 1920s, three-quarters of the infants living in East Coast cities suffered from rickets, a softening of the bones caused by a lack of vitamin D and calcium. Then, in the United States and Europe, food-fortification programs nearly eliminated the major diseases caused by nutritional deficiency, including rickets, goiter, and pellagra. Between 1940 and 1960, vaccines were developed that immunized the public against measles, rubella, tetanus, and diphtheria. Perhaps most remarkable of all was the near-worldwide elimination of smallpox through a persistent program of isolation and inoculation.

In fact, you could argue that the way we now conceptualize childhood, as a carefree time of growth, play, and education in which the most vulnerable members of society are cradled in its toughest protections, is itself a very recent cultural creation. Before child labor laws, many children under the age of ten were working in factories and mines. Formal education was for the lucky. Parenting ideals we now consider a given—establishing close emotional bonds with children, giving them a sense of security—were not widely recognized. Yet as the last century witnessed a doubling of life expectancy, it went hand in hand with a sustained and concerted interest in bettering the lives of children. Childhood was transformed from a time of tentative personhood into a celebration of human potential. In fact, our culture now embraces the preciousness of early childhood so completely that vulnerabilities inherent in the first few years of life have faded into the background of our collective consciousness.

We now view thriving infants as testament to the "natural" course of early life, but this seems natural only because cultural supports for healthy childhood are so deeply entrenched in our lives that they are largely invisible. The foods we buy in grocery stores have been fortified with vitamins and minerals, and milk has been pasteurized, largely for the benefit of growing kids. Healthy baby visits to pediatricians and scheduled programs of inoculation have all become standard practice, reducing the threat of diseases that once felled young children. Sensory functions, such as vision and hearing, are sufficiently well understood to allow very early interventions when problems arise. In recent years, genetic screening and diagnostic ultrasound have made surgical treatment of some disorders possible in utero—before a child is even born! Teachers know more about how to reach young students, thanks to psychological studies of the ways children learn, and parents know more about how to raise them, thanks to child development resources from Dr. Spock to parenting classes informed by developmental science.

If one needs convincing that such life expectancy gains are the result of the power of culture, the proof is in the sad fact that similar increases have not been uniform throughout the world today.

The divergence in life expectancy between the developed and developing world is astounding. Life expectancy in Japan is currently seventy-nine years for men and eighty-six for women; fewer than 1 percent of Japanese children die before age five. In Sierra Leone, life expectancy is thirty-nine years for men and forty-two for women; nearly 27 percent of children die before age five. In some countries, particularly in sub-Saharan Africa, life expectancies are falling. Lack of health care, underdeveloped infrastructures to purify water and food, a high rate of complications during pregnancy and birth, and the spread of HIV/AIDS and other deadly infectious diseases keep infant and maternal mortality high and life expectancies low. The real tragedy is that unlike during earlier historical periods, when ways to improve life expectancy were unknown, today that information exists. What's missing is not knowledge, it's money and political will.

Think of this shift that has allowed more people to survive into adulthood as a massive social revolution, albeit an imperfect one still slowly making its way to all parts of the globe. Here in the Westernized world, I believe we are now in the middle of a second revolution, one that will make adulthood itself longer and healthier. But this time, instead of having to figure out what germs are and how to make drinking water safe, science must confront a mystery it has scarcely seen before: very old age.

I know it sounds odd to describe old age as new. After all, every historical era produced its elder statesmen; you probably have a ninety-year-old or two somewhere in your family tree. But for the first time, old age is no longer going to be the exception, but the rule. The percentage of people on the planet who are over age sixty-five is expected to more than double by the year 2050.

The "oldest old," or people over age eighty-five, are the fastest-growing segment of the population. Yet because information about how people's bodies change as they approach the century mark has been relatively scarce up to this point, we don't have as much insight as we'd like into how the body behaves in very old age. Which aspects of aging are purely biological, and which are due to the impacts of disease or trauma? Which changes are the inevitable stamps of time's passage, and which are the products of a sedentary lifestyle or other culturally learned practices?

From Pyramid to Cube as the U.S. Population Ages

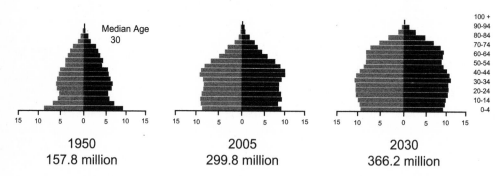

1950
157.8 million

2005
299.8 million

2030
366.2 million

After all, what *is* aging? Milestone markers like birthdays and retirements obscure its slow and gradual progression; they make aging feel like a series of steps. It is as if we are young for a very long time, then wake up one day middle-aged and remain middle-aged for decades. Later still, we look in the mirror and realize that we are old. Nothing could be farther from the truth, of course. Aging begins the day we are born and continues until the day we die. It is as steady as the day is long.

Fundamentally, aging is a biological process that occurs in cells throughout the body. Many scientists believe that aging is the product of an accumulation of damage caused by normal wear and tear on cells as they go about the business of life. Some damage occurs during cell division—every time a cell divides, there is an opportunity for something to go wrong. A piece of DNA can break, a cell membrane can be damaged. Some of this damage is wrought by free radicals, unstable molecules with a single missing electron, which are produced during normal metabolic functions like processing the very air we breathe. To replace their missing electrons, free radicals steal them from nearby cells. This can damage the cells' DNA, causing cellular dysfunction and possibly triggering mutations, which in turn can snowball into cancer. Worse, one stolen electron can set off a chain reaction by producing a new free radical, bent on raiding another electron from its neighbors. Our bodies naturally produce free radical fighters called antioxidants, which can neutralize these runaway molecules by donating an extra electron to them or quashing the chain reaction. But your body can make only so many antioxidants on its own, which is why diets and supplements high in antioxidants, namely vitamins A, C, and E, have recently become popular. However, the effectiveness of taking antioxidants in pill form is still being debated by researchers.

The longer you live, the more cellular damage piles up. And here's the tricky part: since mass survival into old age is such a new phenomenon, evolution has never had much of a reason to select for adaptations that would help us resist this long-term damage, which can ultimately manifest itself as age-related diseases. (On the other hand, it's had plenty of time and reasons to select for adaptations that help us survive until reproduction, the big Darwinian payout.) If our bodies were cars, you could say that we're now driving them long after the factory warranties have expired. No other generation has kept their parts in service this long before, and little is known about how they'll perform once they've had eighty or ninety years to accrue engine buildup. In a way, we've overshot evolution.

In fact, some of the cellular protective mechanisms that developed when humans had a much shorter life span turn out to have negative repercussions during a long life span. For example, cells that sense they are damaged beyond repair may become senescent—they don't die, but they stop dividing. It's a mechanism that hinders DNA mutations from progressing to cancer. When you're young, this is a great trade-off—it diminishes your risk of childhood cancer, helping ensure that you survive long enough to have kids of your own. But it comes at a cost. Those senescent cells spend the rest of your life secreting proteins into the area around them, weakening it and actually making it *more* susceptible to cancer as time goes on. A few of these protein-secreting cells are no big deal when you're young, but as you age and develop more of them, your cancer risk rises.

But even absent a diagnosable disease, an accumulation of cellular damage is a part of normal aging. So is a gradual slowing of bodily processes, which on the whole become less responsive to change. Changes to any given vital organ are modest, but because they occur both within and across organ systems, the body has more difficulty maintaining internal balance or *homeostasis,* the process by which it can readily adjust to changes or stressors in its environment. These changes begin in one's twenties or thirties and continue throughout adulthood.

As time goes on, you can see some of these changes in a mirror; the rest you might feel in your bones. Lung capacity, resting heart rate, and the speed at which nerve cells conduct information all decline fairly steadily. Skin, blood vessels, and muscles lose their elasticity, which accounts for wrinkling and sagging. Bones become more brittle, and your vertebrae settle on your spine over the years; most people have lost two or three inches of height by their eighties. Kidneys are less efficient so it takes longer to rid the body of toxins. It becomes increasingly hard for the body to regulate pulse rate, blood pressure, oxygen consumption, and blood glucose. Lung capacity drops by 2 to 3 percent every year from the mid-thirties onward.

As your body ages, it reacts more slowly to environmental changes, whether that be the time it takes for your eyes to adjust when a room dims, or for your heart to return to a resting rate after being startled, or for you to notice a spike in the ambient temperature. Older people are less likely to detect overheating and adjust accordingly; most of the more than fourteen thousand people who died in Europe during the 2003 heat wave were elderly. It also takes the body longer to repair damage caused by injuries, illness, or exposure to extreme conditions. As one small example, overall loss of muscle tissue means that everyday wear and tear on muscles is repaired more slowly. And unfortunately, as we age, this kind of damage becomes harder to avoid. Less muscle mass, resulting in reduced strength, places people at greater risk for a fall. Decreased bone density boosts the likelihood that a fall will lead to a broken bone.

Sounds bad, right? But remember, this is part of the same long, steady process that has been going on since your twenties—you don't pick up speed at the end. The magnitude of decline from age forty to fifty is approximately the same as the decline from age eighty to ninety. There's no sudden drop-off for these normal aging changes. Decade-to-decade changes are not dramatic, but they are noticeable. Even thirty-year-olds will tell you that they can't pull all-nighters like they could when they were twenty. The good news is that in the absence of biological or environmental stressors, like falls and illnesses, these changes tend not to limit functioning very much. Healthy sixty-, seventy-, and eighty-year-olds do not feel debilitated. Among those who are mentally and physically active, aging changes are pretty innocuous and don't impinge much on daily functioning. The difference is that when the system is stressed, whether by illness, emotional strain, or extreme environmental conditions, older people do not rebound as quickly as younger people.

As troubled as I am when people equate "old" with "sick," there is some truth to it, especially at advanced ages. Poor health and old age are so strongly connected that some scientists say we shouldn't distinguish between normal and pathological aging. I had a fascinating conversation about this one day with Paul Baltes, a former director of the Max Planck Institute for Human Development in Berlin, Germany. I contended that many of the problems of aging are actually problems of illness. He argued, "But there *are* no ninety-year-olds who are free of disease." He was essentially right. Aging is associated with an increased risk of chronic diseases for two reasons: First, it takes time for the problems to develop. For example, the loss of bone mass that occurs in all people with time can eventually become the condition we call osteoporosis, or gradually increasing blood pressure can ultimately become hypertension. Second, the declines in function associated with normal aging increase one's susceptibility to diseases like heart disease and cancer. The longer you live, the greater the likelihood that something could go wrong.

But it can be hard to tell which conditions are purely pathological and which are the products of aging. Diabetes, for example, is a disease that is more common in older people than in younger people, yet most older people don't have diabetes and some younger people do have it. Moreover, it's treatable. Other distinctions are more subtle. Arthritis is a disease that is more common in old age, but normal wear and tear reduces cartilage, too. A loss of flexibility in blood vessels is considered normal aging, but atherosclerosis, a buildup of fatty deposits on arterial walls, is a disease that does not affect only the old. Renal function is compromised in normal aging, but older people are also more susceptible to renal failure in the face of infection.

The same blurriness between what is "normal" and what is considered pathological appears when we consider the aging mind as well as the aging body. Is dementia inevitable if you live long enough? Or does dementia represent an extreme form of the changes seen in virtually everyone as we age? The textbook answer is that dementia is not part of normal aging—it is a disease. But even if this is so, it is clear that some negative cognitive changes occur in even the healthiest of us as we age, which result in mild impairments in recollection, attention, and language. The common thread among all of these is age-related slowing and its ripple effects. For example, it takes longer to learn new information. It is more difficult to concentrate, and to ignore irrelevant material. It is more troublesome to retrieve the exact word that you want from memory. This is particularly true for names and it is especially embarrassing at parties. (Name tags should be mandatory at social gatherings for the over-fifty set.) The most famous slowing-related decline is probably the deterioration of memory. There is an entire class of jokes in which an old person is asked a question and the punch line goes something like "How soon do you need to know?"

However, not all types of memory decline. *Procedural memory*— or memory of how to do things, like how to ride a bike or type on a computer keyboard—is barely (if at all) affected by aging. You don't struggle to remember how hard to press the pedal; it feels as though the memory is in your foot. As a rule, these tasks are so ingrained—what psychologists call "automatic"—that they are performed without conscious effort.

The type of memory that declines most noticeably is *working memory,* which refers to the ability to keep multiple pieces of information in mind while you act on them. We need this type of memory to process and store new information, as well as to solve problems. In order to put two and two together, we have to simultaneously remember both numbers. Changes in working memory appear to be inevitable, and its deterioration, along with a number of other factors involved in processing information, is well documented in people regardless of race, sex, educational background, or wealth. No one who lives a long life fully escapes them. In truth, the decline begins early in adulthood. Like the aging of the body, the aging of the mind is a slow but steady process.

However, as with bodily changes, declines in mental function during normal physiological aging are fairly modest. While they may slow us down, they do not prevent learning or problem solving. For the vast majority, these changes are subjectively unwelcome, but not disruptive to functioning in daily life. Furthermore, the path of change doesn't lead entirely downhill. Some abilities do not decline with age, and some even improve. Vocabulary and cultural acumen tend to increase well into old age as one gains greater knowledge of the world. People over age fifty are also more informed about politics and world affairs than younger people. Tim Salthouse, a cognitive psychologist at the University of Virginia, believes that accumulated knowledge is the key to explaining why people continue to function well in life despite declines in working memory. Older people may be slower on the uptake, but in many instances their knowledge about similar situations, experiences, and topics allows them to outperform their younger counterparts. In one classic study, Salthouse showed that crossword puzzle experts got better with age. It may take older people longer to find words, but they know more of them.

Finally, there's one more X factor that helps blur the line between normal aging and pathology: physical inactivity. Ironically, the social advances of the twentieth century knocked down one set of barriers to long life only to set up new ones. They eased some of the biggest threats to healthy longevity, like malnourishment and infectious disease, and reduced the immense physical strain on the body previously caused by a lifetime of labor on farms, in factories, or running pre-mechanized households. By the twentieth century, we'd created not only a sustainable food supply, but one that is actually too calorie-rich, heavy on the fats and sugars. For many of us, a hard day at work now means eight hours sitting at a desk, and then another hour or two sitting behind the wheel of a car. Even formerly aerobic household tasks like doing laundry and beating carpets have been transformed into less physical activities by devices like washing machines and vacuum cleaners.

And did we take advantage of these labor-saving changes? You bet. Yet our bodies are not evolutionarily programmed to deal with an age of abundance. We still want to eat all that we can, whenever we can—and the fattier the food, the better—because, on a very basic level, our bodies want us to store up fat against the next famine. We want to do things the easy way whenever we can, because our bodies think it's wise to conserve energy. As a result, once we as a society were no longer threatened by the problem of *not enough*, we became fat, weak, and sedentary, threatened by the problem of *too much*. Remember how the major killers in the late 1800s were pneumonia and the flu? Today the top three causes of death in America are heart disease, cancer, and stroke, conditions that are linked to obesity and inactivity.

Exercise makes an enormous difference in how the body ages; recall the twin study in which the twins who exercised aged nine years more slowly than their siblings. In fact, the effects of physical activity are so positive and reliable that some geriatricians question whether "age effects" wouldn't be better described as "inactivity effects." The truth is that we don't know what normal aging would look like if we walked ten or twenty miles a day like our ancestors did on the African savannah. We'd likely be more physically fit, but we would still be slower than youngsters, and eventually we'd still wear out.

We've had so few glimpses of what *very* old age looks like that we really don't know what kinds of behaviors or conditions contribute to it. I suspect this is why we have such a fascination with centenarians. People over one hundred are regularly asked for their secrets to long life, but so far they've failed to elucidate a common theme. Some attribute it to clean living, while others attribute it to a daily stiff drink. I've heard experts say that there are no smokers among them, but even this isn't entirely true. Professor Gene Cohen, geriatrician and former president of the Gerontological Society of America, once asked comedian George Burns (who died at one hundred) what his doctor thought about his cigar smoking. Burns replied, "My doctor's dead." (I still maintain, don't light up. There are some very rare folks who seem genetically resistant to diseases of old age, and Burns may have been one of those lucky few.) Of course, the best retort I've heard from a centenarian came from Gail Courtney Rittgers, who told *U.S. News & World Report* reporter Jodi Schnieder, "It's simple: Don't die, honey."

Much of what we know about centenarians is based on anecdotes or very small, nonrepresentative samples. There are many legends about entire villages of centenarians living in Ecuador or Soviet Georgia, most of which have been shown to be just that—legends. Over the years, many people have claimed to be (and perhaps truly thought they were) older than they really turned out to be. Prior to 1900, birth certificates were not recorded regularly or reliably and population registries, like those that assign Social Security numbers, were nonexistent. Prominent mistakes have been made. Shigechiyo Izumi of Japan, for example, was once listed as the oldest man in the *Guinness Book of World Records* but was later discovered to be merely 105 years old. Essentially, the absence of reliable historical records has rendered large-scale studies of centenarians virtually impossible and entirely ruled out studies of representative samples.

As Thomas Perls, director of the New England Centenarian Study, and his colleagues see it, selective survival is involved. Clinical lore has long held that centenarians, as a group, are even healthier and more cognitively intact than their eighty-year-old counterparts. Perls wondered if people who make it through their eighties may be genetically resistant to the diseases that cause infirmity and death in old age, like heart conditions and Alzheimer's disease. In one study run in collaboration with Bradley Hyman's laboratory at Massachusetts General Hospital, his team examined genetic markers for susceptibility to Alzheimer's disease in healthy people aged 90 to 103 and found that a very low percentage carried the marker. Other research has shown that the marker becomes increasingly rare as people age.

If Perls and his colleagues are correct, people who grow very old may not only live longer but also spend more of those years in good health. When extremely old people die, they tend to fail more quickly than their relatively younger counterparts. Records remain imperfect, but it is widely held that centenarians die most frequently from the flu or pneumonia. Indeed, some longevity researchers hope that as an older society we can eventually achieve what some have dubbed the "salmon model," in which one transitions almost instantly from good health to the grave, rather than lingering indefinitely at death's door. If centenarians truly do have a tendency to stay healthy for most of their lives and then die quickly, this is good news for health care planners: faster deaths are cheaper deaths. In fact, if centenarians are genuinely heartier than younger elderly people, it means that the health care needs of a one-hundred-year-old aren't necessarily a linear escalation of the needs of a sixty-five-year-old, as many have assumed. Estimates of health care costs based on presumptions that the oldest old will become much more infirm than their younger counterparts may turn out to be inflated.

JEANNE LOUISE CALMENT: THE QUEEN OF THE LONG-LIVED SCENE

So far, longevity's reigning champ is Jeanne Louise Calment, a Frenchwoman who holds the title of the longest-lived person ever. Calment died in 1997 at the age of 122. She played herself in the movie *Vincent and Me* at age 114, making her the oldest actress of all time. Prior to her last twelve years, when she was confined to a wheelchair and lived in a retirement home, Calment lived independently. Known for her sharp wit to the end, it is reported that when, at the age of 120, she was asked by a journalist what sort of future she envisioned, she replied, "A very short one."

By the time she died, Calment was blind and nearly deaf. Mentally, however, she was notably intact. Neuropsychologist Karen Ritchie had assessed Calment's mental capacity at the age of 118 and concluded that there was no evidence of progressive neurological disease. Her test performance was like that of a comparably educated 80- or 90-year-old.

My favorite story about Calment's mental acuity in her later years concerns a property deal she accepted at the ripe old age of 90. She owned a house in the French city of Arles, and a 47-year-old lawyer, André-François Raffray, wanted to buy it. He proposed paying Calment $400 a month for the rest of her life if she would leave the house to him upon her death. Calment accepted and a contract was drawn up. Over the next thirty years, Raffray paid Calment more than three times the value of her house. In the end, Calment outlived Raffray by two years; he died at age 77. She is said to have told him on her 120th birthday, "We all make bad deals."

We know that people can make it past age one hundred; if we created the optimum human conditions, how long *could* people live? Can we hope to gain another twenty-eight years in the twenty-first century, as we did in the previous one? Well, we probably shouldn't hope for a second shot at that particular brass ring. The longevity gains made in the twentieth century happened because society attacked the causes of the most premature, preventable deaths. Essentially, we picked off the low-hanging fruit. Eliminating the types of diseases that kill an older population that has already benefited from those basic improvements is going to be exponentially harder. As Jay Olshansky writes, "You can't save the young twice."

Still, there are advances to be made. Scientists generally agree that if cures for the primary diseases of old age can be found, average life expectancy could increase by up to fifteen years. Under *optimal* conditions, life expectancy would probably be somewhere in the vicinity of ninety years, a number we are rapidly approaching. However, just as culture may support longer life in the future, it could work in the opposite direction too. Some researchers believe that the obesity epidemic could end up reducing life expectancy.

This doesn't mean that many people won't blow past ninety with their roller skates on—remember, life expectancy is a population average, not a predictor of individual fortune, and the U.S. Census Bureau is anticipating that there will be 1 million centenarians kicking around by 2050. But life's end probably can't be pushed back indefinitely. People will still age and they will still die. Only if ways were found to slow aging itself could the dramatic increases in life expectancy witnessed in the twentieth century be matched. In other words, we'd have to find the Fountain of Youth.

Let me be clear: We haven't. Despite discoveries that continue to unfold in fields like gene therapy, stem cell research, and cloning, so far these therapies can only hope to treat the diseases of aging and help delay death. Although serious researchers are diligently seeking ways to slow or arrest the aging process, using everything from fasting regimens to organ replacement, there are no existing interventions that can actually turn back the clock. So far, we know of nothing that can push back what seems to be a built-in limit to human life.

This is called "maximum life span potential," or how long humans could live if all environmental influences were optimal and accidental causes of death were avoided—in other words, if the only thing on your death certificate was "died of old age." Maximum life span potential is more a vague concept than a precise mathematical quantity, but if you want to put a number on it, it's likely around 122—the record set by Jeanne Louise Calment.

Nobody knows if the maximum life span is fixed at a certain

point, and if so, where that point might be. It is, however, the subject of a very famous bet. In January 2001, Olshansky and zoologist Steven Austad each contributed $150 to a trust fund, which is anticipated to be worth $500 million when their bet ends in the year 2150. (The jackpot will be paid to their heirs, if the two distinguished researchers aren't still around.) The game: Predict what the world record for long life will be by 2150. Olshansky has placed his money on 130. Austad, drawing hope from cloning technology and stem cell research, has bet that someone already living among us will make it to the age of 150.

Predictions about the very long term are always extremely uncertain; everything that is discussed today about extending life span is highly speculative. Consider for a moment how difficult it would have been in 1900 to predict the changes that occurred during the twentieth century. Yet one hundred years ago, we at least had some clues as to the cause of early death. We just didn't have the solution. Today, we don't even know for sure why people age, whether there is a life span limit, or whether it can be modified. For our purposes, we probably should assume that maximum life span will remain more or less the same as it is now and that life expectancy will simply approach that limit. We seem to have come to the land of old age without having located the Fountain of Youth.

I expect that to come fully to terms with life, we must let go of the fantasy of immortality. This realization is liberating and profound. It redirects our energies to something achievable instead of something in the realm of science fiction, and lets us get down to making the best of the years that we have.

3

Reenvisioning Long Life

'm always asking people where they'd like to insert extra years into their lives. Trust me, no one ever says, "Let's stretch out old age." Yet strangely, this is exactly what our society has been doing as we've added more years to life.

Conversations about aging today, whether around kitchen tables, in corporate boardrooms, or in Congress, are focusing on small questions—like whether full retirement age should be pushed from sixty-seven to sixty-nine—rather than on the much broader question of how to best use extra decades of life. It's true that we're gradually adjusting. The tail end of the twentieth century produced an upward creep in the age at which Americans experience key life events. Since the 1970s, the average time it takes to complete an advanced degree has inched up a year or so. The average age at first marriage and the age at which American women have their first child have both increased by about four years. In some subgroups the marriage age has increased even more: marriage has been delayed so long among African American women, for example, that demographers can't decide if women are marrying later or opting out of marriage altogether.

But society rarely encourages us to radically delay—or for that matter, reshuffle—any of these steps. The partitioning of life into three fixed stages—education, work and family, and retirement—is so well established that "life course" is considered an institution by sociologists. Instead of giving this social script the rewrite it needs to make sense of our newly expanded life spans, we've been fiddling around with details, making minor variations to a plotline written to guide our ancestors through much shorter lives.

Yet, the curtain dropped on our ancestors at about the same point where, today, we're just reaching the break after the second act. You wouldn't adapt a one-act play into a full-length play by keeping everything pretty much the same, then adding a forty-minute intermission between the denouement and the curtain call—the audience would boo and throw popcorn! To make sure that the entire production retains its momentum and builds toward a meaningful end, we should change where the major plot points fall, and give our characters more to do throughout the play. To insist on keeping outdated social scripts simply because we can't imagine any others is entirely wrongheaded; we may be squandering the greatest gift a species has ever been given.

You might wonder what's so bad about sticking with the status quo, even if it's becoming outdated. The way I see it, the current life course model has two major flaws. First, it has created a highly age-segregated society, in which each phase of life is strictly associated with a particular task. The young study, the middle-aged work, and the old rest or volunteer. We're supposed to do things one at a time, and in order. There is very little overlap between life stages, and as a result, not only do members of different generations have limited interaction with one another, which fosters misunderstanding and unease, but it's hard for anyone—of any age—to find a holistic balance between family, work, community, and educational opportunities. There is very little flexibility in our system for the forty-year-old who wants to go back to school or the seventy-five-year-old who wants to keep working.

Secondly, this life script has way too much action in Act II and not nearly enough in Act III. The middle of life is overcrowded with work and obligations, with everyone working at full speed so they can retire as early as possible and with enough money in the bank. Young adults entering this phase of life are not only expected to work full-time, but to really throw themselves into achieving career success, even though at about the same time they may be finding a mate and starting a family. People who try to juggle work and family are often under enormous time pressures, and as a result, care for children and ailing elders is increasingly being outsourced to paid helpers. Civic involvement also suffers. In *Bowling Alone,* Harvard public policy professor Robert Putnam chronicled the sharp decline in community participation in the latter half of the twentieth century, and cites time pressures as a reason for middle-aged people's disengagement from politics, clubs, church groups, and other civic organizations. These timing conflicts make people feel like they must sacrifice one meaningful social role in order to perform another, although in a truly well-balanced life script there would be time enough for all of them.

The flip side of this jam-packed midlife is that leisure is pushed back to a multidecade retirement that few can afford. We have no idea what to do with the millions of old people who are about to find themselves onstage playing out an act of life that no one's ever rehearsed. When faced with a twenty- or thirty-year retirement, many may find themselves at loose ends, particularly if they haven't nurtured much of a social life outside of work or have no meaningful extracurricular interests, or if their spouse is still employed and isn't able to join in a life of leisure.

Since the middle-aged are AWOL from civic life, there is a movement under way to recruit retirees as volunteers. It's a noble idea, but older people don't actually volunteer much more than younger ones do. Worse, the idea that old people should do all the community service not only drains the volunteer corps of the diversity it could have, but it smacks of ageism. Ask any homemaker: unpaid work performed by a stigmatized group has always been devalued. At least volunteering is a better idea than one recently floated in Japan, one of the first nations to confront the aging boom, where finance minister Masajuro Shiokawa suggested shipping elderly people off to nursing homes in the Philippines. That's a fourth act, true enough, but we may want to consider a few other endings before we settle on that one.

It's time to stop tinkering with the old script, and to write a new one optimized for longer life. Let's stretch it out all the way through! Certainly old age will last longer, because *we* will last longer. But we could expand youth and middle age, too. We could give ourselves more than three acts—perhaps four or five—and make them both longer running and more satisfying. We could create a more balanced mix between work, family, and civic life, since cognitive skills and psychological characteristics change over the course of a lifetime, and a new model for longer life could harness the best of each stage at its natural peak.

My suggestion for how to revise the script hinges on a simple proposal: *We should diffuse work across the life span.* We're used to the idea that we should work and save as much as possible when we're young so we can retire as soon as possible when we're old and eke out as many years of rest as we can. Instead, why not spend more of our lives in the workforce, but make those years less of a grind? We can do this by creating an employment "arc" in which employees gradually ease into the workforce as young adults, working fewer hours during the years that they're caring for young children, completing their educations, and trying to find the right careers. Older workers would ease back out just as gradually. Instead of vaulting into full retirement on their sixty-fifth birthdays, staying on for more years, but working fewer hours, would allow older workers' years of expertise to be used to full advantage. A slower, longer work phase would mitigate the time pressures on middle-aged adults and allow people of all ages more options for how to spend their time.

With longer careers but shorter working hours at the beginning and end of our employment, we'd have more time for family, community, and leisure throughout our lives. With more time for community involvement, volunteering would become something people could do throughout life, and subsequently become better recognized as a gift to society, instead of something we foist upon old folks to keep them busy. During the early stages of our careers, when we're working fewer hours, we'd likely earn less money, but overall we'd have more working years in which to save for retirement. Our career ambitions could be just as high, but there'd be no reason to make the climb at a breathless pace. We could exchange speeding through life for a chance to enjoy the journey.

In fact, I think we should plan lives so that people are expected to catch their second wind at age fifty. Think of it as a "fifty-fifty split," in which the first fifty years of life could be spent learning and shaping ourselves into the kind of people who can spend our next fifty years giving back to our communities. You can imagine it as a kind of Social Security system for culture, but one that works in reverse: we'd spend our early years withdrawing knowledge from the system, and we'd spend our later years paying it back in. This is a radical departure from the old script, which holds that life after fifty is a stage of decline—you've already accomplished your goals and are, for better or for worse, sailing through life's "leftovers" on the momentum of your previous actions. In this new model of life, fifty will be when things get really interesting, and when you can make some truly profound social contributions to your community, work, and family.

There's no reason that life's second half couldn't be an era of personal growth or public engagement. The twenty-first century inherited a huge talent pool that never existed before in the history of humankind: older, experienced people who, after age fifty, are in relatively good health, mostly free of child-care responsibilities, and have valuable skills and wisdom gained from good educations and long employment. As my friend Grace used to ask me: what is old age for? One answer may be that a population top heavy with people who are individually accomplished and have already raised their families can make unmatched contributions to society.

Yet our culture and institutions have hardly begun to tap this resource, in part due to the expectation that one should retreat from the public stage at age sixty-five. Think what valuable contributions people could make if we could reshape work to accommodate the diverse health needs, job skills, and leisure preferences of an older population. Retirement could be the pinnacle of life, rather than its "leftovers."

How? I have a few ideas.

I won't pretend that I have the definitive road map for how to navigate long life; I don't think anyone does. Just as our species has overshot biological evolution, we've similarly overshot many of the social norms our society evolved during our history as short-lived people. We have turned a corner so sharp we are still reorienting, struggling to navigate this new terrain.

In fact, I don't think there will be a single road map. The mantra for the future should be flexibility, so that there will be lots of alternate paths on the new roadway that takes people from birth to death. There will be U-turns, and scenic rest stops, and that's okay. The future, if we build it right, will give us more options than we have now. So, think of this as a sketch of where we could go. Feel free to argue, or design your own variations. But just for a moment, imagine this: that the first thing that happens when you're born is you start preparing for old age, that you take a mini-retirement before you work a full-time job, that your career really kicks off around age forty, and that when you're eighty you rule the world.

Act I: The Show Begins

Let's start with the idea of giving every newborn a retirement savings account. In 2002, Britain began presenting every infant born in the country with a Child Trust Fund account; once children turn eighteen they can use the money for education or to launch a business. The government makes the first contribution to the account, but its very existence establishes a way for relatives and friends to give gifts that contribute to the child's future welfare. Setting up accounts early in life establishes what psychologists call a "channel factor"—that is, something that "channels" behavior in a particular direction, by communicating ideas about how people are supposed to behave. Almost overnight it made saving for college a social norm in Britain. (In the United States, by the way, the government encourages saving for college via tax-advantaged vehicles called 529 plans, but guardians must initiate enrollment themselves, and there are no cash contributions from the government to jump-start them, which may be why fewer than 15 percent of Americans participate.)

The Child Trust Fund is a wonderful idea. Better yet, why not make it two accounts—one for education and one for retirement? Maybe these seem like sort of nitty-gritty details that would delight only a tax accountant, but think of them as symbols of a commitment to a gradual progression through life. Even the very young would learn the value of long-term planning, of having faith that they and their tiny bank accounts will meet again once they are both much larger. Knowing that their retirement savings are already growing would take some pressure off of young adults who want to work fewer hours, and make less money, while they raise a family. By beginning retirement planning in youth, we'd also remove a terrific burden from the shoulders of the forty- and fifty-somethings who often wait to start saving until they have finished paying off the big expenses of adulthood—mortgages, their kids' college tuitions, their own educational loans. The vast majority find themselves on the brink of retirement with little in the bank.

Since cognitive skills develop over time, a new life span model that is a better fit for modern, long-lived people should take advantage of these skills when they peak. The old model did do one thing well—it emphasized education for the young. Children have the ability to quickly absorb information and pick up new skills, and they also have tremendous energy and physical agility. What the young have in alacrity, they lack in experience and emotional maturity, so it is critical that adults guide their development. But when it comes to adolescence, the period of rapid learning and emotional development stretching from puberty to maturity, the old model could use a revision. Today, adolescence is generally expected to conclude with the teenage years, or perhaps with college graduation, around age twenty-two. But this cuts adolescence too short. Given that both the brain and emotional maturity are still developing well into one's mid-twenties, adolescence truly lasts until around age twenty-five, when people reach their peak capacity for learning and are at their most physically resilient. One of our first steps as a long-lived society should be to, quite literally, give ourselves a few more years of youth by extending adolescence and allowing ourselves more time to learn.

Some may find this idea a bit unsettling, because we often as-

sociate adolescence with dependence and may think of a prolonged adolescence as a license for laziness, irresponsibility, or
emotional immaturity. Some might worry that stretching it any
further will be giving future generations of slackers carte blanche
to do nothing but endlessly mooch around their parents' base-
ments covered in a fine layer of Cheeto dust. On the contrary, I
think our society can be more productive if we harness the natural strengths of the adolescent mind to do what it does best—
learn and explore. This would be entirely appropriate for an
employment arc in which young people are expected to enter
the workforce in steps. The fifty-fifty split model calls for us to
spend the first half of our lives developing ourselves into the sort
of people who can be community leaders when we are older. In
this increasingly global society, what qualities will a leader need?
I'd say we want people who are well educated, familiar with other
ways of life, and multilingual, and have developed a range of physical skills (some of which, like swimming, yoga, or golf, they can
continue even in advanced age). They will have tried on several
professions until they found the right one for them, have a lifelong history of community service, and see themselves as part of
a broad social network. It seems reasonable that it might take
about twenty-five years to develop such a well-rounded set of life
skills, and anyone who does so will certainly be no slacker.

However, instead of being encouraged to explore the world
and their place in it, teenagers today are intensely pressured to
pick a career and get into the right college. Often, by age seventeen or eighteen they have launched themselves on a career path
without much information about what it's really like. Students
who decide to become businesspeople have never sat through a

sales meeting; students who choose to become doctors have never seen the inside of an emergency room on a Friday night. The opportunity to experience on-the-job training often doesn't happen until several years into a specialized program, and by then there isn't much wiggle room for students to change their mind. This can be enormously stressful; young people believe that the consequences of their career choices at age seventeen or eighteen will set the pace for the rest of their lives.

That pace can be tiring, even at such a young age. I recently taught a small seminar for freshmen at Stanford. These students—granted, all academic stars—were still reeling from the intensity of the academic preparation that got them to Stanford. Here they were, just starting college, and they were already exhausted by their studies. One of my students suggested that high school should be stretched out a bit, so that students could take a hiatus from their studies while interning at a company or volunteering overseas. I think she's on to something. A more flexible education that incorporates opportunities for travel, community service, or work would remove some of the strain caused by asking teenagers to pick a career without letting them try it out first. It could help mold future citizens who are culturally adaptable and have begun to make volunteering a lifelong habit.

These learning experiences could happen during summer breaks, the gap between college and high school, or even sabbaticals embedded within the college years. What if internships, usually reserved for college students, could be frequently offered on the high school level? What if we found ways to help young people travel, and not on their parents' dime—through school programs, youth exchanges, volunteer organizations, or even paid part-time work? These opportunities should be available to all students, not just the children of upper-middle-class families, who don't rely on teenagers as wage earners. In fact, to make sure that young people from low-income backgrounds don't have to decline these opportunities in favor of paid work, or aren't priced out of participation, these programs should be tied to financial rewards like school credits, stipends, scholarship money, room and board while abroad, or a chance to later convert an internship into a paying job.

While adolescence could last a little longer, I think education should last longer still. In fact, it should continue throughout the life span. In contrast to our parents' working days, our nation's economy no longer promises us lifetime employment with a single company, nor even within a single field. Over a lifetime, technological changes will frequently outmode our early schooling. In an era in which your computer is outdated almost before it's out of the box, it's silly to think that all the practical skills and technical information we teach students in their teens and twenties will remain current throughout careers that may span fifty years. We should make sure that universities have "revolving doors" that let students of all ages back in, and that other options, like online classes or employer-provided seminars, are available, too.

Lifelong education would be good for everybody. Employers would benefit from having staffers with up-to-date training. Returning students would enjoy education that's relevant to their occupational success and comes in relatively small doses. Younger students could learn from older returnees who have some real-life experience with the subject matter. Campus life could become less age-segregated. Education would no longer be an intense, one-time opportunity for children and adolescents, something even some of my very bright young students experience as drudgery. It could be interwoven through life's other strands.

Act II: The Action Builds

After schooling, in the current life model young adults are expected to begin full-time work, while also finding romantic partners and starting families. I regularly hear my thirtysomething friends despair that they are behind schedule, pointing out that when their parents were their age, they were responsible adults with solid jobs, a house in the suburbs, and two or three children. Today many Generation Xers haven't even finished school. Some haven't yet decided whether to marry or have children.

I think that's just fine. When my young friends worry that they are deadbeats, I tell them that somewhere in their subconscious they must know that there is no longer a need to rush. After adolescence, we should have an extended period of young adulthood lasting roughly from age twenty-five to forty. During that time, twenty- and thirtysomethings should work less than they currently do. That's right, *less.* Part-time work should be the norm during this period of time. The goal would be to make this life stage a time of finding one's place in the working world while grounding oneself in the community and in the home. It would be an opportunity to try more than one job before settling with a full-time employer, and round out one's work experience with related community service. For those who choose to start families, this ability to take a mini-retirement before starting full-time work would give young parents more time to spend with small children.

Given how pressed most young parents feel trying to fulfill the needs of home and office, I can't think of a stage in life that could benefit more from additional time. Indeed, research shows that two committed, loving adults in a young child's life are better than one. (For the record, there is no evidence that two moms or two dads wouldn't work just as well as one of each, nor an aunt or uncle who steps in to help out a single parent.) The first five years of childhood are pivotal ones for cognitive, social, and emotional development, and there is no doubt that very young children really like to be with their mothers and fathers. Gradually, as parents' gender roles blur, fathers are finding that they, too, would like to share in the kind of hands-on parenting that was once the sole duty of moms.

Let me make this clear: I'm not advocating that moms and dads stop working. I'm saying that the working world needs to give young adults and their children a break, so that *both* parents can work part-time, trading shifts at home with their children throughout early childhood, and not just during a brief period of parental leave. Part-time work could be arranged in any number of ways to suit different kinds of employers and workers: as shorter workweeks, shorter daily shifts, flextime or work-from-home jobs that can adapt to erratic schedules, job shares that allow two to do the work of one, or alternating periods of full-time work with sizable chunks of paid time off, as primary school teachers do, for example. Part-time work doesn't have to be mandatory, because not everyone will prefer it or find it practical, but it should become a socially acceptable, widely available option.

Everyone, including people who choose not to raise children, can gain from slowing down the early phase of work life. A slow, steady ramp-up to full-time work would provide a valuable "getting to know you" period for both employer and employee; employees would build expertise while learning what it's like to work in a particular field or for a certain company, while employers could make truly informed decisions when deciding on a full-time hire. Young people could use the flexibility of part-time work to pursue an advanced education, travel the world, start a business or nonprofit enterprise, practice an art form, or do something else that adds to personal development. Today, we are too often urged to delay travel and artistic and cultural pursuits until after retirement, because work must come first. There's no reason why we couldn't experience them more than once, during different life phases, when they're bound to have different results. I guarantee that the way you travel will not be the same at seventy as it was at thirty. Besides, why put off all the good stuff until the end when—even in an era of very long life—we know that the future is promised to no one, and tomorrow may not come?

Local communities stand to benefit, too. In *Bowling Alone,* Putnam observes that making it easier for both men and women to work part time would be a great boon for civic engagement. Community service in young adulthood could be combined with one's area of career interest, so that they reinforce one another. For example, imagine a young schoolteacher who co-teaches several days a week at a suburban elementary school but volunteers on others at one in the inner city, or imagine a young dentist who spends some time each year fixing teeth in impoverished nations.

I realize that part-time work, like volunteer work, has a bad reputation. Employers often feel they don't get all that they should from part-time workers. There is the cultural perception that full-time work is more worthwhile or prestigious, partly because it's our workforce norm and partly because it usually comes with the biggest paycheck. Reserving health and retirement benefits for full-time workers also reinforces the idea that their labor is more valuable.

But establishing part-time work as a cultural norm for young adults would help ease this stigma, and companies that adapt could realize concrete benefits. For example, hiring twice as many half-time workers could mean that twice as many minds are available to attack complex research, engineering, or creative challenges. Being able to choose full-time hires from a large pool of young trainees would give employers greater flexibility in adjusting their long-term workforce. Companies that offer part-time work might have better success retaining well-educated, highly trained young parents (traditionally women), whose expertise would be lost if they permanently left the workforce to raise children. A greater number of workers on different part-time shifts—days, nights, weekends—would suit the needs of twenty-first-century businesses that run around the clock. Overall, a company full of people with fewer conflicts between work and family obligations could be a calmer, saner, healthier place to work.

Some might argue that in this system, parents who choose a slow career ramp-up will be outgunned in the workplace by the single and the childless. But that's always been the case, although the burden of trading rapid career success for time at home with the children has historically fallen more heavily on mothers than fathers. Making part-time work a social norm removes the stigma—and the gender stereotyping—from the equation. Others may argue that it's more difficult nowadays to raise a family on the combined equivalent of one full-time salary, even though single-salary homes were the norm for decades. After all, life has gotten more expensive: houses are bigger, families own more cars, college tuitions are sky-high.

It's true, young part-time workers may make less money, but longer careers provide more time for their savings to accrue compound interest. Likewise, the considerable expense of child care will be reduced or eliminated by having parents home more often—some families now end up paying nearly one parent's entire salary to day care or a nanny. We already have acceptable models for living on less money in early adulthood: Look at graduate and medical students, young artists, or entrepreneurs starting up their own businesses. Most of them have living standards barely above the poverty level, yet society understands—even lauds—this temporarily spartan lifestyle because it's understood that they are investing in their futures. Isn't raising children another kind of investment in the future?

Act III: Taking Center Stage

In a new model for long life, full-time work life would begin around age forty. If the first four decades of life are a long, slow process of accumulating learning experiences, the decades that follow are when this incredible investment in developing human capital begins to pay off. By about forty, people are well shaped by life and work experience, and they have developed the emotional stability that guides them as leaders. Developmentally, middle-aged people are much more suited to skillfully practicing a trade than to learning one.

Middle age is when people shift from primarily consuming social resources to providing them, a transition that starts in young adulthood as people begin to care for their own offspring and to take on more responsibilities at work and in their communities, but flourishes as they gain tenure in the workplace, becoming mentors, managers, and business owners, responsible for the welfare of their coworkers. This is also when emotional maturity peaks. People are better able to take the perspective of others, appreciate the uncertainty of life, and see grays in situations that once appeared starkly black and white. Gisela Labouvie-Vief, a life-span developmental psychologist at the University of Geneva in Switzerland, argues that midlife is a time when cognition and emotion blend optimally in ways that give people insights into themselves and others. People think with their hearts and their minds simultaneously, and when emotion informs thought we make better decisions. This idealized picture of midlife is not achieved by everyone, of course, but on the whole, middle age is characterized by expertise both at work and in life.

However, there is an inevitable trade-off inherent in human development: experience brings expertise but just as surely limits new ways of thinking. This isn't something that starts to happen in old age; it starts at the beginning of life. For example, having acquired one language, it's more difficult to learn another. Scientists use theories to help guide them to answers, but merely having a theory can also mean that contrary evidence is overlooked.

It's what psychologists Paul and Margret Baltes called "selective optimization with compensation," and it's based on the general observation that development always entails gains and losses. A young man of twenty is far more competent than he was as a boy of ten, and by thirty he will have acquired more specialized knowledge and many more skills. By fifty, he will likely have more authority at work and be more seasoned by life experiences. That's not to say that the ten-year-old boy wasn't better at some things. Indubitably, he had more energy and physical agility, and could have acquired a second language faster than he could as an adult. Many more paths were open to him then than to the man of fifty. But the man of fifty walks whichever path he has chosen with greater surety than the boy.

The traditional life span model utilizes this expertise to a certain extent. Anyone who's been in an office building knows that middle management is chock full of the middle-aged. But the key difference in my life span model is that because entry into full-time work would be delayed, the prime working years would both start and end later. In my fifty-fifty split model, people in their fifties or sixties would still be in mid-career, rather than on the cusp of retirement.

A bunch of you might be ready to protest that by fifty or sixty people have had more than enough work—they've survived decades of office politicking, stultifying meetings, crabby bosses, and life-sucking commutes. Who wants a life plan that makes middle-aged people run on that hamster wheel even *longer*? But practically speaking, longer life, combined with a larger population of old people drawing benefits from the Social Security common pool, very likely means that everyone except the very rich, or those who voluntarily choose a bohemian existence, will need to work longer. I think the most successful model for long life isn't going to be the one that gets everyone off the wheel faster; it'll be the one that makes work feel less like a hamster cage.

Most people actually enjoy their professions and would be willing to work longer if their health permits. When we do burn out on the nine-to-five world, it's often because of a job that is repetitive, without many opportunities to take breaks, change tacks, or learn anything new. Outside of academia, very few jobs offer sabbaticals and not all employers encourage workers to go back to school. We Americans work very long hours with few opportunities for relaxation. We put in more hours in a week, and more weeks in a year, than the Japanese or Western Europeans. According to the Center for Economic and Policy Research, the United States is the world's only advanced economy that doesn't require employers to provide paid leave or paid public holidays to workers. Fully a quarter of U.S. workers don't get any paid vacation at all. Workers in the European Union, by contrast, get at least twenty days of paid leave mandated by law. And if you think it's just the Europeans, think again: China mandates paid vacation to workers.

Increasingly, American workers view time off with ambivalence, often opting not to take vacations because they worry they will fall behind in their work or compare unfavorably to their coworkers. Vacations are sometimes seen as being for people who aren't really "serious" about their jobs. In the United States, among employees who do get paid vacations, the average worker takes only eleven days although fourteen are usually offered. Worse, some of us who venture outside the office for the occasional long weekend or family outing don't really unplug; we end up dragging our PDAs and laptops along.

If we like work so much, why should this matter? The Centers for Disease Control and the National Institute for Occupational Safety and Health maintain that it matters very much to our health. Very long working hours (that is, over forty hours a week) are associated with unhealthy weight gain, diabetes, heart attacks, and poor cognitive performance. Psychologically, vacations help prevent burnout and actually improve the performance of workers. Indeed, studies have found that employees who have returned from vacation sleep better and have quicker reaction times than they did before they left, and that risk of heart disease goes down as vacation time goes up. That's good for employees, and possibly even better for the bottom line of company health insurance plans.

We need to rebuild the full-time work phase so that it not only falls later in life but comes with built-in breaks for family purposes, for community service, and for employees to give themselves a little rest and enrichment. I'm not saying that employers should give us all yearlong paid vacations so that we can go slack off on the beach. But adaptations like sabbaticals, shorter work weeks, more flexible working hours, or longer vacations that employees would actually be encouraged to take could make employment less of a brain drain. These arrangements respect workers by giving them time to attend to their personal lives, and reward employers by returning to them people who feel fresh and ready to be productive again. These would be substantial changes to the American business culture, but they make sense in the context of the much longer employment arc occasioned by greater life expectancy. What was once a sprint will now be a marathon. We'll need to pace ourselves accordingly.

Ideally, periods of rest, work, community service, and continuing education could be intertwined so that they support one another. Imagine a history teacher who uses his sabbatical to visit Italy and brings back materials for his class to study, or a businesswoman who uses a bit of her summer off to teach herself the newest accounting software. Imagine a civil engineer who uses some of his half days out of the office to shore up his skills at the local college, or to donate his expertise to a charity that builds bridges in developing nations. Or imagine a parent who takes time away from work during her child's difficult adolescent years to guide the teen through a rough patch—an eating disorder, a drug addiction—just when some additional parental involvement is needed. Most important, imagine that people get enough breaks during their working years so that they don't feel like their biggest chance to enjoy life is a distant retirement that a car accident or a cancer diagnosis could ensure that they never see.

Just as inserting a mini-retirement into early adulthood would relieve some of the stress that work imposes on young families, it would also remove some of the stress that raising a family imposes on the pursuit of career success. By the time workers hit forty, those who started families in their twenties or thirties would have children old enough to be in school during most of the workweek, who need less constant parental supervision. This would help free the parents to devote more time and energy to work without worrying that chasing a corner office was a direct assault on family time. It would be a great gift—particularly for women, who have long struggled to deal with the conflicting priorities of supermom-dom—if workers felt that they could achieve career success *and* quality time with their children without sacrificing one for the other.

Act IV: The Turning Point

Work wouldn't last forever, even in this elongated model of life. So when, exactly, should we begin retirement? As strange as it is to think of old age as a new phenomenon, the concept of retirement is newer still, and even less well defined. The introduction of the Social Security Act in 1935 profoundly changed our culture. It created a new phase of life, and made sixty-five a magic number for many folks. Nowadays we think of retirement in overwhelmingly positive terms: as a reward for a lifetime of hard work, or as our personal "golden years." But this was not always the case. The idea of making retirement a time of leisure dates back to an era when rest was pretty much all an older person *could* do, given ill health and frailty.

Today, retirement can mean very different things to different people, depending on their health, wealth, and how they feel about work. For some, retirement is a permanent vacation. For others, it's a welcome relief from the stresses of a competitive office, the tediousness of a job they never liked, or the physical wear and tear of manual labor. The very poor may be looking forward to the stability of Social Security, Medicare, and other government programs aimed at seniors, which will provide steady incomes, safe housing, and health care to them, perhaps for the first time in their lives. In contrast, some of the working poor feel unable to retire because their personal savings are so small that Social Security isn't an adequate supplement.

So let's not get rid of retirement, or crank up the age limits across the board—that would be a terrible disservice to people who are truly too sick to work, or truly sick *of* work. Social Security is solid enough to support this segment of the population if they leave the workforce at the traditional age. But in general, we need to push full-time retirement back—way, way, back—for people who are willing and able. In many cases, we'll be able to phase it in around age eighty.

Yes, I said eighty. And yes, I said "phase it in."

When Social Security was designed, it was intended to provide a minimal level of security and comfort to people at the very end of their lives. Its purpose was not to help developers populate Sun City with shuffleboard players. It was not supposed to be a decades-long government-funded vacation to which everyone was entitled. On average, people nowadays who make it to sixty-five can expect to live another eighteen years. People who can work—and would enjoy doing so—are nevertheless stepping aside at sixty-five because it's the social norm to do so. We are losing an incredible amount of skill and experience simply because of this outdated standard. In fact, as the average life span gradually moves closer to that projected maximum of 110 or 120 years, and an increasing percentage of octogenarians remain cognitively sharp and in good physical health, we may find that even eighty is too young. If we do not adapt to our new life expectancies, society is about to find itself staring down the barrel of a forty-year retirement. That's longer than childhood, adolescence, and young adulthood combined!

Instead of sending older people the message that their usefulness is over at age sixty-five, society should encourage them to continue working in the ways that best suit them. Rather than a firm cutoff age for retirement, I propose a gradual phaseout of work that makes use of long-practiced job skills, yet makes work increasingly less physically demanding and time intensive. To bridge the gap from full-time work to complete retirement, a process that could proceed at any pace, employers could once again provide opportunities to job-share, work flexible hours, or work from home—much as they could do for young adults easing into careers.

If thoughtfully constructed, this phaseout stage of work could be highly desirable for workers and employers. Today, employers are sometimes anxious to get rid of older employees because they draw the highest wages. But there is no reason that salaries couldn't be gradually reduced as time on the job is phased out, perhaps by converting annual salaries into hourly pay. Because employees will be partially self-supporting, able to withdraw from their 401(k)s and IRAs during this phase of work, the reduction in salary should be manageable. Employers would get to keep their most seasoned staffers in-house and available to mentor younger hires, and employees could increasingly distill their efforts to the parts of their jobs they like most and perform best.

Social Security already comes with gradations: the longer one stays in the workforce, the larger one's Social Security payments will be. I think this should simply be stretched out, with top dollar being paid to people who work into their eighties, rather than until age seventy. People who want to opt out of the workforce earlier could do so, if they are content to collect smaller payments. Those who do stay in the workforce would benefit more than financially: their well-being would get a boost from the continued mental stimulation that work provides, from the perks that come with seniority in the workplace, from having ongoing social interactions with a wide network of people.

This doesn't mean that everyone has to spend their entire career working in the same office, or even in the same discipline. Maybe you've already heard the buzz about "encore careers," as my friend Marc Freedman, CEO of the think tank Civic Ventures, calls them. Encore careers call for a second, deeply personal, stage of work life. After retiring from a primary career, a person would next apply their job skills in a new field that they find personally meaningful. The idea is to mobilize this massive form of human capital to address social problems. Imagine, for example, a former corporate finance officer who becomes a grant writer for a nonprofit group, an engineer who turns into a math tutor for kids with learning disabilities, or a retired police officer who aids a group that combats domestic violence. They'd still be working, but without the financial demands that accompany middle age—child rearing, mortgages, tuition—they'd be free to choose more altruistic, less lucrative pursuits. Freedman puts it this way: "The old retirement dream of the freedom *from* work needs to be replaced by a new vision: the freedom *to* work—in new ways, on new terms, to even more important ends."

For those who do not have the educational background or professional skills to support an encore career, or to make them particularly desirable job candidates in a working world that often discriminates against the elderly, we also need to reward the informal, unpaid labor that older people already contribute to our communities. Sociologist Gunhild Hagestad has characterized grandparents as a kind of "National Guard" for child care—well trained, kept to the background, but available in a crisis.

(Indeed, grandparents are the most likely candidates to assume care for their grandchildren if parents die.) But even when not serving as emergency backup for their own families, older people have been very good at providing the kind of help that millions of Americans of all ages need: someone to pay attention to them. You don't need to be a retired CEO to help your community with the ordinary functions of life; all you need is real-world experience. Community needs range from looking out for children after school to accompanying a neighbor to a doctor's appointment to helping with errands. Experienced homemakers, in particular, are a superb but underutilized resource. They are seasoned experts in preparing hot meals and boxed lunches, navigating the health care system, getting deals on purchases, tending community gardens, mending and sewing, and organizing church, charity, or school events.

What if older people could earn credits for this kind of work via a barter system? They would contribute their services, and earn credits for services that they need. For example, if Mary earned credits for sewing the costumes for the local elementary school play, she could cash in her credits to have Phil drive her to the grocery store every week. Phil, in return, could use his credits for Angela to give his granddaughter guitar lessons. Similarly, think of how many grandparents could be enlisted if they could earn college tuition credits for their grandchildren in return for their work. Imagine federal, state, or county grants for programs that would reward participants for helping out with neighborhood beautification programs, local watchdog groups, or providing parenting classes for young couples. But let's not insist—as we do now—on trying to lure older people into volunteering with the premise that they have nothing better to do. Let's encourage community service throughout life, and reward older people for their help by giving them the resources they need to stay independent and functional in old age.

Some might find it shocking to expect older people to work longer in any capacity, or for any reward, but it's already becoming a social norm. In 2005, Rutgers University's John J. Heldrich Center for Workforce Development declared the traditional no-work retirement "obsolete" after conducting a national survey in which nearly seven in ten respondents said they intended to work full or part time after retirement. While financial anxiety was a driving factor for some respondents—12 percent thought they could never afford to retire—money didn't seem to be the biggest motivator overall. When respondents over age fifty-five were asked about their postretirement plans, only about a fifth of them said they'd need to work part-time for financial reasons, while a full third said they'd do it for fun, and another 15 percent said they hoped to volunteer, presumably for free.

It's important to realize that practitioners of some professions often *don't* fully retire—and thrive that way. It's a tantalizing hint about the value of long careers and ongoing intellectual and civic engagement. Professors, for example, usually become "emeritus professors" after they retire, but they do not necessarily stop their research, writing, or lecturing—and interestingly, their life expectancy is longer than comparably aged members of the general population. Catholic nuns, symphony conductors, and other musicians, all of whom tend not to retire, also live longer than average. Scientists, journalists, artists, actors, and clergy often continue to work until they can no longer do so or the work is no longer available. Physicians sometimes retire very gradually simply by declining new patients and maintaining a naturally shrinking medical practice until very late in life. It's interesting that although artists and clergy may fall on the opposite side of the income scale from doctors and scientists, these professions have many similarities: Their practitioners tend to be educated, to live healthy lifestyles, and to find deep personal meaning in their work. In some sense, work is a part of who these folks are. When a physicist retires, she's still a physicist.

The flip side is true, too: sudden retirement can lead to feelings of disorientation, and blue-collar workers in particular tend to make the transition from employee to retiree overnight. I remember a man who told me that, each day at lunchtime, he drove to the factory where he had worked. He would park his car across the street and watch his coworkers as they sat around a bench and chatted over lunch. He was lost without their companionship. Sudden changes aren't just hard on the retiree—Nubuo Kurokawa, a Japanese physician, coined the term "retired husband syndrome" to describe a serious psychosomatic illness suffered by homemaker wives in Japan from the stress of catering to domineering retired husbands who prompt them to work harder than ever.

Act V: Resolution

Whether or not one stays in the workforce, or for how long, in an ideal world I imagine the years closing in on eighty as a sort of "autumn crescendo." By this time, you have paid your debts to society, raised your family, and are ready to enter a life phase in which you do whatever you want. I love the story about a 104-year-old woman who was asked, "What's the best thing about being over one hundred?" Her reply: "No peer pressure." When my dad, a professor emeritus of biomedical engineering at the University of Rochester, turned eighty-five, he said that he had reached an age where he could get away with anything. Now eighty-nine, he pretty much does what he wants—including attending lab meetings at the university, counseling young graduate students and faculty, and writing scientific papers—but only the things he really cares about.

Keep in mind that most Americans in their eighties are in reasonably good health; they live on their own and largely enjoy life. True, they are likely to have some chronic health issues, as well as some changes in memory. But there are gains that come at this stage in life, and as with every other stage, we should try to harness its natural cognitive strengths. Researchers are finding some significant, perhaps serendipitous, benefits of the kinds of cognitive changes we've viewed traditionally as deficits. Sometimes being distractible helps people find creative solutions in unusual places. Being slower to anger, as many older people are, can be a very useful skill for mediating interpersonal problems. Older people are less likely to hold a grudge, more likely to forgive. They come to know "when to hold them and when to fold them," and experience insights into the preciousness of life that are largely inaccessible to those who see seemingly infinite futures. This makes them excellent candidates to serve as facilitators who can help different members of a group see the bigger picture.

In fact, this might also be a good reason to seriously team the young and the old in community service efforts. Mixing the eightysomethings with the twentysomethings who are traveling the world and learning about different cultures could produce a powerful international peacekeeping corps. You'd combine wisdom and perspective with youth and vigor. It's an idea that the Gray Panthers offered years ago, insisting that middle-aged people create the worst obstacles and that the young and old have more innovative and progressive ideas. As with encouraging older students to return to campus, mixing old and young in the volunteer force would help break down the communication gap between generations. Instead of seeing people over eighty as needy or dependent, younger people could start seeing them as capable of great leadership and of contributing to the good of society, and as the kind of people they would someday like to be.

In this new life span model, very old age would offer you time to look back on your life and use your long experience to make the sweetest, most beneficent offering possible to society. If you were a musician you might write your most beautiful pieces. Maybe you would be a better grandfather than you were a father, or become the friendly neighbor that all the latchkey kids dropped by to visit on their way home for a snack and some help with homework. No matter what you did, people would never expect you to stop contributing to the world. Thanks to this unprecedented gift of extra time, life could be one long, slow process of gradually distilling knowledge and expertise and deploying it in ways that would enrich society and bring you great satisfaction. There is a beautiful Greek proverb, "A society grows great when old men plant trees in whose shade they know they shall never sit." What more selfless gift could one give to society than using life's last act to make the world better for generations to come?

4

The Social Side of Aging

Now that we have been given extra years, we'll want to make them healthy, happy, functional ones—and that will depend a good deal on our social lives, including the choices we make about them now. For most people, family and friends are what make life worth living, so it is not surprising that people who are deeply and happily embedded in their social worlds live more pleasant lives and enjoy better mental health than those who are not. But would it surprise you to know that the strength of your social bonds is also tied to your cognitive functioning, disease risk, and overall longevity?

Increasingly, scientists are uncovering evidence that our social worlds influence not only our happiness in everyday life, but the ways that our brains process information, the levels of hormones circulating in our bodies, and our physiological responses to stress. These changes have a profound impact on health outcomes, including whether or not we get sick, and how quickly we will either worsen or recover. Though it's normal for social networks to narrow with age, they can shrink too much. Having fewer than three people in your social circle with whom you feel emotionally close is a risk factor for all sorts of physical and psychological problems. In fact, feeling socially isolated is as great a risk factor for poor health and death as cigarette smoking! So it's important that we start thinking now about how social connections like marriage, families, and friendships may fare in the face of very long life.

It's inherently human to be social. Our strong desire to connect to other people is hardwired into us, because simple survival depends upon interaction with other human beings. It has ever since we lived on the African savanna in small bands of twenty or thirty people, with the older ones ensuring that the younger ones stayed alive. Newborns would die within a matter of hours without the devotion of at least one committed adult. That social smile from the tiny baby melts our hearts and keeps us providing care despite all the frustrations of midnight feedings and diaper changes. We've all been stuck in traffic behind cars with bumper stickers reminding us that it takes a village to raise a child, but the fact is, we need that village to see us all the way through. Even as adults, we need other people to share our labor, to help us reproduce and care for our children, to aid us when we are sick or injured, and to pass on the knowledge and skills we accumulate during our lifetimes. Those ancient people who struck out on their own—or who simply failed to form strong attachments— are unlikely to be among our ancestors.

We care for those who care for us, but the instinct to care is not so specific that it extends only to our biological relatives. When a young boy alone on the playground falls and scrapes his knee, virtually all of the nearby adults will turn their heads until someone attends to him. It's automatic. Even less personal events draw us to others. For example, if you witness a car accident, you'll likely begin talking to the stranger standing nearby on the sidewalk. Even strangers can reassure one another that the accident was a bizarre fluke, unlikely to happen again, or better yet, that it was the fault of the victim, which assures us that the world is predictable and controllable.

As anyone living in New York City in the wake of the September 11 attacks knows, entire neighborhoods suddenly felt strongly connected. People checked on their frail neighbors and shared the latest information with anyone who cared to listen. For a time, New Yorkers were especially kind, patient, and pleasant to one other. You could ask anyone on the street a question and get the type of helpful answer you'd expect from a good friend. Churches and synagogues swelled with people who were comforted, not irritated, as more and more people squeezed together in the pews. There was an instinctive understanding that we stood a better chance if we stood together. Scientists do not credit nationalism for this sudden surge in neighborliness—they credit the fundamental human impulse that, even in modern times, prompts us to band together for our own good.

Human survival is rooted in our relationships to others, and when these bonds are shaken we respond on a visceral level. Even babies understand that there's an unspoken social contract. Susan Johnson, a colleague of mine in the psychology department at Stanford, has shown that one-year-olds already have mental representations of how social relationships are supposed to work. In very clever experiments, she shows babies animated video clips that feature large and small objects moving around on a computer screen. Even though they are only abstract shapes, the babies can see stories unfold in their actions. At one point the tiny object shakes rapidly and cries out, and instead of approaching the little one, the larger object moves away. When the large object fails to approach the little one, as an adult would rush to a distressed child, the babies recognize that something is amiss. Their eyes widen and they look intently at the screen. These babies cannot talk or walk, yet they display rudimentary knowledge of a sophisticated social system.

We seem to know instinctively whether or not we are valued by the group, and where we stand in the social hierarchy. Our beliefs about our social standing translate directly into observable cognitive effects. For example, anyone who has ever squirmed in agony while waiting to be picked for the dodgeball team at recess—picking order being an obvious barometer of schoolyard social status—knows that young children monitor their popularity. At very early ages, children who are unpopular internalize their outsider status. They aren't just unhappy; their brains process new information about their social worlds differently than the brains of popular children do. In one study, popular and unpopular children were shown a list of words and asked not to read the word, but to name the color of the type the word was printed in. This experimental approach is called a Stroop test, and it's widely used to assess cognitive sensitivity to particular stimuli. People who suffer from irrational fears are slower to name the color when the words on the list include *snake* or *spider.* Depressed people are slower on trials with words like *sad.* Unpopular children are slower to name the color when words like *lonely* or *re-*

jected appear, because they are distracted emotionally. These children wouldn't notice that they are slower to respond—it's all very subtle, only milliseconds of difference—but their brains are sensitive to the meaning of words that relate to their vulnerabilities.

Adults, too, are deeply aware of their social standing. Nancy Adler, a psychologist at the University of California, San Francisco, developed a simple and ingenious measure of perceived social status: a picture of a ten-rung ladder. Adler tells participants that the most advantaged people in society are represented by the top rung and the most disadvantaged are on the bottom. Then she asks them to tell her where they fall on the ladder. People easily relate to the ladder metaphor and can quickly place themselves on it. What's amazing is that where they place themselves on the ladder predicts not only their physical and mental health—for example, how likely they are to have angina or suffer from depression—but also how long they will live! Adler's subjective measure of social standing predicts health outcomes better than more objective indices of social status, like income and occupation. It's a compelling indicator that health isn't just predicted by how many resources people have, but by how they relate to other people.

Scientists have asked, what is it about social isolation that links it to poor health? Does *feeling* isolated make you sick, or is it a function of actually *being* isolated—for example, lacking a supportive social network to help you recover when you fall ill? After all, some of the positive effects of being part of a social group are straightforward and behavioral. People who share meals with others are more likely to eat a balanced diet instead of day-old pizza out of the box. They are more likely to go see their doctor when they get sick. In many cases, being nagged by loved ones is exactly what makes us take care of ourselves. Even without nagging, the knowledge that other people depend on us improves our habits. I know lots of new parents who started exercising or quit smoking after their little ones were born. Recognizing how vulnerable their children would be without them, they established regimens to improve the odds that they will see them through.

But increasingly, scientists are finding that the subjective sense of isolation actually prompts physiological changes that can be detrimental to health. "The social world remodels your body," says UCLA psychologist and hematology-oncology researcher Steve Cole, who has done particularly stunning work showing that HIV infections progress faster in gay men who are closeted than in those who live openly. Cole's work hinges on the fact that your brain's perception of the threat level of your surroundings translates into body chemistry that affects your health and well-being. Your relationships with the people around you profoundly influence whether you perceive the world as a safe, comfortable place, or as one that is threatening and uncertain. "As long as your brain thinks that everything is fine, your body is going to be running a program of long-term investment, general maintenance, and rebuilding," says Cole. "But if your brain perceives that you are in an uncertain or threatening environment then it's going to activate stress responses in the rest of the body that trigger changes in gene expression." All of us are born with basic fight-or-flight stress responses that help us deal with the challenges of everyday life, but when people are very sensitive to their social environment, or feel threatened by it, they repeatedly activate this response. That, says Cole, leads to changes in the body's molecular composition that make it more vulnerable to damage and disease.

To understand this relationship between our interior and exterior lives, Cole built on work done by Sally Mendoza and John Capitanio, primatologists at the University of California, Davis, who had been studying monkeys infected with simian immunodeficiency virus, or SIV. Every day, Mendoza and Capitanio's monkeys got two hours of playtime. Some of the monkeys were always allowed to play in the same groups, so that they socialized with familiar monkeys. Others spent two hours with a different group each day. In a matter of months, the mild social stress of having to frequently interact with strangers drove the virus to reproduce faster in those monkeys.

Cole's research team already knew that there was a link between stress and viral replication; they'd found that exposing human T cells infected with HIV to the stress chemicals produced in a fight-or-flight response allowed the virus to replicate three to ten times faster than normal. With the monkeys, Cole wanted to understand what stress was doing to their immune systems that made them more vulnerable to the virus. Cole focused on neural fibers that run from the spinal column and into the lymph nodes, where the body coordinates its immune response. He found that the stressed-out monkeys had grown twice as many of these fibers, which were acting like soaker hoses, releasing the stress hormone norepinephrine into the surrounding cells. Nearby T cells were two to three times more likely to be replicating the virus than cells farther away from the fibers. Because the monkeys had twice as many fibers pumping out stress chemicals, they were replicating the virus twice as fast.

Social stress can be a reaction to our surroundings, but the way

our bodies handle social situations is also partly a function of in-
born temperament, and of the worldview we develop thanks to
a lifetime of experiences. These form a self-reinforcing cycle. For
example, a naturally shy, introverted child may hang back on the
playground, get picked on for doing so, and become even more
likely to withdraw. These variations in individual temperament,
says Cole, "are relatively small differences to start off with, but
they can propagate into big differences over time by shaping the
pattern of social choices you make." Consistently choosing one
way over the other solidifies your outlook on whether other people are generally good and trustworthy, or unfriendly and threatening. If your worldview leans toward the latter, says Cole, you're
more likely to build a more autonomous, independent life for
yourself. "That in turn propagates this perception that the world
is a distant place, that there's no one else you can turn to," he says.
"And that really does seem to be correlated with long-term increases in health risk."

These risks can be for illnesses both large and small. Feeling socially isolated makes you two to three times more vulnerable to
a cold. While it's clear that stress alone doesn't cause cancer, the
stress response can aid the growth of blood vessels that feed tu-
mors, accelerating their growth. It can even impact the speed of
aging. Working with John Cacioppo, a professor of psychology at
the University of Chicago, Cole studied the differences between
adults in their fifties and sixties who were socially satisfied and
those who consistently felt lonely over several years. The lonely
people's immune systems tended to overexpress an array of inflammation genes, which control immediate tissue-repair processes but also drive the wear and tear we know as aging. If you

compared two fifty-year-olds, one with a happy social life and one who felt isolated, the lonely person would have an "older body" in that it would show greater chronic inflammation. In his study of HIV-positive gay men, Cole concluded that being in the closet was sort of a "marker" for social isolation, for what he terms "essentially shy, sensitive people who felt like they couldn't necessarily count on other people responding in a positive way to their gay identity." Because feeling like an outsider is stressful, and because that stress accelerates viral growth, he concluded, the closeted men sickened faster.

It's important to emphasize that a lack of positive social relationships doesn't *cause* disease. But think of stress as an accelerator that speeds up damage from a disease you already have. By contrast, positive social relationships that keep stress at bay are "modulators" that can slow down its progression. In 2000, epidemiologist Laura Fratiglioni of the Swedish Kungsholmen Project came to an extraordinary conclusion: having a satisfying social network may delay the onset of dementia. Geriatricians have known for a long time that people with dementia are more socially isolated than others, but the assumption was that isolation is a consequence of the disease, not the cause. Fratiglioni embarked on a different sort of study. She recruited more than a thousand elderly Swedes, none of whom were showing signs of dementia. She assessed their social situations, including whether they were married or single, lived alone, and enjoyed their social relationships. Then she tracked them. Three years into the study she observed that people who had strong social networks were 60 percent less likely to have symptoms of cognitive impairment than those who did not.

THE PROOF IS IN THE PRONOUNS

Researchers have developed some clever ways of trying to see the overall impact on longevity of having close relationships. For example, in one study, Sarah Pressman and Sheldon Cohen, of the University of Pittsburgh Medical Center and Carnegie Mellon University, respectively, analyzed published autobiographies. The study participants included a group of distinguished psychologists who had contributed their autobiographies to an eight-volume series on the history of the discipline. Another group of writers included poets, as well as fiction and nonfiction writers. The researchers counted the number of relational words that people used in their autobiographies, words like *father, brother,* or *sister,* as well as inclusive pronouns like *we,* compared to individual pronouns like *I.* Pressman and Cohen then charted the correspondence between the frequency with which people had used relational words and their age at death. They found that the authors who heavily referenced social roles in their life stories lived, on average, five years longer than those who did not.

But do you have to be a social butterfly to reap the benefits of social connectedness? Not at all. Cole points out that in his studies of older adults done with Cacioppo, the people who became the sickest were the ones who *felt* socially isolated—not necessarily the ones who had the fewest friends. Compared to socially satisfied people, the adults who felt lonely, he says, "have slightly smaller social networks, but not dramatically smaller—yet they do have dramatically different biological responses." It's your brain's subjective calculation of how safe your social world is and what the future may hold for you that determines whether or not your stress responses are activated—not how big that social world actually is.

Anneli Rufus, the author of *Party of One: The Loners' Manifesto*, points out that those who identify as solo fliers can feel well connected and content with a very small but deeply valued social circle. "Most of us have a few relationships that really matter," she says. "Apart from those few—perhaps these include the spouse, the best friend, the parent, the child, a mentor or another relative—then the entire rest of humanity, all the would-be friends and all the chattering masses, can just never say another word to us again and we would be fine. Maybe even more than fine!" And although those relationships might take a slightly different form from those of an extrovert—more e-mailing, fewer large group outings, and certainly not as many "drop-in" visits—they're no less cherished. "It would matter enormously to us to lose any of those few—not so much because we need company, but because that person . . . means a lot to us," says Rufus.

Just as it's possible to be happy with a few close bonds, it's possible to feel alone in a crowd, and for your body to pick up on the resulting stress. Here's a striking example: Fratiglioni's study observed that people with strong social networks are less likely to show signs of dementia . . . but only if their social relationships are *positive*. Dementia risk was higher for people who had lousy relationships with their children than for childless people. Indeed, bad relationships may be more harmful than good relationships are beneficial. Additionally, the study found that the relationships we often think of as the linchpins of a socially well-adapted adulthood—marriage and children—were not required to have a low risk of dementia. Lisa Berkman, an epidemiologist at Harvard University, puts it this way: "Being alone is what is risky, not living alone."

And, for the most part, we don't live alone. Toni Antonucci and Robert Kahn, psychologists at the University of Michigan, coined the term "social convoys" to characterize that core set of people who accompany each of us through life. These convoys are not terribly large, and they're usually heavily constituted by close kin. Convoys can grow or shrink over time. Early in life our childhood friends join our convoy. Later in life, so do our own children, and sometimes particularly well-liked colleagues and neighbors. As the years go by, new people join the convoy, and others are dropped. If you've ever wondered what became of some of the once-close friends who made up your bridal party or who used to live around the corner, you've seen how your social convoy can change. This doesn't mean those bonds you shared weren't real, just that even our core social group has some flexibility to shift over time.

Social spheres generally contract with age, so you may have fewer people in your convoy at age eighty than you did at age fifty. For years, the prevailing view among social scientists was that this narrowing of the social world was a problem for older people. Attrition was often chalked up to the deaths of friends and loved ones, or alternatively to pervasive ageism that discriminates against older adults on multiple levels. Later views came to see older people as uninterested in, or disenchanted with, the social world. "Disengagement theory," prominent in the 1960s and '70s, posited a mutual withdrawal between society and individuals—it was suspected that older people were pulling away from close relationships in preparation for death, while at the same time society pulled away from them in preparation for the loss of its citizens. Many policy makers and scientists have reacted to this perceived loneliness with consternation and thrown a good deal of time and effort into designing interventions to remedy it. But smaller social circles are not a problem as long as the relationships within them are emotionally strong—and this is in fact what tends to happen in old age. Indeed, though elderly people have smaller social spheres, they report higher-quality relationships than younger people do.

Is this another paradox? I don't think so. People engage in a natural pruning process as they age, removing people who are not so satisfying from their social circle while retaining the ones they enjoy. Most people in early and middle adulthood have many acquaintances and regular social contacts that they do not choose: a cubicle mate at work, the other moms in the PTA, friends-of-friends-of-friends. These people don't necessarily become part of your life because you find them particularly compelling, it's just that their lives overlap with yours. You go to the same meetings, you live on the same block, your kids play the trumpet in the same marching band. As people age, however, social networks are distilled and peripheral relationships are voluntarily discarded until the network retains only its most important connections.

I remember witnessing a particularly compelling example of

this phenomenon in action one year when a well-meaning group of students tried to set up an "adopt-a-grandparent" program because they thought older people in Stanford's surrounding community would be cheered up by having some young visitors. They had no problem getting students to sign up for the program. But it was harder to recruit grandparents. Why? Because unlike college students, most older people aren't trying to expand their social horizons; they're trying to deepen the relationships they already have. Rather than going through the getting-to-know-you process with a college-age stranger, most of the seniors would have preferred spending time with their own college-age grandchildren.

Older people also spend more time alone than younger people and they appear to be quite comfortable with that fact. It's not that they dislike others, just that they have less need to be with people. This often leads others, like my well-meaning students, to speculate that seniors are hurting socially, even when they aren't. Keep in mind, older people have lower rates of nearly all mental health problems, including depression and social anxiety, than younger people do. I think people often forget that both positive *and* negative emotions are generated in the context of social relationships.

This narrowing of the social world with age is perfectly healthy, provided that the relationships you maintain are truly a source of emotional enrichment, rather than driven by habit or obligation. I've urged many adult children over the years to stop nagging their parents to go to the local senior center or, worse yet, to start playing bingo. There is no evidence that these types of superficial social contacts confer health benefits. To the extent that they make people uncomfortable, they may do just the opposite.

However, findings from my own research team, and by others who study healthy aging, do suggest that having too few close contacts can be risky. We can only speculate as to why, but for older people three seems to be the magic number. Fewer than three connections is just too few for comfort. Better yet, these relationships should be a diverse mix—friendships, kin, a romantic partner, professional alliances. Berkman points out that it's not sufficient to be wrapped up in a single, intense social bond. Having only one close relationship that overarches all others, say, an insular romance, is precarious since that bond can always be broken. You can see why social network resiliency would be particularly important in aging, a process that tends to gradually separate people from loved ones as older members of their social group pass away and younger ones leave home.

Older people are particularly vulnerable to losing their whole network if all of their close relationships are with people in their own age group. I vividly remember a woman in a nursing home telling me that she'd lived her life with three wonderful friends. She didn't feel like she needed anyone other than these women. But then she got a phone call telling her that the last of the three had died. What hit her hardest, she told me, was that there was no one to tell, no one to phone. She had never felt so alone.

At the heart of this transition from acquiring new connections to taking care of the ones you already have is the perception that the future profoundly influences our goals, the basis for a model my students, colleagues, and I have developed called socioemotional selectivity theory, mentioned briefly in chapter 1. When we are young, and time seems to stretch limitlessly before us, we make choices that we hope will help us expand our social pool, broaden our worldview, and give us the experiences and resources we'll need to make a life for ourselves in a complex, crowded society. We go to mixers and parties, we join teams and clubs, we accept blind dates. We are open to meeting lots of new people, and if it turns out that we don't click with them, oh well, plenty of time to meet others that we might find more satisfying.

Yet as we age, and the time before us grows more constrained, we begin to prioritize and savor the relationships we already have. That's not to say that older people don't join clubs and make new friends—in some cases they do. But overall, older people are less motivated to make new social connections and more interested in the upkeep of the ones they already have. They start to focus on the big picture, to ignore the more trivial interpersonal problems that engulfed them in their twenties and thirties, and to be more open to reconciliation. I often think of musicians Paul Simon and Art Garfunkel, who when they turned sixty-one—many years after a split that divided the once-close friends—decided to put the acrimony in their relationship aside and embark on a reunion tour. Aging reminds people that they don't have all the time in the world to "get it right." This refocusing doesn't represent "disengaging" from society. On the contrary, it's about engaging in a way that values quality over quantity.

The effect of socioemotional selectivity is powerful, but old age itself isn't necessarily the cause. This reframing of social relationships can be prompted by anything that forces us to recognize the fragility of life and the inevitability of endings. Aging is a powerful reminder that life doesn't last forever, but so is disaster. I was in New York during the September 11 terrorist attacks, and I vividly remember sitting in my sister's apartment, glued to the television news, wondering what would come next and worrying about my niece, Rubyanna, then just a baby sitting on the apartment floor, completely unaware of the tragedy unfolding around us. The world had changed in a matter of minutes. The phone rang and it was a call from a former student of mine, Helene Fung, who is now a professor at the Chinese University of Hong Kong. She was excited about the prospect of collecting data to see if people's goals would change in the wake of this disaster in the way our theory predicts. I remember telling her that I didn't give a hoot about research, a first in my adult life! I only wanted to be with the people I loved—which, of course, was exactly what our theory predicts people will do.

Fung decided to go ahead and collect data in Hong Kong, presenting participants with a simple question that we have used in many studies over the years: "If you had thirty minutes free, and the following three people were available, with whom would you choose to spend your time?" The alternatives were: a member of your immediate family, a recent acquaintance with whom you seem to have much in common, or the author of a book you just read. The first option represents someone with whom you are emotionally close (for better or for worse). The second is someone who, over time, could become important to you. The third option is someone you'd be likely to learn something from, but with whom you probably won't form a close relationship.

In all of our studies, we've found that older people show a strong preference for spending time with a member of their immediate family (or when we use a different set of alternatives, a close friend). Younger people, in contrast, are just as likely to pick any one of the options—with one important exception. Younger people who are sensitive to potential endings, whether anticipating a geographical relocation or living in the midst of the SARS epidemic, respond just as older people do. Following September 11, even as far away as Hong Kong, Helene Fung found that the event reminded people of the fragility of life. Young and old alike desired emotionally meaningful social contact.

During the year following the September 11 attacks, which had reinforced people's feelings of vulnerability to unforeseen catastrophes, many newspapers reported cases of young couples who decided to marry, or single people who became more interested in seeking a spouse after their brush with danger. Some newspapers trumpeted this as a triumph of life in the face of death, and some went even further, speculating that there would be a resulting "baby boomlet" and that more women would start giving up their careers to stay home with their children. (Both phenomena failed to materialize.) But although some people doubtless did decide to wed in the wake of September 11, during the same time frame anecdotal accounts were also appearing about lovers who looked each other straight in the eye and realized that they were not right for each other. Whether people reacted to September 11 with an urge to make up or break up, our point is the same: when people are powerfully reminded that our time together ends, they make choices about who they want in their social network. Sometimes that means saying "I do." But sometimes, it means saying "I don't."

On campus, we see this selection process every year in the difference between the social lives of college freshmen and seniors.

Freshmen, who know they have four years of nonstop socializing in front of them, aggressively pursue new friendships and new interests. Seniors, who anticipate that they will soon be leaving campus life behind, are more focused on their own area of study and the close friendships they have already established. In one study, my former student Barbara Fredrickson, who is now a professor of psychology at the University of North Carolina at Chapel Hill, asked graduating seniors and returning undergraduates to keep daily diaries about who they spent time with and how involved they were with their social relationships. There were no differences in the types of contact that seniors and returning students reported day to day. But graduating seniors were significantly more emotionally engaged when they were with their close friends. Even at the tender age of twenty-two, in terms of social connections college seniors behave much more like senior citizens than their fellow undergraduates.

You can expect to have fewer—but deeper—connections in old age. But with whom? And what will those connections be like? Core relationships, like marriage and family, will likely change in an era of very long life. And that's okay. Social conservatives often fret about departures from the traditional, but in truth, what we've come to regard as "traditional" arrangements have actually come and gone over history. Richard Saller, a professor of history and classics at Stanford (and dean of the School of Humanities and Sciences), puts it this way: "When we lament the fact that families today are falling apart, it is generally understood that this represents a deterioration from a better past when families were healthy and whole—the image of the Cleaver family in *Leave It to Beaver* with a gentle father, a wise housewife-mother and two basically decent but mischievous sons." Yet this nuclear family norm has perhaps more often been seen on TV than in the real world, where even in ancient times, Saller points out, both early death and divorce were common, wreaking havoc on family stability. So realizing how flexible the family has been over time, let's take a look at some of these most basic social ties and consider how they might adapt in the new environment of a hundred-year life span. In particular, let's examine three very important kinds of relationships: marriage, family life, and grandparenting.

Marriage

Though marriage is becoming increasingly optional as a social institution, the vast majority of Americans—better than 90 percent—still marry at some point in their lives. American couples tend not to cohabit for long periods; they either break up or marry. They seem to use cohabitation as a trial marriage, rather than as the enduring alternative to marriage observed in Europe.

Just as Americans are more likely to marry, they are more likely to divorce. But divorce doesn't seem to deter Americans from marrying again, usually within just a few years. Among the younger set, terms like "starter marriages" are becoming part of the lexicon. In our inimitable way, Americans are eternally optimistic about marriage. Whether unmarried or married, we idealize it. It's ironic that some people express great concern about granting marriage rights to gays and lesbians on the grounds that it may undermine the institution of marriage. You could look at it another way: marriage is so popular that everyone wants to get in on it.

For most Americans today, marriage is a partnership of one's own choosing that is based in romantic love and establishes two people as a legal, economic, and social unit. Only one hundred years ago, marriage was primarily about children. Couples married with the explicit intention of procreating and raising their biological offspring, although shorter life expectancies meant that there were lots of orphans. Siblings and cousins would often be shuffled around to extended family members during tough times. The family was not only a social unit, it was an economic one. Children contributed labor to the family farm or general store, or to their fathers' trades. Marriages were functional; you didn't expect your spouse to make you blissfully happy any more than you would assign that role to your business partner. It's not that there weren't great love stories in marriages of the past, but that wasn't the *expectation* of marriage.

In modern times, these expectations are almost completely reversed: a 2001 Gallup poll found that fewer than a fifth of respondents ages twenty to twenty-nine felt that the main purpose of marriage was to have children, while a full 94 percent of them agreed with the statement "When you marry, you want your spouse to be your soul mate, first and foremost." But marriage still has its economic side. When two people share their fates, the arrangement distributes risk, allowing the social insurance people need to take chances. Two-income households are less vulnerable when one earner loses a job, for example. Couples can also execute plans that ultimately result in a higher standard of living. One spouse can return to school while the other pays the bills, thereby increasing the couple's long-term earning potential. As a rule, harnessing two people's efforts to get ahead in life is more effective than individuals doing it on their own. Just as partnerships benefited our ancestors on the African plains, modern humans who share their lot enjoy relative prosperity.

In the movies, women are usually portrayed as the ones who desire marriage. They are the ones who connive and scheme to get their men to the altar. But marriage actually seems to hold more social and health benefits for men than for women. Indeed, sociologist Jessie Bernard once contended that embedded in every marriage are two marriages, one "his" and one "hers." On average, married people live about three years longer than their single counterparts, but the effects are stronger for husbands than wives. Married men live longer than unmarried men, but for married women, the benefits are more qualified. Many studies find no longevity benefit for married women compared to single women, but it appears that it depends on the state of the marriage. Women in good marriages reap advantages similar to those of men, but women in bad marriages do not. (Interestingly, husbands benefit from even bad marriages.) Why might this be? There is considerable consensus among marriage experts that wives tend to feel more responsible for the quality of a marriage than their husbands. It's as if taking care of the relationship is part of her job, so wives experience more distress when the marriage isn't going well. Over long periods of time this stress can take a toll on health.

While wives do most of the emotional work in a marriage, husbands rely on the marriage more. For husbands, wives are generally their primary sources of emotional closeness and support. Ask a husband to name his best friend, and he will likely name his wife. Yet ask a wife to name her best friend, and she'll likely rattle off the name of a female friend. When men lose their wives through divorce or death, they often lose their social net-works right along with them, not necessarily because the old friends are taking sides or losing interest in staying in touch, but because the wife was the keeper of the social calendar, the one who invited folks for dinner and stayed in touch with those cous-ins from Omaha.

You hear about grieving widows passing away shortly after their spouse dies, but that's actually more commonly true for hus-bands, who are also more likely to get sick after the death of a spouse. Psychoneuroimmunologists speculate that it's because the wife's passing is more likely to isolate a husband from the social world. If your wife is your only confidante, you suffer an enor-mous loss with her death. In one study, T-cell counts—indices of the resiliency of the immune system—were measured in men whose wives had terminal cancer. The majority showed steep de-clines in lymphocyte responsivity two months after their wives had died, making the widowers more susceptible to illness, and the suppression persisted for over a year. Wives aren't more likely to die immediately after a spouse does, and researchers suspect that is because their husbands are less likely to be the links to their social worlds.

Younger people regularly say that they want their relationships to remain youthful, not to wear like old married couples' rela-tionships, but they are blind. Mark Twain had it right. He wrote in his notebook in 1894, "Love seems the swiftest, but it is the slowest of all growths. No man or woman really knows what per-fect love is until they have been married a quarter of a century." To many couples, a quarter of a century qualifies one only as a newlywed! Research shows that marriages improve over time;

even unhappily married couples say that they are happier in old age than they were when they were younger. As time passes and couples weather tough times, they are proud that they shared those experiences. They have triumphed, perhaps more than those who had a sweeter time of it.

Indeed, it's quite common for marriages to improve when the couple hangs in there. A 2002 report based on the National Survey of Families and Households concluded that five years after a divorce, former partners were no happier or less depressed than when they were married. By contrast, two in three unhappily married spouses who did *not* divorce were happy five years later. When my research team was studying long-term marriages, we talked with couples who had been married three and four decades, and nearly all of them said that there had been rough patches in their marriages. One older woman I interviewed told me how much it irritated her when young people commented on how lucky she was to have found her perfect mate. "Our marriage is the product of a lot of hard work, not luck!" she exclaimed. Recently, a mother of four who had been married for more than fifty years told me that she and her husband managed to stay together because of a solemn promise they made to each other: whoever leaves first has to take the children.

The "Greatest Generation," the one currently in retirement, has the unique honor of being the longest-married generation—and may hold that distinction in perpetuity. Prior to the twentieth century, when our ancestors courted and tied the knot, couples married for life, but life didn't last all that long. Yet longer life in the latter half of the twentieth century has not necessarily meant long marriages, and the reason is simple: divorce.

Some marriage experts argue that modern relationships crumble under the too-heavy expectation that spouses are responsible for one another's happiness. But economics is probably also at play. Divorce became more prevalent once women entered the workplace en masse, which allowed them to establish economic independence from their husbands and leave unsatisfying unions, something that had been much more difficult in an era when men were the primary breadwinners. Indeed, between 1948 and 2006, the percentage of women who participated in the American workforce nearly doubled, from approximately 32 percent to just over 59 percent. The 1970s witnessed the first time in history that divorce beat out widowhood as the most common cause of marital dissolution. If the divorce rate remains high, sixty- and seventy-year-long marriages could be just as rare in the future as they were in the past.

But while divorce remains common—the best estimate of the national average is 48 percent—it's not evenly distributed throughout society, and in fact the divorce rate is moving along two different trajectories. It appears to be declining among highly educated people who are financially secure, but increasing in marriages between partners who do not have a college education. Princeton sociologist Sara McLanahan maintains that among educated Americans, family life is improving. In most of these households, both mothers and fathers work, so they have more financial assets to invest in raising their children. She also observes a lessening of gender roles, with fathers and mothers sharing parenting roles that once fell almost entirely to women. The result? Mothers and fathers are both engaged with their children and the family has more resources. The shift by mothers from staying home to joining the working world required a difficult cultural transition, but at the other end of the fight, constraints on the gender roles of husbands and wives have eased, benefiting families, which are now wealthier and more egalitarian. On the other hand, McLanahan warns that among the least advantaged Americans, those who are poor and have little education, the family is becoming less stable, with households suffering from a lack of resources, both financial and social.

One last word about marriage: even the best of marriages eventually end. Only in the case of accidents or bizarre coincidences do spouses die at the same time. Nearly always, one spouse is left behind, and because women tend to live longer than men, and to marry men who are several years their senior, women usually outlive their husbands. Let's put it this way: most men are married until they die, but women typically live as widows at some point in their lives. As the difference in life expectancy between women and men narrows, these numbers will change, but for the foreseeable future, widowhood will be typical for women, but not for men.

Outliving a spouse can have serious financial implications in old age, and because women are more likely to outlive their spouses, the problem disproportionately affects them. Caring for a spouse through a prolonged illness takes not only a physical and emotional toll, but it can consume a couple's savings. Laws vary by state, but most require that couples "spend down" personal assets before they are eligible for government assistance for nursing home care. By the time they are widowed, even people who were once financially comfortable may find themselves in a very different situation. If financial problems aren't enough, living alone is a major risk factor for older adults with health problems. It leaves all the household upkeep to one person. It means that if you fall, no one may know, and you have no one to remind you to take your medicine. And of course, loneliness can be a health stressor when husbands and wives have not maintained close relationships outside of their marriage.

Even in old age, Americans are a remarrying sort, but with widows greatly outnumbering the widowers, the odds don't fall in women's favor. Older widowers are far more likely to remarry than widows. It's not clear, on the other hand, that older women even *want* to remarry. Word on the street is that older women are behaving increasingly like young bachelors—eager for romance and companionship, not so eager for marriage. The prospect of being widowed a second time may have something to do with a reluctance to remarry, especially the possibility of another round of caring for an ailing spouse. I recall one widow telling her children, who were urging her to remarry, "I took care of your father for years before he died but I'm not taking care of a stranger"—and the stranger she was referring to was a man she had been dating for more than a year!

Family Life

A short twenty years ago, the typical household included adults and children. Ask any real estate agent—the rule of thumb has been to never buy a house with only one bedroom, because even if you didn't need a second, third, or fourth, the next potential buyer would. Now we are entering an era in which, for most of the life span, family life won't include young children.

At the turn of the twentieth century, the average American woman gave birth to 4.2 children. The birthrate fell during the first half of the century, spiked just after World War II (producing the baby boom), and proceeded to fall again in the second half of the century. Today the birthrate remains half of what it was a century ago. It's not just that women are opting to have fewer children, but that more of them than ever before are opting out of motherhood altogether. In the 1970s, one in ten women didn't have children; today that number is close to one in five. Between delays in childbearing, fewer births, and the decades that parents now spend together as empty nesters, the majority of households in America are child-free.

There is another little-known demographic trend emerging that may have even more profound implications for social life: living alone. Today it's not only one generation per household, it's often one *person* per household. The 2000 census revealed that living alone was more common than any other living arrangement. More than one-quarter of American households include only one adult and no children.

In addition to becoming smaller, families are changing in other ways. It's increasingly common for children to be born to unmarried parents. In 2001, nearly 60 percent of American women were single when they became pregnant with their first child. By the time they gave birth, about half of those mothers were still single. Among African Americans, almost 70 percent of births are to single mothers. Overall, roughly one-third of American births are occurring outside of marriage, but the circumstances surrounding these births can be very different: some are to single mothers who never marry, some are to cohabiting heterosexual couples, and about 4 million American children are being raised by gay and lesbian parents, who are still forbidden from marrying in most states.

Europe is already way ahead of the United States in terms of decoupling childrearing from marriage, but European countries have also been taking strong measures to protect parental relationships with their children. In Scandinavia, for example, parents agree to complicated living and custodial arrangements to ensure that parental bonds with the children stay strong regardless of the state of the couple's relationship. In other words, Europeans are opting out of marriage, but not their commitments to their children. By contrast, in part because childrearing remains so strongly associated with marriage in the United States, the dissolution of a marriage here often means the disappearance of the father. Today just over half of American children live in households with both of their biological parents. Most of the rest live with one parent, usually a single mother, or with reconstituted stepfamilies. Despite our tendency to marry, American children on average experience more changes in their households than European children.

In American households with married parents and children, women are not only having children later and having fewer of them, but returning to work in fairly short order. Seventy percent of mothers of young children work outside the home, and more child-care tasks are being outsourced. About half of parents hire nannies or take their kids to day care; others rely on grandparents for babysitting help.

A widespread myth about the American family is that our national penchant for individualism leads to family disconnectedness once children reach adulthood—that parents strive to launch their children from their homes and that they even measure family success by their children's independence from them. While it's true that some families adhere to this model, it's usually not quite so extreme, and it's certainly not true across different ethnic groups in the United States. Among African, Hispanic, and Asian Americans, weakening ties with adult children would represent a tragic failure of family. But even when children do leave home to pursue schooling and careers, for most families, blood ties are forever, including parental obligations to help their offspring. Older parents function as "insurance" for their adult children, helping them out financially during hard times, taking them in as they go through divorces or financial strains, and giving monetary gifts that help them buy homes and establish businesses. Financial assistance is much more likely to flow from old to young than the other way around. When adult children live with their parents, it's not unusual for the child, rather than the elderly parent, to be the one who is in need of help.

Relationships between brothers and sisters in adulthood haven't received very much attention from social scientists even though they will likely be the longest relationships people will have. What we do know is that although relationships between siblings often fade during young adulthood as everyone heads off on their own, brothers and sisters usually maintain contact with each other through their parents, who function as "communication central" for their scattered flock. It's beginning to look like closeness among brothers and sisters may be revitalized as people age, and that's largely due to the efforts the women in the family put into fostering relationships. Let's put it this way: whether it's sisters, wives, daughters, or grandmothers, women are the keepers of relationships.

The important thing to realize about the future family is that even if it won't look like the *Leave It to Beaver* family, in fact the typical American family never did. Regardless of the family's changing—and shrinking—shape, we can still expect strong connections among family members that will last a lifetime.

Grandparenting

Not many of today's young children live with their grandparents—only about 8 percent do—and most of yesterday's children didn't either. For most of human history, early deaths meant that grandparents were unusual and great-grandparents were rare. Only one hundred years ago, 20 percent of children had lost both of their *parents* before they reached adulthood. So there aren't—and haven't been—a lot of households with multiple generations. Usually co-residence of generations is a function of economic need. Even in regions of Asia where co-residence is socially desirable, the optimum arrangement seems to be having a mother-in-law apartment, or a nearby separate residence, rather than the entire family living under the same roof.

Today, the majority of people who have adult children also have grandchildren. Yet despite the near universality of grandparenting, the role is a supremely flexible one. It's not like parenting, which comes with a strict set of cultural rules about what you must do. For example, it would be illegal for parents to suddenly decide they want nothing to do with their young children, but in the United States, grandparental involvement is entirely optional.

While many grandparents, especially those who live near their adult children, are integrally involved in their grandchildren's lives, others are relatively distant figures who are content to send the occasional birthday card. This is not so everywhere, of course. In China, there are strong expectations that grandparents will participate in their grandchildren's lives. The Chinese have a saying: "Six wallets, one child."

One of grandparents' most frequently reprised roles is that of babysitter. About a third of children under age one, and about one-fifth of preschoolers, are cared for by their grandparents. One in every fifteen grandparents contributes extensive care—that is, the equivalent of a full-time job—for their grandchildren while parents are at work. In times of family trouble, grandparents may even take over as their grandchildren's primary guardians; one in ten grandparents performs this duty for at least six months.

In cases where custodial care is provided by grandparents and the parents are absent, the task can be extremely challenging. It's hard to disentangle the job from the circumstances that lead to the job; under ideal circumstances, parents rarely turn over their children to grandparents to raise. In most cases, this living arrangement comes about because the parents are unable to provide for their children, often because they are habitual drug users, incarcerated, or deceased. Problems that rendered the parents unsuitable to raise their children often affect the kids. For example, the children of drug users often suffer from attention-deficit disorders or physical problems resulting from low birth weight and poor nutrition. They tend to have weakened immune systems, asthma, and hyperactivity. Some are born addicted to heroin; others have brain injuries related to fetal alcohol syndrome or in utero exposure to cocaine. As a result, the children in grandparent-headed households are often among the most challenging to raise, and their care generally takes a physical and emotional toll on the grandparents. Adding to already difficult situations, custodial grandparents are very likely to be living in poverty, without even a spare bedroom for the little ones.

However, when grandparents play an assistive role in child-rearing, instead of completely replacing the parents, the result is usually quite positive. Indeed, Kristen Hawkes, an anthropologist at the University of Utah, believes that grandmothers may be responsible for humans' ability to live well past childbearing age. Most species die shortly after their reproductive years. But humans and a handful of other species that also contribute to grand-child offspring, like lions and vervet monkeys, do not. Hawkes's "grandmother hypothesis" states that survival past the reproductive years held an evolutionary advantage, because it allowed the postmenopausal females, who no longer needed to nurse their own newborns, to shift their attention to ensuring the survival of their grandchildren—and therefore their genetic lineage. They mainly did this by providing the grandchildren with food. So even though—or perhaps because—grandparents were rare, families that included older members had substantial survival advantages.

Evolutionary accounts will always be speculative, but Hawkes supports her claims with data from studies of present-day hunting and gathering communities in Africa. Hawkes observes that when the mother's focus shifts from her toddler to her newborn, the grandmother steps in to help. She has documented a reliable peak in the amount of food grandmothers gather after the birth of the second grandchild. There are some who argue that the grandmother hypothesis would be better termed the grand*parent* hypothesis, but Hawkes prefers "grandmother" because in her work, grandfathers are less likely to share the food they gather.

Longer life means that by the time today's children reach adulthood, it will be commonplace for all four of their grandparents to still be alive. In fact, great-grandparents are the next new thing in grandparenthood. Ken Wachter, a professor of demography at the University of California, Berkeley, is predicting that most young children will have great-grandparents by the year 2030. However, they are such a new demographic phenomenon that although social scientists can tell you that there'll be lots of them in the future, they can't tell you much about the roles they will play in family life. If trends in health improvement continue, great-grandparents may be functionally similar to grandparents today, and a set of eight extra adults prepared to provide the family's youngest members with love, care, and resources could be a very, very positive development for the well-being of children.

What's Next?

So how will this confluence of longer life, fewer births, and the rise of serial marriage, divorce, and nonnuclear households affect the well-being of Americans? To start with, it will change the very shape of the family tree.

Not too long ago, the typical nuclear family tree was a short, stumpy one. Most households were only two generations deep, and usually no more than three generations of each family were alive at any one time. But this family tree had very broad branches spreading out along a horizontal plane, because each generation contained a fairly large number of siblings and cousins.

The nuclear family tree of the future will be shaped more like a beanpole, with each generation having fewer members overall but more generations living at the same time than ever before in human history. It will be typical for four generations to be alive simultaneously; five will not be uncommon and six will be feasible. Yet because there will be fewer children, nuclear families will be smaller in every respect. Children will have fewer siblings and fewer cousins, and if their generation continues current trends, they'll also have fewer children of their own, as well as fewer nieces and nephews.

Many very thoughtful people are worried about this vision of the future family. They're concerned that the continued prevalence of divorce and remarriage will create multiple sets of parents and stepparents, diluting bloodlines and seriously weakening the sense of obligation that family members feel toward one another. They fear that families top heavy with older generations will leave relatively few resources for children. They worry that the trend toward living alone or without young children in the home, caused by the delay of marriage and childbirth, and the extended period of empty-nesting brought about by extra-long lives, will entail loneliness and social disconnection, and that this disconnection will literally make people sick.

But it's important that we don't get distracted by changes in the form of the family, when what really matters is its function. How families are constituted probably doesn't matter a great deal as long as the new structure supports the well-being of its members. What social science is telling us today is that the most important thing is for people to feel embedded in a larger group, a part of something bigger than themselves. They need to know that there are people they can count on if they are in trouble, so that social isolation doesn't wreak its havoc on their mental and physical health. And they need to be needed by others. Stability matters enormously to children; they need to know that there is someone watching out for them and giving them love, not just providing them with food and shelter. Harvard psychiatrist Robert Waldinger puts it this way: "To develop well psychologically, children need at least one person in their lives who is crazy about them." This doesn't have to be a parent or even a relative. It doesn't matter so much *who* fills the role, as long as the role is filled.

In the end, I think the heart of the matter isn't so much the composition or the legal status of those social convoys that Toni Antonucci and Robert Kahn imagined caravanning with us along the life path, but rather their continuity. As parents couple and recouple, and families dissolve and form anew, both children and adults will need relationships that transcend these unions. Whether or not parents marry or cohabit may not make much difference as long as both parents are invested in each other and their children. Blood ties aren't essential either. Whether kinship is legal, as in the case of adoption, or informal, as in the case of "fictive kin," genes don't predict the quality of relationships.

My expectation is that in the twenty-first century, bloodlines will continue to define families, but I also expect that families will increasingly come to include voluntary relatives not related by blood. Because of the lengthening portion of the life span in which Americans live alone or remain childless, they will incorporate close friends into the social space once reserved primarily for kin. While nuclear families with lots of kids were once the norm, there is no longer reason to think that people need to have lots of children (or any) to be happy.

However, it does mean that childless people, or those who live alone, will need to seek connections outside of the nuclear family to moor them to the social collective, so that when hard times hit they do not find themselves adrift. The same thing goes for married couples with children, because they still stand a chance of becoming separated from their partner by divorce or by widowhood, and because they will likely spend a much greater percentage of their lives as empty nesters than their own parents did. Everyone who hopes to enjoy a happy, healthy old age should look for ways to plug themselves into a diverse network of relationships that they form out of affection, not out of obligation, so that if one cherished connection fails, the others will remain intact.

Because the gift of long life is not yet equally distributed throughout society, even people who make it to old age in good health and with a solid network of relationships are at risk of social isolation if all of their connections are only to people their own age, such as their spouse or similarly aged siblings and friends. As a result, one challenge will be to reduce age segregation, encouraging the growth of family and friendship ties *between* generations that are as strong as those within generations. In the best-case scenario, people will find ways to maintain strong family ties but will nurture lasting, close relationships with friends, mentors, neighbors, and coworkers who will become a different sort of family. Human beings make family out of whatever materials are available, and sometimes water is thicker than blood. Families formed by choice have their advantages, mainly that everyone in the group wants to be there.

And while some see the lowering of the birthrate as a liability, I think the best news yet for families in the twenty-first century may be the coming tilt in the ratio of adults to children, adults who hopefully will have a united interest in looking out for the young ones' welfare. History provides important context: Richard Saller observes that over the twentieth century, as fertility rates fell, there was an unprecedented increase in investment in human well-being especially in children and their education. The trend toward adults remaining childless may provide an army of aunts, uncles, neighbors, and family friends who, without children of their own, are happy to play "fairy godparent." Stepparents could also become part of this army. If we could make part-time work more available for young adults, so that new parents could spend more time with their children, we could usher in an era in which we actually do have a village available to raise each child.

I truly hope that healthy aging will benefit from the science of social relationships in the way that parenting benefited from the understanding of child development a century ago. We now have more than individual anecdotes about what contributes to health in old age; we have broad studies that have tracked the lives of thousands of people. It's clear, for example, that long-term relationships are hard work, but the fact that they extend life suggests that they are worth every bit of it. We're seeing what a profound toll social isolation can take on physical health, and that should underscore the importance of providing social support to those among us who are most vulnerable to loneliness. If we're interested in slowing the divorce rate, we should seriously consider the messages of the data showing us that well-educated couples are less likely to divorce, that unrealistic optimism about marriage hurts its chances for survival, and that divorce doesn't necessarily leave people happier several years down the road. Research on conflict resolution, forgiveness, and gratitude—all abilities that seem to deepen with advanced age—is shedding light on skills that could lead to strong, more long-lasting relationships. We're learning that supportive grandparents who assume a "second parent" role appear to have a lot to offer to both their adult children and their grandchildren, but we'll need to work harder to encourage truly vital relationships across increasingly widely spaced generations.

It's important to remember that while these social changes, which are part of our broad collective adaptation to longer life and a modern world, are profound and sweeping, and may feel beyond our control, they still play out in our individual lives in thousands of little choices that we make for ourselves. We will age, and our children will age, in social worlds that we design. It's time to begin thinking seriously about the best types of convoys for journeys that last one hundred years.

5

Collective Supports: Social Security and Medicare

As crucial as supportive relationships with friends and family are to our well-being as we grow older, we also look out for each other in more broadly collective ways. We've built programs and institutions into our culture designed to provide support in the areas where we're most likely to need help in old age: with financial security and access to health care. Social Security and Medicare are the best-known embodiments of this social insurance system, and while they don't make up the entire collective safety net, they are definitely its most durable threads.

Yet, while it's tempting to think of these entitlement programs as stalwart bureaucracies that have existed forever, in historical terms they're practically freshly minted. Social Security was launched less than a century ago, in 1935, and Medicare in 1965. Let's put it this way: the Rolling Stones have been around longer than Medicare. As a result, these institutions don't have much experience adapting to complex demographic changes like the ones that are unfolding as the result of longer life. As the baby boomer generation begins to retire, there will be considerable strain on these systems, and a number of important issues to work out. It's a good idea to start thinking now about what you can expect this system to provide for you, and to realize where you may have to fill in the gaps yourself.

It's also important to understand the implications of potential reforms so that you can be an informed voter. Both of these programs face future financial troubles—Medicare much more so than Social Security—and hotly charged debates about solutions appear almost daily in our newspapers and on our television sets. Inevitably, the debates are framed in monetary terms, focusing on what our aging nation can and cannot afford. When questions are about strained budgets, answers mostly address reducing costs. Yet the ways we think about work and health should extend far beyond budgets to involve thoughtful considerations of how the economic trade-offs associated with reforms would mesh with our national and personal values.

Social Security in the Era of Long Life

We're a nation grounded in cultural ideals of independence, so it's no surprise that at the root of our Social Security system is a very independent-minded premise: older people should be able to survive on their own. While the idea of a formal support system for seniors, administered by the federal government, seems like a no-brainer today, back in the 1930s when Congress was debating such a proposal, the idea smelled, to some, like Communism or socialism. Indeed, the developed world hadn't yet even fully adjusted to the idea that there could *be* a life phase after work. As recently as 1890, nearly everyone worked until they died. In that more agricultural era, retirement could mean merely remaining on the family farm and gradually allowing one's adult children to assume the heavy lifting. In fact, the word *retire* is synonymous with "go to bed," which quite literally described retirement for previous generations. Among those who voluntarily stopped working before they died, the average age of "retirement" was 85.

Historically, families provided most of the support for their elders, which could be a heavy burden if those elders were frail or ill. There were social organizations that offered help here and there: trade unions and fraternal orders looked out for the welfare of their members, and charities and almshouses could provide some measure of relief to the desperately poor, but none of these institutions was equipped to administer support to an entire generation of old people. Company pensions began to be introduced in the United States in the late nineteenth century, but at first the idea was slow to spread. In 1906, the pension program for surviving Civil War soldiers made history when it began allowing veterans to claim benefits based on age, rather than just for disabilities. While it's considered a forerunner to Social Security, the population this program served was minuscule in comparison—less than 1 percent of the U.S. population.

Then along came the Great Depression, which wiped out the life savings of an entire generation and made clear the dreadful toll that poverty could take on the old. By this point, the industrial revolution had already done much to dissolve the structural support families had once provided. Families had become geographically dispersed as younger members left for jobs in the cities, and without their presence older people who were too sick to work could be left with no one to care for them. Since much of the twentieth century's dramatic surge in life expectancy was accomplished in its first half as medical care and the public health infrastructure improved, suddenly there were more elderly people than ever before. Social reformers, outraged by the miseries the elderly suffered during the Depression, began pushing for the adoption of a general old-age pension like the social insurance programs that had taken root in Europe, starting with Germany's in 1889. They argued that the United States owed something to citizens who had labored most of their adult lives, and that old people should not be abandoned to uncertain fates.

President Franklin D. Roosevelt signed the Social Security Act into law in 1935, creating an umbrella program that, in one fell swoop, was designed to aid 30 million unemployed, disabled, or elderly Americans. Roosevelt's statement on signing the law, explaining why it was necessary for the nation's welfare, rings as true today as it did then: "The civilization of the past hundred years, with its startling industrial changes, has tended more and more to make life insecure. Young people have come to wonder what would be their lot when they came to old age. The man with a job has wondered how long the job would last."

Social Security's creation marked a profound shift in thinking about the life span. It made old age a distinct, institutionally recognized phase of life. Robert Binstock, a political scientist at Case Western Reserve University, observes that Social Security led to the creation of an "old age welfare state," a life stage in which the expectation is that government will provide for you. But truthfully, back in 1935 nobody imagined that this welfare state would be particularly generous, or even that many people would be able to take advantage of it. At that time, only about 4 percent of the citizenry made it to Social Security's stated retirement age of sixty-five. People who did live that long in 1935 could expect to live another thirteen years, not another eighteen as the average American 65-year-old can today. As FDR himself pointed out in his radio address on the Social Security Act's third anniversary, "The Act does not offer anyone, either individually or collectively, an easy life—nor was it intended so to do. None of the sums of money paid out to individuals in assistance or in insurance will spell anything approaching abundance. But they will furnish that minimum necessity to keep a foothold; and that is the kind of protection Americans want."

Social Security, which nearly eliminated poverty among the elderly overnight, is arguably the most successful government program in American history. For generations, it has provided real financial security for older individuals and relieved their families of some of the burdens of care, dramatically improving quality of life. It symbolizes humaneness, and a commitment to protecting society's vulnerable citizens. But although it remains one of the most efficient and popular government programs today, Americans are growing increasingly jittery about Social Security's future. Only a minority of young people believe that the program will exist by the time they are eligible to collect benefits.

It's true, there are problems. Social Security was created for a population that died much younger than people do today, and who therefore spent fewer years withdrawing funds from the system. Since 1955, the overall amount of time people spend in retirement has increased by 50 percent! Yet even though life expectancy has increased by sixteen years since Social Security was founded, eligibility age has barely changed. Currently, Social Security's retirement age for someone born in 1950 is sixty-six, and under current law, it will creep up to only sixty-seven by the year 2022.

As the 78 million baby boomers retire, an unprecedented number of people will begin to tap into the system. Barring some sort of widespread health catastrophe, they are likely to remain on the Social Security payroll for a very long time. Not only will the boomers live longer than their parents, they're likely to be more dependent on Social Security than their parents were as well. Many in the boomer generation, and those that follow, will not have the kind of company pension that previous generations received from employers as compensation for their lifelong labor. Instead, they have been expected to supplement their Social Security funds by patching together a postretirement income stream from a variety of voluntarily funded investment vehicles like 401(k)s, Individual Retirement Accounts, and personal savings.

If there's one thing we know about voluntarily saving, it's that Americans don't do nearly enough of it. Only about a third of those eligible to contribute to a 401(k) program do so. In fact, Americans aren't doing well with any kind of savings, even outside of tax-protected retirement vehicles. The personal savings rate, which had been as high as 10.8 percent back in 1984, dipped into negative territory in the year 2005 before creeping back into the black, a nadir witnessed only once before in the nation's history, during the Great Depression. Even among those who did save and invest, the 2008 stock market crash took a toll on their funds and will force some to rely more on Social Security than they had anticipated. As a result, we are approaching a time in which there will not only be more retirees than ever before in history, but they will be more dependent on Social Security than previous generations, and for a longer period of time. For millions of Americans, Social Security is likely to be their *only* source of retirement income.

So where, exactly, does this money come from? In short: out of workers' paychecks. American employees pay a total of 15 percent of their salaries into Social Security and Medicare taxes. No one is exempt. In fact, depending on your income bracket, it may be the only tax you pay on your earnings. It would be comforting to imagine that those taxes are held in a special account somewhere, waiting for the day that you retire. But in fact, Social Security is a pay-as-you-go system, in which the taxes collected from younger workers pay the benefits of retired workers with the implicit promise that the next generation will do the same for them. It is a lovely concept, and historically it has worked because there have always been significantly more workers than retirees. But the balance is about to change. The tipping point, when Social Security taxes no longer cover Social Security payments, will occur in 2016. Current Social Security statements come with a notice that by the year 2037 the program will be collecting enough in payroll taxes to pay only 78 percent of promised benefits.

In fact, since 1993, those Social Security taxes have been just a part of the country's general income stream, along with personal and corporate income taxes. In 2004, the country spent all of our income from all taxes—including those designated for Social Security—and still had to borrow $422 billion to meet the government's current expenses. It is important that we understand that when we speak of the national debt, which had reached approximately $10 trillion by 2008, it makes no allowance for the obligation to pay for Social Security benefits to retirees. According to a report from the Urban Institute, if today we were to purchase an annuity—placed in a real, interest-earning trust fund—that would guarantee promised Social Security benefits to existing workers and retirees, it would cost $13 trillion. In other words, today our federal government owes $10 trillion for its past debts and would still need another $13 trillion to make payments to future retirees. To put this into perspective, according to the World Bank our gross domestic product in 2007—that is, everything we did or made for pay in this country—was approximately $13.8 trillion.

UNDERSTANDING SOCIAL SECURITY BENEFITS

A portion of every dollar that American workers earn is collected by the federal government as a Social Security tax. In this "pay-as-you-go" system, funds contributed by current workers are paid out to retirees, who receive an annuity—a monthly sum paid to them for the rest of their lives. The dollar value of this annuity varies from person to person and is calculated using a formula that considers one's marital status, age at retirement, and average income generated over a lifetime. There is a very loose correlation between one's total contributions in taxes and the value of the annuity.

Your Social Security benefits are based on the average you earned during your thirty-five highest-paid years of employment and are indexed to wages prevailing at the time of your retirement. Much of the strain on Social Security relates to wage indexing, because wages have gone up far more than the cost of living in past decades. In fact, wage indexing has produced an effective annuity for today's Social Security beneficiary that is roughly three times greater in real dollars than it was for those retiring in 1960. Combined with increases in life expectancy, today's beneficiaries will be paid far more than their parents.

Social Security is a social program, not a true investment fund, and its benefits formula favors lower-wage earners. The lowest wage earners receive 90 percent of their wage-adjusted average earnings, whereas the highest earners receive only 15 percent. Beneficiaries with relatively high income in retirement also pay taxes on up to 85 percent of their Social Security income. In other words, taxes collected from the well off fund some portion of the retirements of the less wealthy. In some cases, if there was no Social Security program, higher wage earners could have received a greater return by privately investing the same portion of their income.

Social Security also favors the married. Couples in which only one spouse works receive more benefits than single people do, because *both* husband and wife receive benefits based on the worker. Among the current generations of retirees, many wives were not employed outside of the home, yet they receive Social Security checks worth half of their husbands'. If the husband dies before the wife,

her check is replaced with his. Additionally, because a couples' joint life expectancy is longer than a single person's,
the system further privileges married couples.

You can calculate your retirement benefits on the Social
Security Administration's Web site at http://www.ssa
.gov/planners/calculators.htm, although as every Social
Security statement notes, benefits are subject to the whim
of Congress and could be reduced at any time by a simple
legislative vote. However, historically, Congress has been
remarkably steadfast in its generosity.

Despite these difficulties, it's crucial that we keep Social Security afloat so that it can continue to provide a base level of financial support to American seniors. Some say that there are two old
ages in America, one for the well to do and one for the poor. I
believe that there are probably three or more financial fates in old
age: life is certainly different for wealthy Americans, the middle
class, and the poor. Social Security functions very differently in
each of these economic echelons. In considering these differences, let's leave aside the very, *very* rich. They are the tiny minority who don't need Social Security at all. (However, they do
get checks like everyone else—I've met people who have told me
that they tried to give their checks back, but the government
won't take them!)

Putting these folks aside, for most affluent Americans, Social
Security makes up about a third of their postretirement income.
The people in this economic category worked jobs that paid well,
they saved and invested, and as a result they generally have other

assets and income streams that allow them to enjoy their older years relatively free from financial worries. That gives them license, when difficulties arise, to throw money at their problems. They can hire house cleaners and yard workers to perform strenuous chores, or aides for routine tasks like shopping and bill paying. They can fly adult children in for visits, even if they live in another part of the world, or keep up with them via long-distance phone calls. Relatively advantaged people in our society are likely to have exercised regularly, eaten healthy foods, not smoked, and had consistent health checkups when they were younger, so they arrive at old age in better physical shape. When problems develop, they can afford to enlist medical specialists or shop around for second opinions. While they aren't invulnerable to the financial consequences of serious health crises—only the very, *very* rich are exempt from that particular nightmare—they don't have to lose a lot of sleep worrying about their postretirement finances.

For those in the middle, Social Security makes up about one-half to two-thirds of their monthly retirement income. These are the folks who worked hard and saved what they could but never became truly wealthy. By the time retirement arrives, they may have paid down their mortgages and accrued modest pensions or savings, but it would be very difficult for them to manage without Social Security. Their financial fate is often uncertain; as long as life goes along as planned, they do fine, but unpredictable increases in the cost of gas or food affect them very much. An unexpected loss, such as the failure of their company pension or a serious illness, could easily wipe out all of their assets. In old age the middle class tends to get caught in a financial bind: they are too well-off to qualify for assistance from other government programs, yet not well off enough to rest easy knowing that their savings can cover any need that might arise. As a consequence, old age—and preparing for it—can be a time of financial worry for middle-class Americans.

At the top of their list of anxieties is the possibility of a prolonged illness that would burden their families with providing in-home care, an expense that is not reimbursed by Medicare and is usually not covered by private medical insurance either. Since most middle-class people don't qualify for public assistance and don't have enough expendable income to hire household or nursing aides as needed, family members usually provide whatever day-to-day assistance they can. However, if long-term skilled nursing care is required for one spouse, the expense may place his or her partner in a highly precarious position. Thanks to government programs that require older Americans to "spend down" savings before becoming eligible for assistance, a significant minority of elderly people become poor for the first time in old age. Most of them are widows who are pushed out of the middle class due to the expense of seeing a dying spouse through a long illness.

When medical disasters arise, some middle-class people sell their homes in order to pay the bills, but even so the value of the houses owned by people in this slice of America is usually not high enough to underwrite their expenses for long, especially when nursing homes, on average, cost $70,000 a year. Keep in mind that once people in the middle class lose their homes, they lose the familiarity of their neighborhood, access to old friends, their regular chats with the nice woman at the post office who always asked about their son—all those things that help one feel socially connected and are an integral part of both physical and mental well-being. As a result, for the middle class, Social Security provides sufficient support for ordinary needs but is not enough to provide complete peace of mind, or to stave off the possibility of financial catastrophe.

Finally, the poorest Social Security beneficiaries rely on it for more than 80 percent of their income. Public or charitable assistance provides a good chunk of the rest. People who live in this financial echelon are entirely at the mercy of these support systems, because they have virtually no other income from pensions or savings plans. Worse, because they were typically low-wage earners before they retired, their Social Security checks are smaller than those of workers who had more lucrative jobs. Technically, only one in twelve elderly people lives in poverty, but according to the Center on Budget and Policy Priorities, without Social Security that number would be closer to one in two. Yet Social Security alone provides an income only marginally above the poverty level. In 2008, the official poverty level for a couple was $14,000, while the average Social Security payment for a retired husband and wife was $19,400.

To give you a sense of how financially strapped people in this group are, consider something that happened to a very poor woman I met through my work at the Over 60s Health Center in Berkeley, California. Because I know her as a patient I've changed some details to disguise her true identity, but the story is otherwise accurate. Let's call her Nettie. After the Loma Prieta earthquake that shook the Bay Area in 1989, Nettie had to move and, as a consequence, also changed banks. She requested that the

Social Security office deposit her checks into her new account. However, the switch wasn't made. As a result, Nettie inadvertently wrote several bad checks, and the bank charged her a fee for each check that was returned. Because she didn't have additional savings or income that she could use to cover those fees, those overdrafts meant that Nettie couldn't pay other bills. Both her electricity and phone service were shut off, and even more late fees were charged to her accounts.

To make matters worse, well-intentioned advisers from the bank and utility companies assumed that Nettie must be losing her memory, so they convinced her to turn her bill paying over to a volunteer at a charitable organization. Nettie is very sharp, so it was pretty humiliating for her to be put on a budget by a man not half her age who told her how to spend the little money that she had. Still, her self-confidence had been sufficiently shaken that she went along. In the end, it took her five years to straighten out her finances and get back on track! Whenever I hear people talk about policy changes that will reduce poor people's incomes even by small amounts, I think of Nettie and am reminded of just how financially stretched the elderly poor are in America.

Yet interestingly, for people who have been extremely poor their entire lives, government programs sometimes offer a better life in old age than they have known before. For example, subsidized senior housing may provide them a level of safety and comfort they did not have in their old neighborhoods. Very low-income seniors may be eligible for supplemental income from county programs or assistance from charitable organizations. Additionally, Medicaid—health insurance for which people qualify by income—pays for some services that Medicare does not, including in-home assistance and over-the-counter medications.

For elderly people who have always been poor, health is a serious worry. They are far more likely than more affluent Americans to come to old age with costly and disabling chronic conditions. Both arthritis and osteoporosis are more common for poor women in old age than for their wealthier counterparts, reflecting hard lives, poor nutrition and a lack of medical care. Among the poor, diabetes is less likely to be diagnosed or treated early and consequently is more likely to lead to blindness, amputation, and poor circulation by the time people reach old age. Similarly, unchecked high cholesterol and hypertension increase the risk of cognitive impairment later in life. Even hearing loss is more severe in poor elderly people, especially among men whose occupations exposed them to constant noise. Consequently, even though poor people may need or want to supplement their lower Social Security incomes by continuing to work in old age, they are often physically less able to do so.

It's important also to recognize that race is intertwined with social class. Thirty-five percent of older African American women live at or below the poverty level. More than a third of older African American and Latino households rely on Social Security for *all* of their income. Poverty rates among older Asian Americans are relatively low, although they differ by geographical region and ethnic group; for example, poverty rates among the Indonesian and Samoan elderly are strikingly high. Overall, when Social Security is jeopardized, American minorities are at special risk.

With so many people depending so heavily on Social Security, it's clear that it provides a safety net we cannot afford to lose. The good news is that of the many problems facing the federal government today, stabilizing Social Security is one that we can fix.

True, it will require some adjustments, and we'll have to approach the topic without the emotional heat that often flares when politicians raise the prospect of reform to scare voters, or economists say that the system is unsustainable. Social Security is unlikely to go bankrupt, but if we want to keep it solvent for our grandchildren, more people, starting with the boomers, will have to work longer.

As valuable and successful as the Social Security program has been, it has inadvertently imposed a kind of straitjacket on our work culture by keeping the standard retirement age low, even in the face of extended life span. But we could both ease and delay demands on the system by encouraging productive employment among people who are still able and willing to work past age sixty-five. Let me be clear: I hope we don't raise the eligibility age across the board, particularly during this transitional time when many boomers have been counting on retiring at a particular age. We'll want to protect people who have worked physically laborious jobs or ones that are just so dreary that they count every day to retirement. Let's not create problems for those who lack the physical stamina to continue working but whose health may not be sufficiently bad to qualify them for disability insurance. Instead, the more humane solution is to encourage willing and able people to remain in the labor force by rewarding them for it.

To some extent, Social Security already does this, but in a very limited way. Today retirees may begin receiving income from Social Security as early as age sixty-two, but their monthly benefits are greater if the start date for receiving them is delayed. However, this benefit increase is truncated at age seventy. The program currently provides no incentive for delaying benefits—and continuing work—beyond that age.

Perhaps most important, we should get rid of *disincentives* to work. At present, all workers pay Social Security taxes. In their book *Putting Our House in Order: A Guide to Social Security & Health Care Reform,* my colleagues former secretary of state George Shultz and economist John Shoven suggest that after a certain period of time—perhaps forty years in the workforce—people should no longer have to pay these taxes. This would effectively reward their continued work with a 6.2 percent "raise" created by the resulting bump in their take-home pay. Additionally, employers would no longer have to pay Social Security taxes for these workers, making retaining older employees a more attractive bargain. (Today, employers are often reluctant to keep them on the payroll because of the higher salaries they command.)

We could also reduce the tax rate on the modest amounts of income that some people receive in addition to their Social Security checks. Currently it approaches 30 percent, and if that is earned income it is also subject to a 15 percent FICA tax, making the net tax rate far higher than the income tax rate paid by millionaires. As a result, certain workers between age sixty-two and full retirement age face an almost unbelievable penalty. For every two dollars they earn, one is subtracted from their Social Security payment—effectively a 50 percent tax. Thus, given a certain combination of circumstances, taxes and Social Security codes become grossly confiscatory.

Historically, these tax rates were intended to nudge older workers to clear out of the workforce, thereby ensuring that there would be enough jobs available for young people. But today the economics are clear: in a pay-as-you go system, the more workers there are, the stronger the system. Shoven and Shultz disavow the notion that encouraging older people to work longer will take jobs away from the young. They call this fallacy the "lump of labor" hypothesis—the idea that there is only a set amount of work to be done. Instead, they argue that if people work longer the entire economy will grow. They point out that if today's twentysomethings stop working at the same age their parents will thanks to longer life spans, they will spend even *more* years in retirement than their parents, creating a heavy demand on the Social Security system starting around the year 2050. However, if they stay in the workforce a few years longer and then enjoy a retirement the same length as their parents', the total hours worked in 2050 will grow 9 percent, swelling the GDP by 6 or 7 percent. That means more money for programs like Social Security. "Thinking of the economy as a pie," they write, "we can clearly see that the larger the pie, the easier it will be to allocate money to entitlement spending." In other words, the bigger the pie, the bigger your slice of it will be.

One very sensible part of any Social Security solution should be to move away from thinking that its rules are set in stone. Instead, we need to build more flexibility into the system. For example, Social Security's eligibility age has remained virtually unchanged since the 1930s, but in light of the tremendous financial problems posed by sticking to this outdated guideline, Shoven suggests that the government should regularly revisit eligibility age, basing it on life expectancy at age sixty-five instead of how old a person is. This way, as life expectancy past age sixty-five rises, so will retirement age. These increases could be made slowly, in increments of months, not years, allowing people time to adjust their expectations and plan ahead.

Similarly, adjustments to the amount of money people receive from Social Security have traditionally been indexed to wages, not prices. Yet because wages have risen far more than the cost of living, the absolute value of Social Security for pensioners is more generous today than it was for previous generations—and that gap is growing. John Shoven likes to ask his undergraduate students at Stanford if they hope that they'll get the same inflation-adjusted payout from Social Security when they retire that their parents will get today. Most of them wave their hands to indicate that they do. Then he asks them whether they feel they should get three times more than their parents will. Not one hand is raised. But without changes to the system, wage indexing will likely produce this effect.

I expect that we also need to make Social Security distributions themselves more flexible. The program's current method of allocating benefits is rigid; once a worker decides to begin collecting benefits, those benefits remain fixed for the rest of his or her life. In reality, the need for a safety net increases with age. The older people are, the more likely it is that they will have needs that require out-of-pocket expenses, such as for unreimbursed medical care or hiring assistance for household tasks that become harder to do at advanced ages, like mopping the floor or shoveling snow. If Social Security benefits increased with time, they could at first supplement income for people who are still partially employed, then gradually provide more support as people work fewer hours, and at last, for the very old, fully support complete retirement and finance an assisted-living environment if needed. Although increasing benefits with age sounds simple and reasonable, it would require a fundamental change in Social Security philosophy.

But that philosophy is ours to change. We can and we should strengthen Social Security so that it remains healthy and reliable long into the future. It is arguably the most successful government-sponsored public program ever instituted in the nation: it saves the poorest among us from destitute lives and is an important part of retirement income for the vast majority of middle-class Americans, who would be hard pressed to enjoy a financially stable retirement without it. In debating the future of Social Security we must recognize two things: that Social Security is an insurance program most Americans need, and that Social Security is not, all by itself, a sufficient retirement plan. We depend on it as a safety net, but we also must understand that we should not rely on it to provide all the money we'll need for a comfortable old age. However, if we adapt to our changing demographics by asking the majority of older people to work a few years longer, the Social Security system will not only survive in the short term but still be there for our grandchildren. Just as important, if we can get rid of the antiquated expectation that our full retirement is demanded at sixty-five, talented individuals can continue to make real contributions to the workforce for much longer. As a nation, we cannot afford to lose the talent older workers can provide.

What's Next for Medicare?

Social Security's complement is Medicare, a federally sponsored program that provides health insurance to Americans from age sixty-five onward, implicitly acknowledging that aging brings with it increased needs for medical attention. Medicare was designed to address the plight of older people who, once they were no longer employed, had minimal incomes but faced mounting medical costs that could not be covered by Social Security alone, and who could not obtain private health insurance because insurers deemed them too risky.

Frankly, if you were an insurance company you too might be reluctant to insure older people. The health care expenses of a person over age sixty-five are on average three to five times those of a younger person. In its 2007 *State of Aging and Health in America* report, the Centers for Disease Control and Prevention concluded that at least 80 percent of the elderly have one chronic condition such as diabetes, arthritis, heart disease, or cancer, and 50 percent of them have more than one. Its previous report, in 2004, had estimated that the average seventy-five-year-old takes five prescription drugs. And while technological advances in the twentieth century extended life, in a way they also extended the process—and the cost—of dying. One hundred years ago, the period of infirmity before death was about two weeks and people died at home. Today people are infirm for roughly two years and die in hospitals.

In the 1940s, Harry S. Truman became the first American president to champion the idea of national health insurance—for people of all ages—but the idea was ahead of its time, and was denounced in some quarters as socialized medicine. It was not until 1965, with the nation's growing senior population creating a more urgent need among the elderly for an alternative to private insurance, that Lyndon B. Johnson signed the Medicare Bill into law. (Truman was at his side, and LBJ promptly awarded him the nation's first Medicare card.) Medicare is funded through a payroll tax: employers must withhold and match 1.45 percent from each worker's paycheck. "Through this new law," Johnson promised upon signing the bill, "every citizen will be able, in his productive years when he is earning, to insure himself against the ravages of illness in his old age."

The United States is the only country in the world that follows the practice of guaranteeing health insurance *only* to the elderly. Indeed, Medicare was a remarkable innovation for a society that does not consider health insurance an entitlement; roughly 45 million Americans don't have any health insurance at all. Some of them can't afford it, some would qualify for public programs but are not enrolled, and others—mostly healthy young adults— can afford it but decide to take their chances without it. Ironically, even though American children and young adults are not guaranteed access to health care, it would certainly be cheaper to insure the young than the old, and the long-term payoff in terms of lifelong health and productivity may be greater. Nevertheless, at age sixty-five, American citizens who have paid taxes for at least ten years are automatically eligible for really good health insurance.

THE A, B, C, (D)S OF MEDICARE

Like Social Security, Medicare is a social program, not a conventional insurance policy or an investment. It's another pay-as-you-go system through which younger workers provide for the benefits of older retirees through their payroll taxes. At retirement, all American workers in effect receive a health insurance policy covering a large portion of their medical expenses for the rest of their lives. Benefits are the same for all who are eligible regardless of their previous tax contributions. If such a policy were commercially available, it would be worth several hundred thousand dollars.

Medicare is divided into four sections. Part A is financed entirely through payroll taxes and covers hospital inpatient stays, skilled nursing and hospice care, and very limited home health care.

Medicare's second section, Part B, is voluntary (a euphemism for "costs extra"). It covers doctors' visits and outpatient charges, lab tests, medical supplies, and very limited home health care beyond what is in Part A. Beneficiaries contribute to Part B by opting for a modest deduction from their Social Security checks. Until 2007, all Medicare Part B beneficiaries paid the same monthly premiums regardless of their income; currently premiums are slightly higher for a small percentage of beneficiaries who have relatively high incomes.

The most recent additions to the Medicare program are Parts C and D. Part C, commonly referred to as "Medicare+Choice" or "Medicare Advantage," was added in 1997 to include managed care plans. Under Part C, patients agree to stay within a selected network of doctors and hospitals, and in return they get additional benefits not included in traditional Medicare, such as dental, foot, and vision care. Roughly one in five beneficiaries takes advantage of Part C; the majority decline it in favor of being able to choose any doctor or hospital that takes Medicare patients.

Medicare Part D, first available in 2006, is the biggest and costliest expansion in coverage since the program was created. Under Part D, Medicare provides beneficiaries coverage for prescription drugs that they take at home. (Drugs administered in a hospital or doctor's office have been covered from the beginning.) This is a significant boost in coverage, considering that about 30 percent of all medication prescribed in the United States is for people over sixty-five years old, even though they currently make up only 13 percent of the population. Part D is financed much like Part B, partly through beneficiary premiums and the rest through taxes. The Prescription Drug Act gave rise to a proliferation of specialized insurance companies to administer the program; beneficiaries in some parts of the country have more than twenty individual drug insurance plans to choose from, each with different benefits and different premiums.

Unfortunately, Medicare is in serious jeopardy today, far more so than Social Security. Medicare currently covers one in seven Americans, either because they are older than sixty-five or because they are disabled, and those numbers will balloon thanks to the retirement of the boomers, who started becoming eligible for benefits in 2008. By 2030, Medicare enrollment will have nearly doubled to an estimated 79 million people, drastically increasing its overall cost. Many of these new beneficiaries will be previously uninsured people who arrive at age sixty-five with untreated chronic conditions that have worsened their overall health. After years of untreated diabetes, for example, neuropathies can develop, skin is more easily injured, and wounds take longer to heal. Similarly, left untreated, elevated levels of cholesterol thicken the walls of blood vessels and increase the risk of stroke, heart disease, and cognitive decline. Economists agree, however, that the biggest problem isn't just the sheer number of boomers who are about to become eligible for coverage, or that so many were previously uninsured. The elephant in the room is the enormous cost of providing continually innovative and technologically sophisticated care to a very long-lived population.

Something has to change in the way we approach health care, or else as a country we will face a financing crisis. While the Social Security program is $13 trillion behind in the funds needed to make payments to retirees, the corresponding figure for Medicare is around $30 trillion. While our Social Security obligations can be satisfied through relatively minor changes to the benefits schedule and by providing incentives for longer workforce participation, the solution to the Medicare funding problem cannot be realized without addressing the much larger problems inherent in our health care system itself. No benign tweaking of taxes or benefits rules will solve the problem, and you can't ask people to delay medical care the way you can ask them to delay full retirement. Unfortunately, American health care financing has gradually become a messy, complicated, inefficient hodgepodge, with Medicare for the elderly, Medicaid for the very poor, employer-based health insurance for those who work at large companies, and nothing for tens of millions of families. There are few incentives for providers, patients, service industries, or companies that develop new medical technologies to reduce the cost of care. For solutions, we must look critically at the way the entire health care system is funded in the United States.

In 2007, the Stanford Center on Longevity gathered a number of the nation's top economists, along with Republican and Democratic political experts, and began a project exploring different proposals for health care reform. The number one problem, the gathered experts agreed, is that American health care is too expensive. The United States spends more per capita on health care than any other industrialized nation—in excess of a quarter more than any other country, and close to 90 percent more than the Western European countries to which we generally compare ourselves. If Americans were healthier than other populations, we might conclude that the extra costs are worth it. But we're not. If we lived longer or had lower infant mortality rates, that might be worth it too. But we don't. In Western Europe, where many countries offer universal health care to their citizens, life expectancy is longer and infant mortality rates are lower than in the United States. Let me be clear: The *quality* of American health care is generally excellent. The country boasts superb physicians and leads the world in the treatment of certain diseases like cancer. The problem is in the bloated and inequitable way that the system delivers health care to the population as a whole.

Because Medicare operates within the U.S. health care system, a few general points about the broader system bear mentioning. Our system ostensibly operates as a free market in which providers and insurers vie for customers, but several factors dilute the very forces that make markets work. Both inside and outside of Medicare, our financing system has a perverse set of disincentives to containing costs. Doctors and hospitals, for example, are paid by the number of patients they see and procedures they perform, so they have incentive to dole out procedures without concern for expense. If you've been in the hospital, you know this. Nurses, aides, and doctors come in and out of your room telling you that this or that test has been ordered. They offer you various medications, order X-rays and other types of scans, put you on treadmills, and decide whether to keep you a day longer or not. No one talks with you about whether it's worth the money. Some 30 to 40 percent of medical procedures are ineffective or redundant. An estimated thirty thousand Medicare patients die each year from unnecessary or unproven care. Peter Orszag, former director of the Congressional Budget Office and now head of the Office of Budget and Management, maintains that ineffective or redundant medical procedures cost the nation roughly $700 billion each year.

Because of this lack of transparency, and because such a large portion of the charges are absorbed by insurance providers, very few patients know what the medical services they receive actually cost. Insured patients may see big numbers on their medical bills, but they quickly skim over them to the bottom line indicating what they must pay, which is usually a small slice of the total cost, thanks to the magical discounting that results from agreements negotiated between the insurer and the provider. The last medical bill I received stated a price that the provider billed and a new price that the insurance company renegotiated with the provider, and then printed in the bottom corner was some fraction of the original price that I was expected to pay. Compared to the cost billed at the top of the form I was paying a pittance, so I felt like I got a great deal. But in fact it is hard for us to know the true cost of our medical care. If, like most Americans, your employer is absorbing much of your health care insurance expense, you pay an invisible price in the form of lower wages. Not only that, but employers who are shouldering the burden of high health care insurance costs pass them along as price increases on the products they manufacture, making them more expensive for local markets and less competitive on the world scene.

As you may imagine, there is lots of behind-the-scenes finagling between providers and insurance companies, and this costs money too. Roughly 20 percent of health care costs are attributed to administrative expenses associated with this complex system of payment. Because there are often two or three rounds of approvals, rejections, and negotiations about who pays for what before payments are made to the care provider, the system is top heavy with paperwork. The only people who are charged full sticker price for health care are the uninsured. Of course, uninsured people rarely shop for care at all; they either get treatment in hospital emergency rooms when a crisis arises or don't get any at all.

Even worse, not only is health care in America already more expensive than anywhere else on earth, but our roundtable of experts pointed out that costs are escalating faster in the United States than anywhere else. All of the economists participating in our project agreed that expensive new technologies, medical procedures, and drugs are the principal reason for growing health care costs. In 2005, Dana Goldman, director of health economics at the Rand Corporation, and several of his colleagues published a fascinating article in which they forecasted the arrival of several innovative medical treatments that could conceivably come on the market within the next thirty years, like a new generation of pacemakers that could reduce the risk of stroke by 50 percent and a telomerase inhibitor that could cure cancer in half of the patients who take it. However, such very high-end technologies would cost a *lot* of money, and adopting them would substantially increase the cost of care. The price of that pacemaker that Goldman described, for example, would be $30,000. The telomerase inhibitor, which would need to be administered for the rest of a person's life, would cost $177 a month. These are just two small examples of why economists are so sober about the prospects of a "silver bullet" that would both improve health and bring down costs. We don't want to stop innovation, but without containing costs we'll sink the health care financing system. It is, frankly, a terrible mess.

So, with Medicare fully entrenched in the mire of the larger health care system and 78 million baby boomers headed its way, how on earth do we keep the system afloat? How can we tighten our belts when new cutting-edge medical technologies are extending life but escalating costs? You might suspect that better preventive health measures could be the solution to Medicare's woes, because they would head off—or at least delay—illness and perhaps mitigate its severity, and the amount of care needed. Surprisingly, however, while prevention is a highly worthwhile endeavor, it isn't an especially good way to reduce costs.

It's a little shocking, but it makes sense once you give it some thought. First, although some prevention efforts, like colorectal screening, both improve health and save money, the majority of prevention efforts don't. In a review of more than one thousand studies, Joshua Cohen, professor of medicine at Tufts–New England Medical Center, and his colleagues concluded that fewer than 20 percent of preventive health measures accomplish both objectives. Screening all people over age sixty-five for diabetes, for example, costs far more than treating those people who actually develop the disease. Some preventive measures, like prostate screening in men over age seventy-five, actually worsen health outcomes because they can lead to unnecessary interventions. Second, when prevention measures do work, people end up living longer and thus consuming even more medical care over the course of a lifetime. And finally, most health care dollars are spent in the final two years of life when people are in the throes of serious illness. Even though this moment may be postponed by good preventive care, death ultimately comes even to long-lived people, who face the same end-of-life costs. Pondering this paradox of prevention, I once asked Dana Goldman, a very patient friend, "You're saying that the only way for the health care system to save money is for people to die?" He nodded like I was *finally* beginning to understand and then quickly added, "I'm not saying we shouldn't do it. Prevention is great, but understand: it costs money."

Since preventive care is such a double-edged sword, it alone cannot be our main method of reducing the strain on the Medicare system. The key to keeping Medicare solvent is going to be bringing down the cost of treatment and wisely spending the Medicare dollars we do have on the treatments that give us the most bang for our buck. Currently, Medicare pays for virtually any medical service that is effective, even if one procedure is far more expensive than its alternatives. Take spinal fusion surgery, for example, used frequently as a treatment for lower back pain. It's expensive, painful, and only sometimes effective in reducing pain. Recently evidence has surfaced that it appears to have no better outcomes than noninvasive procedures like exercise and cognitive therapy, which teaches strategies, like relaxation exercises, to ease pain. But from a Medicare reimbursement view, it's just as legitimate an option as far less expensive alternatives.

Historically, cost-effectiveness has never played much of a role in decisions about Medicare coverage. In fact, the government's track record on negotiating prices is lousy. If you're skeptical, consider that in 2004, when the government approved the largest expansion of Medicare in its history (Part D, the prescription drug bill), it accepted a truly remarkable provision prohibiting it from negotiating prices for the drugs that insurers supply to their customers. As a result, drug manufacturers get whatever price they choose.

My colleague Alan Garber, a professor of both economics and medicine at Stanford, chaired the advisory committee for the Medicare Evidence Development and Coverage Advisory Committee for the Centers for Medicare and Medicaid Services, the national committee that advises the government about what Medicare should cover. As a physician, economist, and government adviser, Garber sees the problems from a vantage point that few of us have. He maintains that we need to stop the magical thinking that health care should be free and find fair ways to make hard choices. Medicare cannot continue to pay for any and all medical procedures that enter the marketplace, especially ones for which there is little or no evidence of therapeutic value. Garber argues that it's time to consider not just evidence about the effectiveness of procedures, but their cost-effectiveness.

However, we currently have no systematic way to achieve this. The Food and Drug Administration watches out for drugs that pose a danger to people, but no one monitors new drugs and technologies to make sure they are cost-effective. Some people will maintain that any existing procedure should be made available to any patient who needs it, but we should understand that this entails trade-offs too. If we were to adopt that thinking, we'd need to raise taxes dramatically to pay for the costs of health care. Even worse, this approach encourages spiraling costs. Why should any drug or medical technology developer care about cost-efficiency if there are no market incentives to do so?

Virtually everyone would agree that neither Medicare nor private insurers should have to pay for ineffective treatments. The harder calls to make will be about whether they should cover procedures that might be slightly more effective than their alternatives but cost twice as much. Who makes those decisions? The insurance companies cannot be the arbiters. Given their obvious conflict of interest, their choices would always be suspect. Most patients want doctors to decide, but doctors aren't necessarily concerned about saving money for insurance companies or the government either. Remember, most doctors are paid by methods that factor in the number and expense of procedures they perform. (In large part, this accounts for the rather dramatic differences in income between surgeons and pediatricians, since surgeons perform more expensive procedures.) Perhaps even more important, with new kinds of drugs, surgeries, devices, and diagnostic tests constantly becoming available, doctors often don't know which are the most cost-effective to choose.

Our Stanford experts endorsed an idea that is gaining ground in Washington. We put it to the public and they liked it too: an independent health care board. This nonpartisan board would be constituted of a group of distinguished health economists and physicians who would consider the cost and effectiveness of new and existing technologies, medications, and procedures. The board would need to have substantial funding to do the necessary comparative research, and it would be very important that membership not be tilted toward political appointees, just as it would be important not to stack the membership with representatives from any one industry, like pharmaceuticals. My preference would be for the board to be appointed and managed by the National Academy of Sciences, which is an organization of scientists that operates outside of government but advises it. These experts would rank procedures based on how they stack up against their alternatives, both in terms of effectiveness and price. For example, they would compare not only the relative effectiveness of two drugs but also the relative effectiveness of drugs versus surgery. Their recommendations would not be binding on patients or insurance companies. However, the status and independence of the board would give it expert credibility.

I expect that, for physicians, the board's recommendations would become a guide to "best practices." For insurers, they would guide coverage decisions, giving them helpful information about which treatments are most efficacious but also holding them accountable for reimbursing high-value care. (Such a board might ultimately recommend, for example, that insurers reimburse services like in-home care that are currently not covered but are highly cost-effective and very much desired by consumers.)

Finally, knowledge generated by the board, properly translated for a consumer audience, would help individual patients understand what works and what doesn't, giving them far more confidence in the system. When insurance companies refuse to cover particular treatments, patients often worry that the grounds for denial are purely financial and have nothing to do with the treatment's efficacy. Mind you, sometimes these suspicions are valid. However, having an independent board rather than the insurance companies evaluate which treatments are worth paying for would help people understand why some aren't covered, and make it very difficult for insurers to refuse to pay for effective procedures. The point would not be to withhold good treatments because they are too expensive, but rather to save money by reducing the use of ones that don't work, or don't work as well as other less expensive options. No matter what was recommended, individuals would be free to pursue expensive treatments if they preferred them, but their insurance companies might choose not to fully reimburse them.

Patching the Holes in Our Collective Safety Nets

Together, Social Security and Medicare have changed the quality of life for older Americans, but these venerable institutions need adjustments as we move into a historically unprecedented era of long life. Because these programs are so valuable, the prospect of changing them makes Americans nervous. And to be clear, longer, healthier lives are important to the economy. However, if we hold on too tightly and refuse to change, in less than twenty years Medicare and Social Security together will consume more of the federal budget than all other federal programs combined. The programs could place so much strain on the federal budget that we would have less funding available to pursue other endeavors like reducing pollution and improving our schools and highways. We've reached the point in the road where economics must intersect with ethics. Many argue that the measure of a society is the way that it supports its elderly citizens, but without changes to our current system we are headed toward a culture with great inequities.

The 2008 financial meltdown may be just what the baby boomers needed to reawaken their generation's proclivity for activism. Little did we know back at Woodstock that changing health care entitlements and Social Security could be an enduring mark we leave on society. But it is the boomers' responsibility to make sure these programs are changed so that they are fair, even if it means working longer. Today's sixty-five- to seventy-five-year-olds are hardly different in health and capabilities from those aged fifty-five to sixty-five. It makes no sense for young workers to support other *healthy* people so they do not have to work.

In my mind, the most pressing reason that people should work longer is that they can! It's a great achievement, and people are happiest when they are needed. Instead of urging competent workers to retire and losing the contributions they make to productive societies, surely at this point it makes sense to rid Social Security of disincentives to work. We should develop new policies like phased-in benefits, tax breaks for longtime workers, and flexible working hours that allow for "semi-retirements," all encouraging people to stay employed longer.

As for Medicare, the biggest change we must make will not be encouraging boomers to enter the system later, but thoughtfully evaluating what the system should provide for them. Victor Fuchs, professor of economics at Stanford, argues convincingly that national discussions need to proceed from a set of facts, not political assertions, about health care in America. We must not let runaway prices drain Medicare financing by making the system pay for treatments without proven benefit, or for those that provide the same benefits as their alternatives but at many times the price. We will need an independent board to carefully and fairly review these options. Making sure that Medicare pays for only the most effective, cost-efficient treatments will encourage pharmaceutical companies, medical technology developers, and other innovators to compete with each other, using market forces to drive prices down. We will need to build incentives for individuals to be more price conscious so that they too contribute to the market forces that bring costs down. We'll also need to assure the American public that a more limited set of options will not mean being forced to choose among the lowest-quality treatments.

At the same time, we should encourage Medicare to cover services it currently does not that would be truly useful and would alleviate a good deal of financial strain on middle-class Americans, like in-home assistance for gravely ill people who wish to stay at home, so that their loved ones are not unduly burdened with their care. Additionally, although high-quality preventive care throughout the life span entails its own costs, it will help us ensure that people come to old age in the best physical condition possible. Surveys suggest that most Americans believe everyone should have access to basic health care, and indeed that would be another way of alleviating the problem we are about to face today as millions of boomers retire after lives of hard work and minimal health care, with chronic conditions that have progressed unchecked and will now require extensive, and expensive, therapies.

In revamping the system we should think not only about fixing the looming financial problems of today—though that is essential—but also about how to structure a new system that best encourages long, healthy, and productive lives. Let's think ahead to questions about long-term sustainability, and how we can change the system now to help our children and grandchildren be healthy, engaged, and productive in their golden years. I would like to see a set of national discussions occur so that we can learn more about what Americans actually want from their social insurance system. We should have town hall meetings so that people can talk about why they want to retire, and what could entice them to stay on. I would like to see a systematic evaluation of new medical procedures and technologies, along with open debates about their cost-effectiveness and desirability. We need to get members of all generations—not just those on the verge of retirement today—to talk honestly not only about how they envision their retirement needs, but what they are willing to do today to make sure those needs can be met later.

Considering the importance of what is at stake, it would be untenable not to make adjustments so that we can avoid easily foreseen problems. Understanding the choices and making his or her voice heard in the public discourse is every citizen's responsibility. It may also be the boomers' most lasting legacy.

6

Investing in Our Future: The Case for Science and Technology

The scientific and technological advances of the twentieth century revolutionized the way we live; it was the era that gave us everyday wonders like the television, the airplane, and the Internet, and of course the panoply of hygiene-related technologies that helped make long life possible, like refrigeration, safe water supplies, and sanitary waste disposal. Yet ironically, the notion of extending the human life span was rarely the driving force behind any of these innovations. For the most part, they were simply meant to improve the general living conditions of people who hoped to live out their traditional threescore and ten. Likewise, many of the twentieth century's great advances in medical science were precipitated by the need to address an immediate threat, like quashing an epidemic, rather than the desire to extend life itself. Nevertheless, these fundamental advances, along with broad cultural changes primarily meant to protect the health of the young, had the largely unexpected consequence of stretching out adulthood. This has presented the scientists of the twenty-first century with an entirely new frontier to explore: old age itself.

Still, it would be a terrible mistake to conclude that increased life expectancy should translate into a call for more research concerning only—or even principally—the diseases of old age. More broadly, we need to ask: How can we use science and develop technologies to optimize human functioning so that we can live in good health for nine or ten decades? This will require an entirely new perspective my colleagues and I have been calling "longevity science." Longevity science is a collaborative, interdisciplinary approach to resolving the difficulties and questions posed by old age. It is concerned with the prevention of disease and improvements in quality of life but recognizes that we've pushed willpower and self-discipline just about as far as we can. If we've learned anything over the last fifty years of proclaiming the merits of healthy eating and exercise to a nation that has easy access to drive-throughs and hundreds of channels of cable TV, it's that asking individuals to choose to behave one way in a world that encourages quite different behaviors *does not work*. We'll need science and technology to construct environments that encourage healthy lives.

The Stanford Center on Longevity was established in 2006, and our hope is that Stanford can do for human aging around the world what it did for communications technology in Silicon Valley. Since the center's inception, we have added more than one hundred faculty members to its ranks from a wide variety of disciplines. We believe that longevity science will not operate within the traditional scientific silos of today. It will be at its best when it marries physical and biological sciences with social sciences and forms partnerships with law and business. The overarching purpose will be to test new ideas and consolidate answers from multiple fields. We'll need social scientists to understand which factors predict health in old age, biologists and medical scientists to solve physiological conundrums, and engineers to design the solutions we envision. We'll need lawyers to work with policy makers to build systems that encourage beneficial behavior, and we'll need psychologists and economists to help us dismantle the barriers to effective planning for old age.

Longevity science isn't an entirely new idea. On the contrary, the NIH (National Institutes of Health) has been instrumental in accumulating a massive knowledge base about human health upon which to build. However, rather than being organized around studying specific diseases, as national research efforts often are, longevity science will explicitly focus on identifying and then systematically changing environmental conditions that contribute to long-term outcomes. No doubt, longevity science will lead to advances in the prevention and treatment of problems that we already associate with old age, like arthritis, osteoporosis, and sensory losses. End-stage interventions in these diseases so far have been only modestly effective. Yet perhaps more important, longevity science will search for clues throughout the life span about what leads to positive outcomes in old age so that we can provide the optimal physical, social, and biological environments for people as they develop throughout their lifetimes. It will pose questions like these: How does education early in life change brain function late in life? How do biological processes in infancy contribute to well-being in old age? How can engineering be applied to health care to bring costs down?

We want to learn more, for example, about the genetic differences that make some individuals susceptible to diseases and others resilient despite bad health habits. We'll want to discover which periods in the body's physical development are the most critical for optimal lifelong performance and how to influence this development at opportune times—for example, we'd love to know more about which exercises are best for muscles and bones at different ages so that we can help people reach old age in good condition. We'll want to understand more about how psychological stress affects long-range mental and physiological health, and how to keep stress levels optimized throughout life.

Admittedly, the complex processes the body undergoes as it ages are mysteries that scientists are just beginning to unravel. Scientists still lack a deep and total understanding of why and how we age or what we might do to counter that process. They've identified gross behavioral influences on aging like eating right, exercising, and avoiding chronic stress and are increasingly realizing that aging, disease, and social isolation are overlapping phenomena. Yet we still lack a detailed molecular model of both the mechanisms and the nexus of these powerful forces.

When it comes to dealing with age, I'm reminded of a parable that illustrates the difference between managing a problem's cause and its effects. In this old story, a villager standing by a river is shocked to see a baby floating by. He jumps in to rescue the baby, but as soon as he does, along comes another baby, and then another. Soon the whole village is devoting itself to rescuing babies from the water, but no matter how fast they work the babies keep coming. Finally someone hits on a much better idea: instead of rescuing the babies one at a time, they must go upstream to find out who's throwing them in. With aging, we've been similarly stuck on the lower banks, trying one desperate rescue maneuver after another, addressing the effects of aging but not its causes. Aging is a systematic breakdown of the body, but we're treating that breakdown's symptoms rather than its source because we just don't know enough about what's going on upstream.

That's not to say that scientific and technological advances over the preceding centuries haven't done an unprecedented job of mitigating some of those symptoms, allowing us to dodge bullet after bullet that used to fell our ancestors at early ages. Nobel Prize–winning economist Robert Fogel and his colleague Dora Costa coined the term "technophysio evolution" to refer to improvements in biological functioning that are a consequence of technological advances. Treatments for acute illnesses like heart disease and measures to reduce the spread of contagious diseases, like vaccinations for polio and smallpox, have prevented millions of premature deaths. Injuries that were once permanently debilitating and illnesses like gout or scarlet fever that previously left people with lifelong disabilities are now treated so well that in many cases people recover and live out their full lives. Basic problems like not getting enough to eat have largely been allayed in the developed world. In the two centuries since Malthus wrote his gloomy *Essay on the Principle of Population,* in which he predicted that population growth would surely outpace food production, the world population indeed increased by a factor of six. Yet thanks to agronomic science, yields are greater, more land is under cultivation, particularly in the Western Hemisphere, and a smaller fraction of the world's population suffers from malnutrition than two centuries ago. In the last century, improvements in nutrition were so dramatic that average body size in the developed world increased by 50 percent, the working capacity of vital organs greatly improved and, of course, life expectancy nearly doubled.

Yet we are in some ways the victims of our own success. As food has become more plentiful and life has become less physically demanding, people have become heftier, more sedentary, and increasingly vulnerable to the kinds of chronic diseases our ancestors rarely had the chance to develop. (In contrast, malnutrition was once so common that governments had trouble finding people who weighed *enough* when they needed strong, healthy young men to fight in wars.) Behavioral patterns like overeating or spending life as a couch potato just weren't possible for most people, and even those who lived in kingly fashion were often felled by trauma or infectious disease before chronic conditions like heart disease or diabetes could take their toll.

Today, the situation is quite different. Some scholars estimate that if current trends continue, in fifteen years 80 percent of Americans will be overweight or obese. We're also living long enough that we can now see the effects of advanced age on the human mind and its functioning. If the prospect of 106 million cases of Alzheimer's disease worldwide by 2050—one in every eighty-five people—can be said to have a silver lining, it's that such a major public health crisis will spur research into prevention and cures. To be blunt, back in 1900, when only 4 percent of the population lived past age sixty-five, the status of the elderly— good or bad—was not terribly relevant to society. Today it is. We're facing a very different old age than any generation of humans has before, and we will need the collective intellectual efforts of a global scientific community to work out the host of problems posed by an ever-lengthening life span.

If we apply the same energy, ingenuity, and commitment to improving the health and well-being of older adults that we applied a century ago to infant health, we will significantly improve the functioning, engagement, and overall quality of life for long-lived people. Specifically, I think we'll need to pay special attention to three key areas of research:

- Studying the factors that affect development in utero and in early childhood
- Mitigating the chronic diseases that become apparent in middle age
- Constructing everyday environments that support long life

Starting from the Beginning

Interestingly enough, longevity science will need to start with pediatrics, not geriatrics. Indeed, the starting point may actually precede birth. The Human Genome Project was a spectacular accomplishment that laid the groundwork for a new understanding of individualized risks for disease, and for gene-based therapies that may change the delivery of medicine over the next several decades. However, many scientists expected that cataloging the genome would give us the answers to almost everything; we'd find the heart disease gene, the colon cancer gene, or perhaps the "bad decision gene," and we'd be able to disable them at will. But we didn't. In a way, the human genome turned out to be far simpler than many had imagined it would be, closer to that of chimps, monkeys, and even fruit flies. Yet it was also more complex than expected, because it soon became clear that single genes just don't explain what many scientists hoped they would.

Even identical twins, who have the same DNA, don't always have identical health trajectories. Scientists began to ask, If simple genetic explanations alone don't account for the remarkable variation in human profiles, what does?

This is when genetics turned from the study of Gregor Mendel's simple algorithms to a field called epigenetics, which will be a key part of longevity science for years to come. The famous Canadian psychologist Donald Hebb would smile had he lived to see epigenetics emerge as one of the most fascinating and important areas of biology; Hebb made the prescient observation that debates about the relative influences of nature versus nurture were as useful as arguments about whether width or length contributes more to the area of a rectangle. The exciting new field of epigenetics is revealing a new perspective on our DNA—that our environments shape how our genes are expressed.

Although the genes that we inherit from our parents are hard-coded into all of our cells and remain there all of our lives, the way those genes are instructed to behave is influenced by outside factors like nutrition, exposure to toxins, and even our environments in utero and in infancy. Instructions are delivered by chemical tags that can change the way DNA is expressed by turning genes on or off. Dr. Randy Jirtle of Duke University came up with a tremendously apt metaphor when describing the process for a 2007 *Nova ScienceNow* program: think of it like computing—the DNA is the hardware, and these chemical instructions, the epigenome, are the software that tells it how to run.

These epigenetic changes start in the womb. If you were born to a chain-smoking, hard-drinking mom, your genes may get different instructions than if your mom had been a teetotaler and tobacco free. There is growing evidence from population studies that these alterations may even be passed on through several generations. Since the egg your mother contributed to your conception was formed in the uterine environment of *her* mother, your grandmother's exposure to viruses, toxins, or poor nutrition may have affected your genetic inheritance. In other words, if your grandmother, say, lived through a famine, the effects can be passed on to you even if your mother was perfectly healthy throughout her pregnancy.

Here's a compelling example of how even a small environmental factor in the womb can change one's long-term health: Jim Vaupel, founder and executive director of the Max Planck Institute for Demographic Research in Rostock, Germany, found that life expectancy past age fifty varies according to the month you were born, largely because of seasonal changes that affected your mother's eating habits during her pregnancy. In the Northern Hemisphere, people born in the autumn live, on average, a few months longer than those born in the spring; the reverse is true for those born in the Southern Hemisphere. Vaupel's study suggests that mothers who are pregnant throughout the colder months of the year have less access to fresh fruits and vegetables, and this "seasonally inadequate nutrition" is enough to change the environmental conditions affecting their babies' development. That's not to say that modern mothers are totally malnourished throughout the winter months—grocery stores, refrigerators, and prenatal vitamins mean that women today are less dependent than their ancestors on the season or on a successful harvest for nutrition. (Interestingly, the study notes, as fresh food becomes more readily available year round, the relationship between birth month and longevity seems to be becoming less significant.) Nevertheless, these seasonal shifts in food availability are still enough to subtly alter development in a way that affects life events decades later—and all without changing a single part of the baby's genetic blueprint.

Doug Almond, an economist at Columbia University, uncovered a similar phenomenon by studying children born soon after the 1918 influenza epidemic. The epidemic was fierce but, thankfully, short-lived. It played out mostly during the fall of 1918 and was over by January 1919. Many millions of people died, but millions of others who contracted the virus survived; a subset of those survivors were pregnant when the epidemic hit. Because the epidemic was so circumscribed, children born mere months apart during that period developed in very different gestational environments—those whose mothers had the flu while they were in utero, and those whose mothers had been healthy.

Like a detective, Almond set out to see if there were any reliable differences in the fates of those children once they reached adulthood. Looking at adult men whose mothers were similar by every objective measure except viral exposure, Almond found that those whose mothers had had the flu were worse off as adults across a range of outcomes, including heightened risk for schizophrenia, diabetes, and stroke. Yet it wasn't just their health that was affected—they were less likely to have graduated from high school and their wages were lower. Their odds of being poor were 15 percent greater, and their disability rate in later life was 20 percent higher. Why? Because exposure to the virus in utero left these infants more sickly and vulnerable, their health as young children suffered, and subsequently their schooling suffered as well. Without a good education, they were less able to secure productive employment, and without resources, their health grew worse. In the end, they needed help from society to get by. Almond makes an important point: the state of these children's environment before birth didn't just take a toll on them—it cost society, too.

The epigenome alters the way our DNA behaves throughout our life span. Even identical twins, who start off with exactly the same genes, will have DNA that acts very differently in their later years, thanks to thousands of gene silencings and activations that have occurred in reaction to their various life experiences and environments. After all, similar genetic heritage does not mean similar lives. (The typical population study aimed at separating heredity from environment presumes that if you live in the same house you live in the same environment, but anyone who has ever shared a home with another person appreciates that this is not true.) In many ways, we've done a better job of characterizing the genome than the environment. We're only beginning to identify which environmental factors make the most significant differences in biological responses.

Yet the fact that our DNA's expression is influenced by life events has so far offered us some valuable clues as to how we can modify gene expression with behavior. For example, together with his students and colleagues, Michael Meaney, who directs the Program for the Study of Behaviour, Genes and Environment at Canada's McGill University, is revealing the biochemical mechanisms by which early life experiences change the way genes are expressed even in old age, altering cognitive and emotional responses. Nurturing mothers, he argues, can alter the way their children's genes behave throughout their lives. The starting point for Meaney's team was the observation that rat pups whose moms frequently lick them—a form of maternal grooming—are less fearful and anxious, even as grown-up rats, than those whose moms are not the licking type. Exposure to licking produces a chemical that affects the hypothalamus and subsequently the production of stress hormones. Meaney's team next conducted an "adoption" study by switching the offspring of the moms that licked their pups frequently and those that did not. The adopted pups, whose new moms promptly set about licking them, showed the same biochemical alterations and became less anxious, proving that this aspect of their temperament was a reaction to their environment, not simply their genetic heritage. In this case, maternal behavior had a clear effect on the pups' biochemistry, and therefore their behavior.

So how does this environmental change during infancy affect rats in their old age? Several key regions of the brain—the amygdala, hypothalamus, and pituitary gland—communicate with hormone-secreting glands outside the brain that regulate emotional, cognitive, and stress responses in the short term and ultimately affect metabolism and general health. The intricate influences among these regions are orchestrated by neurotransmitters and hormones governing key survival mechanisms that help us to adapt to our environment: immune response, sweat glands, memory, and heart rate. Scientists refer to the communications network that supports this basic survival system as the hypothalamic-pituitary-adrenal (HPA) axis. Meaney and his colleagues have shown that early life experiences, such as nurturing from a mother, that affect the functional organization of the HPA system in enduring ways also affect cognitive functioning late in life. Meaney has shown, for example, that old rats treated with drugs that positively alter the HPA axis perform better than untreated rats in learning to run mazes. So it's quite possible that even after Meaney's rat pups become old geezers, the ones that had nurturing mothers will run mazes faster because of enduring changes in their brains' development.

This kind of investigation into how nurture can trump nature promises to find answers to puzzles like why one identical twin may develop Alzheimer's disease when the other does not, or why some people are resilient in the face of stress and others fall apart. Most exciting, of course, will be the next step of modifying behavior to turn off gene expressions that do harm and turn on the ones that protect us. Take depression: Risk for this disease has a genetic root. Recent studies have shown that many daughters of women who suffer from depression carry a specific configuration of a gene that has been implicated in the onset of depression, the serotonin transporter gene. Every one of us has two alleles (alternative forms of a given gene) in the promoter region of this gene—one from each parent—and each allele can be either short or long. Having two short alleles increases a person's likelihood of becoming depressed when faced with life stresses. Significantly, 50 percent of girls whose mothers who have a history of major depression will themselves become depressed.

Stanford psychology professor Ian Gotlib and his colleagues have studied these young girls before they show any evidence of depression. They find that, compared with girls who have one or two long alleles in the promoter region of the serotonin transporter gene, girls with two short alleles are more biologically reactive to stressful tasks in the laboratory. For example, the researchers ask the girls to count down from four hundred by sevens for three minutes. If the girls slow down, the researchers tell them to speed up, and if the girls are especially good at the task, they ask them to start at four thousand and subtract by seventeens.

Anyone would find this task stressful, but Gotlib and his colleagues are trying to capture how the girls with the genetic link to depression differ from those without it in their degree of discomfort. Gotlib's team measures the girls' output of cortisol, a hormone people release in response to stress. Cortisol is important for energy and homeostasis, but too much cortisol can impair cognitive functioning and lower the body's immunity to disease. People who are depressed have higher levels of cortisol than people who are not, and indeed, Gotlib finds that under stress, girls with two short alleles secrete more cortisol, and for a longer time, than do girls with at least one long allele. Now that Gotlib's lab knows stress responsivity is an important aspect of genetic risk for depression, they are developing preventive programs that teach high-risk people how to deal more effectively with stress in their lives. For example, people could learn how to react more effectively to difficult situations by interpreting the onset of stressors as "cues for action" rather than as signs of an inevitably unmanageably stressful situation.

Another challenge for the field of psychology is to understand how early education—an extremely important environmental factor for development—has such a strong health impact over a lifetime. A growing and compelling body of literature suggests that even relatively small increases in education pay off in real improvements in the quality and length of life. Independent studies agree that even one additional year of education very likely increases life expectancy by more than a year, and others have linked increased education to better memory skills, better self-management of chronic diseases, and delays in the onset of cognitive changes later in life. But why, exactly, is this true? Are the effects primarily social—that is, does education simply route people toward a more affluent, well-informed life trajectory that allows them to make better decisions as they age, affords them more control over their life circumstances, and gives them greater access to healthy environments? Or does the process of becoming educated itself cause concrete neural and cognitive changes that have beneficial effects? After all, there is reason to believe that education confers direct improvements in brain development and subsequently leads to lives that include more mental stimulation, more intellectually engaging occupations, and even leisure activities that are more cognitively challenging.

BILINGUALISM ON THE BRAIN

Although it's still controversial, some scientists maintain that learning a second language early in life also protects people against cognitive decline decades later. In old age, bilingual people appear to perform better on cognitive tasks and have a lower incidence of dementia. Ellen Bialystok, a psychologist at Toronto's York University, and her colleagues suspect that bilingualism modifies brain function in enduring ways.

In particular, they argue, brain inhibition improves. In order for people to act or think in focused ways, they must activate certain neural responses while they inhibit others. Bialystok and her colleagues believe that people who speak multiple languages persistently activate inhibition centers when they speak—that is, they inhibit words in one language while they speak another. Inhibitory centers degrade with both normal aging and with dementia, and the greater use of these centers by bilingual people helps to maintain their health with age. In other words, if you use it, you don't lose it.

So in addition to its practical value of giving people more than one language in which to converse, greater emphasis on bilingual education may have long-term benefits for cognitive health. This learning process can be started early in life; very young children acquire languages with great ease and precision, and without much in the way of explicit teaching.

Ken Langa, a professor of internal medicine at the University of Michigan, expects that both are key. In an important and optimistic report published in 2008, Langa and his colleagues suggest that the frequency of age-related cognitive decline in the American population is dropping and that education may partially explain the trend. Langa studied a nationally representative sample of thousands of people over age sixty-nine in 2002 and compared their performance on several kinds of tests—including counting, object naming, and recall tests—to that of a similar group that had been studied at the same ages in 1993. Cognitive function was measured on a thirty-five-point scale, in which scores below eight were considered "impaired." The team found that for the 2002 group, the percentage of people showing impairment dropped by nearly a third, from 12.2 percent to 8.7 percent. Two key differences between the groups were education—the more recent group had one more year of schooling on average—and net worth. This type of study cannot completely disentangle the effects of education from income as they are too strongly intertwined, but both are associated with improvements in cognitive function. Indeed, most studies of education are inherently plagued by similar selection effects and extraneous confounds. It's very hard to rule out completely questions like whether smart people just get more education, or wealthier people live in more stimulating environments that sharpen cognitive function. But if education can delay the onset of dementia—and correlational studies like Langa's suggest that it may—the implications for society are profound.

Modifying the Medical Problems of Middle Age

While early childhood offers scientists some fascinating clues about what contributes to healthy old age, I think we should also be paying close attention to changes that begin to manifest themselves in the middle of life. Although much attention has been given—and rightly so—to treating and preventing the deadly diseases often diagnosed in middle age, like heart attacks, strokes, and cancer, chronic nonlethal conditions begin to surface at this time too. These include conditions like arthritis, bone density loss, and muscle atrophy. Each may start with subtle symptoms but can steadily progress with age until they significantly diminish one's quality of life and undermine the ability to function independently. Think of how different the middle and end of life would be if we could squelch the physiological problems that make us tired, achy, weak, or slow to heal. Imagine how wonderful it would be if we didn't have to make the trade-off that traditionally happens in middle age, when we expect to lose our strength and agility but comfort ourselves with the knowledge that at least age has brought us experience and wisdom. Wouldn't it be great to have *both*?

Yet divining how the body changes in middle age is a subtle and complex field of inquiry. Many of the problems that develop during this stage are hard to distinguish from the process of aging itself. They're not caused by infection or trauma; they're the result of wear and tear on the body from a lifetime of activity. So, if they are basic biological processes that affect us all, can we do anything to modify their progression? Stem cell biologist Tom Rando, deputy director of the Stanford Center on Longevity and chief of neurology at the VA Palo Alto Health Care System, thinks so. He studies sarcopenia, a deterioration of skeletal muscle that occurs even with normal aging. Sarcopenia affects muscle mass and strength and is associated with the body's inability to repair injured tissue. It perpetuates a vicious cycle: Because muscles are weaker, people are more likely to injure themselves, and when they injure themselves, they take longer to heal. That makes their muscles weaker during the healing process, which in turn leaves them even more vulnerable to future injuries.

Rando is determined to find ways to maintain muscle tissue

into advanced age and thinks there may be biological tricks that could solve the problem. When muscle tissue is injured, an infusion of stem cells moves into the damaged area to repair the tissue. In both young and old animals (and presumably young and old human beings), the same basic processes occur, but the stem cell activity in older animals is far less robust. Scientists had previously assumed that the problem was with the integrity of the stem cells themselves, that they became damaged with age and less able to make repairs. Rando's team wondered if the stem cells were, in fact, not the problem. Their first clue came when they took muscle stem cells from young and old mice and grew them in a tissue culture dish, only to find that under these conditions the old cells grew just as well as the young cells. The team then hypothesized that the reason stem cells in old animals are less effective in repairing tissues has something to do with the biochemistry of the blood that surrounds them.

To test this hypothesis, Rando's team exposed injured muscle tissue from an old animal to the blood supply of a young animal, and something incredible happened: the stem cell activity around the old tissue was as great as that in young tissue. Weeks later, when they reexamined the injured tissue, it had healed just as well as the young tissue had. Rando's conclusion was that stem cells do not become irreparably damaged as they age; rather, they go dormant. On further study, he was able to identify a substance in the blood of older animals that suppresses stem cell function. Rando expects that one day injured older people will be able to take a drug to block these suppressors, permitting faster and more effective repair by essentially modifying the biochemistry of the blood and rendering it "young" again. "Maybe in this case, you really can teach an old dog new tricks," he says. Rando and his colleagues have evidence that the same processes may be at work not only in the bloodstream but in places like the brain, bone marrow, and liver.

Are there other reinvigorating processes that medical science could stimulate or mimic biochemically? We know that the effects of exercise on health are indisputably positive. For years, geriatricians have been saying that if a pill could accomplish what exercise does, it would put Viagra sales to shame. That pill may be closer to existence than previously thought. In 2008, Ronald Evans, a professor of molecular and developmental biology at the Salk Institute in California, reported that his team had identified a drug called AICAR that increases the exercise endurance of mice by more than 40 percent. It both activates a protein that produces high-endurance muscle fibers, and then tricks cells into thinking that they are out of energy so they'll "turbocharge" that protein. Evans's team envisions a pill that could one day induce metabolic changes that improve stamina, increase muscle mass, and burn fat even without exercise. Now, let's be clear: they're not after a pill that would allow us all to sit on chaise longues and eat bonbons all day. For healthy people, such a drug would not supplant the need to actually exercise. But for people who are physically unable to move around much, it might remove the barriers that fatigue and muscle wasting impose on fitness.

In other cases, scientists are looking into ways to mitigate the effects of chronic illness not by stimulating the body's internal programming, but by designing better external hardware for it. Perhaps you've heard of some of the more far-out, futuristic applications of this kind of technology, like robotic exoskeletons designed to fit over the legs as supplemental braces to help frail people walk. The idea of using hardware add-ons to enhance natural abilities is truly an old one—if you're wearing glasses or contact lenses right now, you're already doing it. In fact, there is already a huge array of wearable accoutrements designed to amplify older people's faculties or to replace function that's fading: hearing aids, pacemakers, even dentures. But most of these devices merely treat the symptoms of aging; they don't halt the progression of age-related problems themselves.

What if they could? My colleague Tom Andriacchi, a professor of biomechanical engineering and orthopedic surgery at Stanford, has spent most of his career designing artificial devices to replace the diseased joints of folks who have end-stage arthritis. Arthritis is a classic example of a disease that stems from a lifetime of strain on the joints. Day after day we run up flights of stairs, walk around the neighborhood running errands, and chase after our kids. The righteous among us even jog early in the morning or enter marathons on the weekends. Yet all this exacts a gradual toll on the knee, and once you're past the age of about two, cartilage doesn't regenerate. With people living longer than ever before, more of them are facing the end result of all of that knee movement—serious limitations on their mobility because of the pain associated with advanced arthritis. Aside from cortisone injections and anti-inflammatory medications like ibuprofen, which treat the symptoms rather than the disease, joint replacement is the only medical option available for this condition.

Andriacchi and his team in the BioMotion Research Group at Stanford wanted to find a way of modifying the natural course of the disease that wouldn't require people to go under the knife. They used motion analysis to gain an in-depth understanding of gait and how it relates to bone disease. They found that, most commonly, osteoarthritis of the knee occurs because of the way that people walk, putting most of the load of each step on the same place in the medial compartment of the knee, over time wearing down the cartilage. Several years ago, instead of making another artificial joint, Andriacchi decided to make a shoe. The shoe has a variable density sole that alters the gait of the wearer, shifting the weight slightly, protecting the cartilage, and offering immediate relief from pain. Perhaps even more exciting, Andriacchi's data suggest that wearing the shoe may reduce the progression of arthritis. "I've spent most of my life making joints to treat a disease at its end stage. Then I got really excited about the prospect of preventing it," he tells me. Andriacchi's excitement about the shoe is palpable, but already he's moved on to another project: using blood chemistry to detect evidence of the earliest stages of the disease. "The earlier we can identify it, the better," he says. "People clearly have arthritis before they suffer symptoms. If we can detect the disease at a very early stage we might be able to use interventions like the shoe to delay or prevent symptoms altogether."

Indeed, finding new ways to enable the early detection of serious illnesses is a key component of longevity science, because it can have a profound influence on disease outcomes. Melanoma is the deadliest form of skin cancer, yet it is easily detected by simple visual inspection, and if found early and removed surgically, the survival rate is around 90 percent. On the other hand, there is no useful screening test for pancreatic cancer, so only about 5 percent of cases are detected early enough for treatment. As a result, the survival rate is only 20 percent, even if the tumor has not metastasized by the time of discovery. We'll need to create sensitive, inexpensive tests that are readily tolerated by people, so that they can be screened—and warning signs caught—before significant symptoms develop, and while treatment or lifestyle changes can still have a beneficial impact.

Early detection could also play a huge role in managing liver disease. Our livers can take some fairly serious insults, including too much drinking, the effects of medication, or chronic infections like hepatitis, and are among the few organs that have significant powers of regeneration when they suffer damage. However, after years of inflammation, many of the liver's cells die and are replaced by collagenous fibrils. An extensive invasion of these fibrils is called cirrhosis. The collagen that replaces healthy cells stiffens the liver—a cirrhotic liver may be ten times more rigid than a normal one. By that stage, liver function is severely compromised and the probability of developing liver cancer increases at a rate of about 5 percent per year. An experienced physician can actually feel the effects of advanced liver damage by palpation but would be unlikely to detect the subtle changes needed for early detection of disease. Worse, normal and cirrhotic liver tissue look very much the same using most conventional imaging techniques. So, presently, biopsy is the principal way patients learn whether they have significant damage to their livers. Unfortunately, biopsies are expensive and unpleasant, and because of the possibility of hemorrhage, one person in one hundred dies from the procedure itself.

However, elastography, a relatively new extension of biomedical ultrasound, has entered the picture as an early detection alternative. FibroScan, a product of the French company EchoSens, precisely determines the stiffness of the liver by using conventional diagnostic ultrasound to measure the velocity of a shear wave pulse traveling through the organ. The procedure is painless and noninvasive. Already more than a dozen independent investigations have demonstrated a strong correlation between results garnered from using traditional biopsies and from using FibroScan. Now that this breakthrough idea has been turned into a commercial product, the goal for development should be to make this instrument so simple and pleasant to use—and sufficiently inexpensive for clinics to purchase—that it will become a standard tool for all hepatologists and perhaps even many primary care physicians. When that happens, early detection and treatment of liver disease can avert patient suffering and reduce the overall cost of patient care.

From a psychological perspective, I can see enormous potential in trying to detect problems while patients still have a chance to heal if they change their behavior. So often smokers, drinkers, or even overeaters say that *if only they had known,* they would have changed their behavior, even though, deep down, they knew that they were behaving badly. Or alternatively, they may think they are the exceptional ones who will dodge the bullet. You know the type, the guy who tells you every time you see him that his Uncle Albert drank every day of his life and lived to be ninety. Denial is harder to maintain when you see a picture. Allowing patients to witness proof that they are in early stages of a disease but letting them know that its progression could still be averted would be an excellent way to motivate people to change their habits. Imagine, too, the reinforcing value of showing people who have quit abusing alcohol or drugs that their bodies are visibly healing.

Changing the Everyday Environment

We can find more sensitive methods of detecting the onset of illnesses, try to treat the body's insides to make repairs, and develop wearable technologies to strengthen our functions when they weaken, but even with all of these technologies, aging will inevitably bring with it some forms of decline. Arguably, the bigger problem is not that our bodies eventually lose power and ability, but that our built environments—the housing, transit, and other structural systems that we must navigate in order to survive each day—are not built to accommodate that decline. When older people begin to have trouble getting around or accomplishing quotidian tasks, we tend to fault them, rather than their surroundings. We feel that they've failed if they're too weak to open the twist-off bottle, not that the bottle's design has failed by being too difficult to use. We sigh that they can't easily race up the stairs anymore, rather than considering that the stairs themselves pose a problem. We deem people handicapped when they can't manage that first tall step required to get on a city bus or into an SUV, when the fault truly lies with those vehicles' manufacturers. Instead, we need to ask: how can we modify environments so that they support long life? When we do, we will come up with far better, more creative, and, I believe, more satisfying solutions that will improve environments for young and old.

My colleague Lee Ross, a psychology professor at Stanford, has a keen nose for these sorts of reframings. As he points out, in the 1980s, when women were beginning to make inroads into many traditionally male occupations, there was concern even among well-meaning supporters that some jobs should remain limited to men. The argument was that women were simply not big or strong enough to perform certain tasks. For example, it was commonly assumed that women wouldn't make good firefighters, because they'd have trouble lifting heavy water hoses, traversing ladders, or climbing into the trucks. In general, they were seen as being too tiny and too weak to handle the large, heavy tools needed to fight fires. Yet women and their smaller bodies weren't the problem: the design of the firefighting equipment was, even though design is something that is infinitely malleable. As Ross puts it, in a land where men averaged five feet, four inches tall and 140 pounds, as women do, they'd find a way to design firefighting equipment for smaller people. "They wouldn't shrug and say, 'No one can lift the hoses. Let the buildings burn!' " Ross points out with a laugh.

As it is, the built environments that surround us were designed with the young in mind. Outdoors we find steps without banisters, and long stretches of urban sidewalks that have no place where one can stop and sit down, or that become icy in winter months. At the store, there are items on high shelves that are hard to reach, doorways too narrow for wheelchairs to go through, or automatic doors that close too quickly. When we travel there are airplanes with overhead baggage compartments that require heavy lifting, buses that are hard to get onto, or cars with airbags that when activated can crush a frail person's thin bones. At home we have houses filled with throw rugs that slip on wood floors, soft cushioned furniture that people sink into and then have trouble getting up from, split levels that make it difficult for a person who has trouble walking to move around a house, and bathtubs that require people to squat down on wet surfaces—not to mention getting up again! These are just a few of the barriers built into our everyday environments because the users are tacitly presumed to be fit and young.

I remember witnessing a profoundly moving example of this in the life of my friend Grace. Until Grace was ninety-five years old, she lived in her own home in Berkeley, California, the same house where she lived with her parents and siblings while she was growing up. It was a large, gracious home and her dance studio sat behind the house on the same lot. Like many old homes, the house was in need of repair. The electrical system required a major overhaul, but Grace failed to show concern that you couldn't run the washing machine at the same time as the microwave oven. She didn't even see the cracks in the wall and the need for paint. Instead, Grace saw the ghosts of times past. She remembered a sweetheart calling at the front door, the argument with her sister. Grace got by in the old house with a little help from her friends and a hired house cleaner, even though her doctors told her she should move into an assisted-living facility. Despite the piecemeal social system on which her independence was based, Grace managed just fine for years.

But over time, it became clear that the house contained hazards that Grace couldn't always navigate safely. One day when I was visiting, I thought I smelled gas. Grace said that she didn't, but I knew that a diminished sense of smell is a typical part of aging, so I persisted until I convinced her to phone the gas company. They sent someone over within the hour, and indeed, the stove was leaking gas. Grace was happy to have a pretty new stove that stood out among her older appliances, but I couldn't shake from my mind the darker possibilities of what could have happened. After all, Grace's friends couldn't always be around to watch out for signs of danger.

And things got steadily worse; Grace was diagnosed with cancer, and after a surgery that was technically successful, she spent several months in a nursing facility before being allowed to return home. Those two months of bed rest resulted in a profound loss of mobility for her. Two months after Grace came home from the hospital, she still couldn't walk more than a few steps on her own, even with the help of a walker. After her physical therapy insurance coverage ended, she used her own money to hire someone to help her improve, but she never recovered enough to walk independently again. The biggest problem she had was with getting to the toilet. She'd not only have to walk to the bathroom, but then make the transfer from her walker or wheelchair to the toilet and back again. For someone who is frail, this can be a precarious task. Falls are the third leading cause of death in the elderly, and Grace couldn't risk it. In the end, she opted to hire round-the-clock care, at the cost of $5,000 a month. To be fair, these helpers did many other tasks for Grace, including cooking and light cleaning, but her main motivation for this monetary outlay was her concern about getting to the toilet safely.

Many times, Grace and I imagined the ways that engineering could have solved her problems. We talked about stair-climbing robots that she could step onto, letting her ride up her stairs, and robotic arm extensions with pincer claws on the end that could help her reach things far away. (Imagine how frustrating it is to drop something on the floor when stooping down is impossible!) We wondered about electronic reminders that would tell her to take her medication, and then warn that she had already taken it if she forgot and tried to take it again. I told her about the cutting board developed by researchers at the University of Rochester's Center for Future Health that detects bacteria so that people don't eat spoiled food, which is another unfortunate consequence of the loss of smell, and of their other projects like bathroom mirrors that can detect melanomas, and "smart bandages" that monitor and assist wound healing. Grace had hoped that I could persuade some engineering students from Stanford to come over and fix her house, but of course, as an isolated case, fixing one elderly person's home would be prohibitively costly. Yet as a general technological challenge, if houses were designed from scratch with the safety and comfort of elderly and disabled people in mind, their needs could be met ever more efficiently with economies of scale. These homes would be safer for children and young people, too.

In fact, some engineers are envisioning ways to create "smart homes" that care for their owners, instead of the other way around. Scientists have long imagined houses that adjust the lighting depending on who is in the room, turn down the thermostat after residents have gone to bed, turn off stoves mistakenly left burning, and even play music when owners arrive home. Much of this technology is currently available—though relatively unusual—in today's marketplace. More recently, smart house planning has been tuned to the needs of older people, and revealed interesting possibilities, such as personalized monitoring systems that will detect gradual shifts in vital signs or bring aid in emergencies. For example, sensors could passively record health information while residents sit on the sofa . . . or on the toilet. Japanese researchers at Toto, a giant in the toilet manufacturing world, in conjunction with Daiwa House, a major home-building company, have developed an intelligent toilet system that samples the urine stream and can measure glucose levels in diabetics or reveal whether someone on a strict medication regimen is taking the proper dosage. Within arm's length of the toilet is a cuff into which users can put their arm for their blood pressure to be taken. Then, while they wash their hands at the sink, their weight is measured. All of this information can be sent to the person's health care provider, who can alert them if anything seems troubling.

IS YOUR MIND IN THE CARDS?

One of the more imaginative monitoring ideas I've heard about involves using computer-based games to track cognitive functioning. Holly Jimison, a professor of medical informatics, and Misha Pavel, a professor of biomedical engineering and computer science, both at the Oregon Health and Science University, are using game-playing performance to track very early changes in cognitive status.

One of the computer games they use is a card game called FreeCell; it's similar to solitaire but requires significant planning and strategy. Cards are distributed in a set of columns and the task is to rearrange them in a particular order using the fewest moves possible. FreeCell requires complex decision making—what psychologists call "executive function"—because the game frequently demands planning several moves in advance in order to perform well. By monitoring game performance, Jimison and Pavel can detect very early signs of cognitive decline, which can be signs of neurological or other types of disease. Potentially, this kind of early heads-up would allow for proactive treatment of some of the disease's underlying causes.

If you want to get really excited about some potential technologies in the works, talk with Eric Dishman, director of product research and innovation for the Digital Health Group at Intel Corporation, which is researching new uses of networked sensors. Among the projects on Intel's drawing board is a *really* smart carpet, designed to prevent older people from falling. Falls are a major problem for people over age sixty-five, not only because they can be injured but because there is a risk of subsequent hospitalization and a downward spiral that too frequently leads to death.

This carpet is embedded with a network of sensors that collect information about walking patterns, including being able to identify the gait patterns associated with newly developing Alzheimer's or Parkinson's disease. The sensors are so sensitive to changes in gait that the carpet can detect subtle changes from hour to hour, even ones so small that an individual may not notice. This is important, Dishman explains, because Intel's research has revealed that in a number of cases a person's gait changes shortly after their morning medicine. Indeed, he says 50 to 60 percent of falls are related either to medications or to muscle atrophy. Once the sensors in the carpet pick up on these changes, they can signal the user to phone his or her physician or pharmacist to see if medication or dosages should be changed. After adjustments are made, the carpet monitors improvements. Early stages of Parkinson's and Alzheimer's can look similar behaviorally, but measurements taken by a carpet like this could help to make the diagnosis clearer and result in different medications being prescribed.

Dishman says Intel is also exploring other self-monitoring solutions, like perhaps using cell phones to remind people to take their medications. Another very cool prototype is for a ride-sharing system. Using GPS technology and Google Earth, Dishman's team is exploring a bulletin board system that tells one older person who is about to get in a car that someone else nearby needs a ride. It's win–win, says Dishman—the driver can do a good deed while running an errand, and a homebound person can get out and about.

Transportation clearly should be reenvisioned for older users. The automobiles we drive today are designed with the premise that all drivers are flexible and strong, can hear and see well, and have quick reaction times. Once people get older, our societal inclination is to take them off the road. After all, drivers over age seventy are more likely than younger drivers to die if they are in a car crash. But older people, particularly those who live independently, aren't any more likely than people under thirty to get *into* accidents, and they still need to get around. While public transportation is a reliable option in some cities, it is sadly under-developed in most parts of the United States, and even when it is available it nearly always requires a good bit of walking. Users of public transportation also frequently encounter the predictably unpredictable "out of order" signs on escalators and elevators. Taxis and shuttle services are slow and irregular, oftentimes requiring that people wait outside in bad weather. For those who opt to hoof it, there are always the physical hazards of being a pedestrian amid traffic and bicycles.

Let's face it: we live in a nation designed around the idea that most people use cars. Why not instead design automobiles that accommodate older people's needs? Some changes would be relatively easy to make with technologies that already exist today. For example, when all cars have rear-mounted cameras and seats that swivel in order to make entry easier, they will be safer and more comfortable for drivers of any age. A more revolutionary idea might be to produce cars that don't need drivers at all. I asked my colleague Sebastian Thrun, a computer science professor at Stanford, about the potential to one day create cars that drive themselves. He should know: his team produced Stanley, the autonomous robotic car that won the race across 132 miles of rugged Nevada desert to win the $2 million DARPA Grand Challenge in 2005. Indeed, he says, the research divisions of automobile companies around the world are already trying to develop cars that compensate for older drivers' vulnerabilities. These cars, sensing a near impact, could automatically pull off the road, or they might have sensors that could detect when a driver has fallen asleep, had a heart attack, or even hit the gas pedal when they meant to hit the brake.

Thrun imagines that self-driving cars could eventually replace the ones we drive today, saving commuters time and trouble. "The highway system is grossly inefficient," he says. "The average worker drives one hour a day." Worse, costs stemming from automobile accidents absorb 1 to 3 percent of the world's annual GDP. Rather than fiddling with improving cars as we already know them, Thrun and his team envision a truly automatic driving system that is more convenient, far safer for young and old alike, and more environmentally friendly. "Those cars would drive under computer control," he says. "Rather than owning a car, we might just order them using cell phones. They would come to our door and deliver us anywhere—just like a taxicab without a human driver. This would make driving cheaper, safer, and also more comfortable. Who, after all, enjoys driving in traffic jams day in, day out?" For older adults, self-driving cars would essentially eliminate concerns about sensory or cognitive limitations and remove the real prospect of social isolation and dependence that threatens older people who are unable to drive.

Likewise, present-day communications technology only hints at the opportunities the twentieth century will bring to people in their bonus years, but it will likely play an enormous role in helping older people remain safe, independent, and able to interact with the outside world even if they are less mobile than they were as youths. Look at how far we've already come in making it easy to find information without leaving home and to interact with people who are far away. Less than thirty years ago, letters or expensive phone calls were the primary way relationships were maintained across the miles and physical trips to libraries were required to gather information. Today videophones make face-to-face distance communication a reality, long-distance telephone calls have become extremely inexpensive, e-mail is nearly free, and family and friends scattered around the globe can touch base many times a day via cell phones. Thanks to the Internet, an ocean of global knowledge has become instantly available to the average citizen, and you can have just about anything delivered to your door with only a few clicks of the mouse. In other words, instead of going out into the world, now you can make the world come to you.

This could have very useful applications for older people in the workplace (not to mention parents of young children who may need to work from home occasionally). As the concept of abrupt retirement fades, better communications technology that lets older workers participate in daily office matters without actually having to be there all of the time will help them ease from full-time employment to retirement while still making a valuable contribution to their workplace. This can make it possible for people to remain not only independent but productive in their own homes for many more years than they do today. Other kinds of communications could help close the gap among family members who live far away from one another, fostering that sense of social embeddedness, including the ability to watch out for one another, that is so crucial to well-being. I know of grandparents who read bedtime stories to their grandchildren on the other side of the globe via videophone. The grandkids take to this much more naturally than those of us who grew up without comparable technology.

Admittedly, technology good enough to simulate actually being there is still in its infancy. At present, video communication remains a poor substitute for face-to-face interactions. Very likely, it's because the subtlety of facial expressions gets lost and the millisecond delays make conversations seem awkward, giving these interactions an artificial feel. Once these glitches are addressed, long-distance communication will have made major strides. Surely, the development of virtual reality technologies will bring additional nuances, like touch, to long-distance communication, enhancing its realism.

The potential for improvement in health care delivery through technology is enormous, particularly if it gives patients better access to their own health history information. Dr. Calvin Hobel at the Cedars-Sinai Medical Center has been working on a life-span data management system that will allow individuals to save their own medical information—every X-ray, diagnosis, and treatment throughout their entire lives—on a small memory stick. Imagine being able to take that sort of information along with you every time you needed to see a new specialist or get a second opinion. Doctors of patients who have seen multiple specialists, who may have prescribed many different medications, will be better informed. Patients will become more knowledgeable about their own medical histories and will be better able to participate in decision making with their physicians.

Technology can change the culture of health care by making patients more active participants in their treatment. The Internet serves as a readily accessible storehouse of knowledge that increasingly is being used by people to acquaint themselves with information relating to their health problems. It helps them be better informed when interacting with their physicians, ask better questions, and understand the answers better than they would without their Web-acquired background. Encouraging patients to become familiar with their options for tests and procedures could actually improve treatment effectiveness. My colleague Albert Bandura, a Stanford psychology professor, has shown in numerous studies that beliefs about performance directly influence whether or not people set goals and what sort of goals they set. The beliefs people hold about their ability to stay healthy and, when necessary, stick to treatment plans directly influence how successfully they achieve positive outcomes. It is reasonable to believe that the more patients understand their own physiology and illness, the better decisions they will make in their daily activities.

But of course going out there willy-nilly to search the Internet for medical advice would be a fool's errand. So much material on the Internet is of questionable validity, and it can be difficult for people without a medical background to evaluate its accuracy or its author's intent. Instead, I'd propose developing a complete, publicly accessible compendium of medical knowledge, sponsored by the National Academies or a medical association and actively used in patient practice. Very simple explanations could be linked to more detailed, in-depth discussions. The compendium could be interactive so that if a patient fails to get an effective answer to a question, the program will be modified to correct the problem.

Distributing the Benefits

As we develop new technologies, we will need to ask not only what can be accomplished, but also what is ethical and cost-effective. Today 90 percent of designers market their products to the richest 5 percent of people in the world. When you think about innovations like stem cell treatments and smart houses that adjust to residents' needs you have to wonder how on earth we will be able to afford these wonderful technologies and who will get them. In health care markets, there are few, if any, economic incentives to bring down costs. On the contrary, as long as private insurance companies or Medicare will reimburse, there are real incentives to keep costs high. It is essential to keep in mind that the skyrocketing financial costs threatening Medicare are not only due to the real costs of innovation but also to a culture that offers no incentives to lower the cost of new technologies. Yet in order for these technologies to have widespread effects on society, they must be affordable for the typical older person.

There are glimmers of hope that this culture can change. The concept of "extreme affordability" is becoming increasingly popular at universities like Stanford and MIT, with cutting-edge companies like Ideo and Ignite Innovations, and with social entrepreneurs aiming to improve the world through business. This idea was originally developed to bring affordable technologies to the poorest regions of the world, controlling costs by making the design, production, and transportation of products as simple and efficient as possible. It's now time to apply this concept to health care and all sorts of other technologies that would help older people everywhere live independently and safely while participating fully in community life.

There must be simple, elegant technological solutions for everyday problems that plague millions of older people, like difficulty negotiating stairs, opening jars, detecting gas leaks, alerting others in emergencies, traveling to a friend's house for a visit, or getting to the toilet in the middle of the night. Problems like these are currently being solved one person at a time and at the cost of sleepless nights for family members, or many thousands of dollars each month for hired assistants. Even some of the more complex technological solutions that are becoming available today could be simplified for easier affordability. If you were to design a smart home today for yourself or for a loved one, it would cost a small fortune, but there's no reason a scaled-down off-the-shelf version couldn't be made available at a lower price. I can imagine kits being sold at Home Depot for less than $500 that would include a video monitoring system, a system of sensors to detect falls and gas leaks, and a few other cool gadgets that together could make homes and people far safer.

Why Science Matters

The United States has an important leadership role to play in producing the kinds of technologies that support long life. American science and technology led the world throughout most of the twentieth century, propelled in part by the social freedoms that nourish science and by the needs created by two world wars. But the benefits didn't all stay within our borders. Medicines, diagnostic tools, and basic research developed in the United States have been utilized all around the world, and American universities have trained top scientists from across the globe, many of whom return home and make long-term contributions to the economic development of their countries. It is a mutually rewarding process: our knowledge base is enriched by the contributions of these students and postdoctoral fellows while they are here, and having thousands of U.S.-educated scientists around the world may well be the best foreign relations effort the country has achieved.

In the last fifty years, science—more than any other sector—has fueled economic growth for the nation. University of Chicago economists Kevin Murphy and Robert Topel put the dollar amount on the increase in national wealth that came about due to medical research conducted between 1970 and 2000 at a staggering $3.2 trillion *per year.* To put this number into perspective, the gross domestic product of the United States in 2007 was about $14 trillion, so Murphy and Topel's numbers indicate that about one quarter of the GDP is attributable to medical research. In the past two or three decades, a surprisingly large percentage of high-quality job creation arose from small-tech enterprises that grew as spin-offs of research centers.

There's another way that medical research bolsters the country's GDP: healthier people are more productive, they have more wealth, and they consume more resources. In other words, good health is good for the economy. In fact, some of the eagerness about science in developing regions of the world stems from recognition among government leaders that science and technology can be paths toward improving their nations' standards of living. The fact that China and India are producing great numbers of engineers will help their economies. As a consequence, a global collective intelligence is emerging that will speed the discovery of solutions through the sharing of ideas. Because science largely ignores borders, no matter where new knowledge originates, we'll all benefit.

But now that scientific and engineering expertise is widely distributed and the entire world is poised on the brink of a technological explosion, will the United States continue to be the leader of this greatest of enterprises? After all, there are so many urgent problems that merit our attention—wars, education, health care, the latest tainted food scare—that, for most of us, support for science ranks far down on our list of priorities. Unfortunately, as a nation we are now beginning to run on the momentum of our past achievements.

Ironically, while we move rapidly toward a society in which knowledge is the central currency, a growing complacency about science is coming over the country. American schoolchildren are performing relatively poorly in science and math compared to students in the rest of the world. The steady increase in high school graduation rates has leveled off. Relatively few college graduates are opting for careers in science and engineering compared to a generation ago. It comes as a great surprise to many that there are more workers in their early sixties—those folks heading into retirement—with advanced degrees than workers in their early thirties. The difference is small, only about 2 percent, but in countries like Korea, Japan, Russia, and Canada, the numbers of younger people pursuing advanced degrees is steadily increasing. As other countries catch up to the United States, our relative competitiveness on the world scene may decline. Real federal research funding—that is, after adjusting for inflation— has been decreasing. As the line between church and state erodes, subjects such as stem cell research have become so embroiled in national politics that a first-ever brain drain *out* of the United States is under way to places like Singapore.

I expect that, in some ways, our complacency reflects the breathtaking success of science in America. Our day-to-day lives have been sculpted by advances in technology so exquisitely embedded in ordinary life that they are invisible. We don't think twice about the safety of the eggs or juice we serve our children at breakfast nor the intricate system of sensors we activate when we turn the key in the ignition to drive home from work. We take for granted the fact that our doctors can generate images of our insides, analyze the contents of our blood, and protect us from diseases that could otherwise kill us. Science has prepared the environments into which we are born, making them so safe, comfortable, and supportive that decades have been added to life. But because we take the gifts of science for granted, we are beginning to neglect the work that makes those gifts possible.

I worry greatly that our children will suffer in many ways if they are not at least science literate, and I hope that many among them become leaders in the world of science. Optimizing longevity demands that people understand, support, and, in a very general sense, direct the course of science and technology. The positive correlation between levels of education and health undoubtedly comes in part from an individual's ability to interpret and apply the discoveries of science. So even if your children and grandchildren decide not to become scientists, they will need to have some basic understanding of the scientific world in order to keep up with the pace of change their futures will hold.

You may ask if it really matters in which country the most cutting-edge scientific research is done. Other countries have benefited from American scientific and technological advances for decades. Why shouldn't they lead innovation for a while, so that we can benefit by consuming products of their creation? Objectively, there's no reason the United States has to be number one. It's hard, it's challenging and it's expensive to be the leader. A half century ago, we were first by default as the rest of the world recovered from devastating wars. Today, the developed world is economically and technologically nearly flat.

Yet I believe that it's valuable and worthwhile for the United States to maintain its place in this international high-tech competition that grows stronger every year. By and large, this competition is healthy and beneficial to the consumer as well as the developer and supplier, and it is, of course, an enormous engine that propels our economy. Most of all, the United States still has much to offer the scientific community. We have a disproportionately large number of the world's outstanding research centers, we have significant sources of venture capital available for tech start-ups, and we have a research industry that is ready to expand. We have funding mechanisms that have been honed over the years to be relatively objective and free of fraud, and most important, we have a strong culture of intellectual freedom. All that we need is a scientifically literate populace and a willing national leadership that can carry us forward to find innovative solutions not only for longevity science but for the needs of all humankind.

If we can harness the scientific community's energy and brainpower to address the challenges of long-lived people in the twenty-first century, we can take on the health issues of aging people and societies the way we took on the health problems of babies and young children at the beginning of the twentieth century. Our future great-grandchildren may shake their heads and try to imagine a time when dementia was rampant, just as we do now when we think about the former prevalence of infant mortality and nutritional disorders like rickets. They'll talk over coffee with friends about the old days when muscles wasted as people aged, when people's knees gave out, and when the elderly couldn't live in their own homes because doing so was too dangerous. Our great-grandchildren will say how lucky they are to live in 2050 instead of 2010. In fact, if we apply extraordinary efforts, we may be able to have those conversations, too.

7

What Might Go Wrong?

Where long life is concerned, I am basically an optimist. It strikes me as oddly funny that we complain about growing old given the obvious alternative. But I am not entirely naive. It's far too early to rest on our laurels. Long life came about because we profoundly changed the world we live in, but we still have many changes left to make. We have an unprecedented opportunity before us, and in order to ensure that added years are a gift and not a hardship, we'll have to adapt to new circumstances and to health threats our ancestors could have never foreseen.

So what do I mean by "go wrong"? Well, what if today we are at the pinnacle—not just the forefront—of healthier and longer lives? The twentieth century's trends toward better health could still be halted or reversed, leaving future generations with shorter lives and in worse health. Poverty could increase, creating wider gaps than ever between the rich and the poor in old age, and ensuring that millions of people don't survive long enough to enjoy it. Our failure, both as a culture and as individuals, to realistically assess how much a multidecade retirement will cost, and save accordingly, could leave future generations even less financially prepared for old age than the baby boomers. During the twentieth century, the length of the average retirement grew dramatically thanks to longer life, but it could shrink once again due to an unhappy combination of worsening health and people being compelled to work longer than ever, not because they find it rewarding but because they have no choice. In short, retirement could revert to what it once was before the prosperity, leisure time, and health gains of the mid-twentieth century allowed it to become anyone's "golden years"—a brief, unenjoyable period of sickness and infirmity that buffers the time between work and death.

Though I take dire forecasts with a grain of salt, I still do take them seriously. You should, too. Thinking about what might go wrong helps us to prepare, so that we can avoid calamities that we might otherwise face. The baby boomers, who as a group will enter old age in larger numbers than any other generation in history, will almost certainly be trendsetters. They will set the cultural stage for entitlements, contributions, and family roles for years to come. In order to fully prepare our society to make the best of very long life, let's take a look at some of the obstacles we might encounter.

Scenario #1: We Fail to Imagine New Models of Life

I spend a lot of time thinking about scientific breakthroughs and technological advances that could fundamentally alter the way people experience old age. What if we discover ways to maintain the muscle strength we have in young adulthood all the way through old age, or we find ways to reverse cognitive slowing so that we get wiser *and* faster as we grow old? It's a great way to use those spare moments waiting in traffic jams or sitting on airplanes before they let you open your laptop. Try it! After all, there are engineers who maintain that if you can imagine it, they can build it.

Yet one of the greatest barriers to modifying aging is a lack of imagination. It prevents us from picturing what we could do to make old age richly satisfying. As a culture, we don't have a vision of what it would be like to live a really great life that lasts one hundred years. At the core, our society has a widely held belief that aging follows an intractable downward spiral. This belief is as pernicious as it is ubiquitous, because it stops us from having those daydreams that are the necessary precursors to real change. It's the opposite of the engineers' promise: if we can't imagine it, nobody will ever build it.

I often ask undergraduate students to imagine themselves at age thirty, forty, and fifty, and then eighty, ninety, and one hundred. They can handle thinking about thirty just fine. At age thirty they imagine themselves as continuations of their current selves at age nineteen or twenty, only better—with more money and independence. But the lights begin to dim around fifty, and by the time I am asking them to imagine life at ninety and one hundred only flickers of light remain. Most report that their minds go blank when they try to picture themselves as old people. Those students who can do it generally see themselves in wheelchairs. Those who have positive conceptions of aging see their wheelchairs outside under a tree. The more negative ones see their wheelchairs in nursing homes or hospitals. But virtually all of the images—among those who can even generate them—involve frailty.

It's easy to understand why many of us associate old age with frailty, because we have likely witnessed it. But when your idea of success in old age is basically not being so weakened that you need help getting yourself to the toilet or eating on your own, it's not aiming very high. As a result of this shortsightedness, we don't tap a lot of creative potential or inspire many sacrifices early in life so that we can aim for loftier ideals.

Not surprisingly, almost all of the technology development around aging is focused on providing for the basics of health and independence. These are worthwhile pursuits, of course, but I'm still waiting to hear about new technologies that ninety-year-olds will really *love,* that will help them enjoy life and participate in society, rather than just survive. I'd love to see someone like Sebastian Thrun succeed at making an automated car with really comfortable seats and 360-degree windows so you can enjoy the view. I can't wait for communications technologies that make you feel like you're physically with your loved ones, and electronic devices that can be operated by just saying what you want instead of making your way through incomprehensible manuals. Why couldn't iPods come with settings that collect old songs from the 1930s or '40s? Yet we aren't preparing for the vast range of things that make life worth living, because we have a hard time imagining one-hundred-year-olds who still want to drive and use gadgets and download music.

But if it's hard for you to wrap your head around this new kind of old age and start imaging what kind of person you could be as you near the triple digits, well, don't blame yourself too much. It's not you: It's your brain. The human mind has some quirky limitations when it comes to long-term planning. Frankly, we're not wired for it. While the Misery Myth that I mentioned in chapter 1—that hard-to-shake cultural notion that old people are lonelier and more depressed than young people—has given us plenty of negative images of old age, I don't think our failure to richly imagine our long-term futures is entirely a function of aging-related dread. Yes, maybe our mental images of our older selves are unflattering and distorted. But the real problem is that most of the time, when we think about the distant future, we don't relate to our future selves in a very realistic or empathetic way. We see our future selves at a great remove, as though they have stolen our faces, added a few wrinkles, and come up with worse hairstyles. And because of that, we plan for our future selves in a sort of impersonal way, the way we plan for strangers.

As humans, we give priority to our present state. Our emotions, instincts, and immediate urges help us know what (and who) to avoid and when to eat and rest. But our brains aren't wired to contemplate the distant future, much less figure out how we'll be feeling once we get there. It's part of our heritage from our short-lived pasts; anything past, say, the next planting season tends to be a hazy blank. Imagining ourselves several decades in the future—not to mention planning ahead for what we should be doing then—is a really tall order.

Even worse, the farther ahead we try to imagine the future, the less detailed the picture is and the less reliable we are at predicting how we'll feel when we get there. When we think about future possibilities, we tend to imagine how we'll feel about them in sweeping generalizations—we imagine that if we retire to Bermuda, we will always be happy, or that if our true love breaks our heart, we will never be happy again. But in reality, even after big life changes, life is a much more subtle blend of good and bad moments, and that's harder for us to appreciate from a distance. In his book *Stumbling on Happiness,* which examines why we are so routinely awful at predicting our own desires, Harvard psychologist Daniel Gilbert writes, "Seeing in time is like seeing in space." We can see the "fine grain" of emotional detail up close, but things far away look fuzzier and somewhat monochromatic. This is something psychologists call affective forecasting, and the reason it's important to a discussion of longevity is simple: it seriously gets in the way of life planning.

Because of this lack of ability to clearly see—or more precisely *feel*—the future, we are likely to make lousy choices about what our future selves will need. Carnegie Mellon economist George Loewenstein came up with the idea of a "cold-to-hot empathy gap." We have a hard time imagining how we will act in the future under the influence of "hot" conditions like hunger, anger, or sexual arousal if we don't happen to feel that way now, and vice versa. We instead make decisions by projecting our current "hot" or "cold" feelings into the future, and we are very often wrong. After eating a large meal you feel confident that you can diet because you are not hungry, just as everything in the store looks good if you are shopping on an empty stomach. If you're feeling chilly in the morning you overdress, knowing full well that the weather report says the temperature will rise to ninety degrees later in that day. If you have the flu, you believe heath care is more essential than on days you're feeling fine. As Gilbert puts it, trying to imagine tomorrow while experiencing today is "a lot like trying to imagine the taste of marshmallow while chewing liver."

Don't misunderstand—it's not that people mispredict the future entirely. We know we'll be happy if we win the lottery, and we are. But here is the catch: We're not as happy as we think we'll be for as long as we think we'll be. After a very short time, lottery winners return to their former levels of happiness. The *New Yorker* magazine once ran a fantastically amusing piece called "Mr. Lucky" about a performance artist struggling to deal with winning $45 million in the lottery, partly because it had done something to undermine the credibility of his off-Broadway one-man show, *A Short Puerto Rican Guy Sings Songs of Angst,* and partly because he knew he could no longer put off dental surgery by claiming that he couldn't afford it. These are details that, no doubt, he'd never envisioned when he bought that winning Lotto ticket. Similarly, even when life deals us blows, after we recover from the initial shock, we are not as sad as we think we'll be. We adjust.

There's another kink in our wiring that impedes our ability to imagine the future, and that's our blindness to cultural norms. As a group, we are enmeshed in a collaboratively written life script that is intensely, but invisibly, powerful. Even though it's forcefully shaping our ideas about aging and where certain events should occur in our life span, we rarely realize it's there. My colleague Hazel Markus, a Stanford psychology professor, likes to use the metaphor of fish in water to point out how oblivious we can be to our social medium until something suddenly changes. Just as a fish is indifferent to water until it drains out of its bowl, we rarely notice our immersion in culture until we're no longer on our home turf, like the disconnect we experience when visiting a foreign country. As just one example: We expect middle-aged adults to be reasonably self-sufficient. The forty-year-old man who lives with his mother, never having left home, makes Americans uneasy. This is because of a cultural proscription; it is not so in Mexico, India, or Greece, where it is typical for households to include adult children and elderly parents. We feel a similar shock here in the United States when we see people in their seventies or eighties who are still in the workforce. How badly did they mismanage their finances, we wonder, that they have to be here greeting shoppers at the mall? Our close adherence to the script prevents us from seeing that it *is* a script, and from questioning how it is written.

To make matters worse, we really like the status quo and will usually defend our ways. Our basic human tendency is to do what we see other people do, and to go on living each day as we did the one before. We don't question whether it is right, and because of that we tend not to see problems with the ways that we live. My mother strongly identifies with her southern heritage, but it still horrifies her that she was just reaching her teenage years before she realized how wrong the Jim Crow laws were. As a child, she had not questioned them because segregation was the only way of life she knew.

Humans have a strong preference for the familiar, no matter whether it's good or bad for us, or for society. In our personal lives, we like the music that we are accustomed to and faces that look like ones we've seen before. In fact, we prefer things that we've seen before even if we can't recall having seen them! Psychologist Robert Zajonc, another of my colleagues, illustrated this phenomenon with a fascinating study in which he presented research participants with drawings of Chinese characters using a tachistoscope, which allows glimpses so brief they are not consciously perceived. Some characters were presented more often than others. Later he asked participants to look at the characters and tell him how much they liked each one. The more frequently a character had been presented, the more the participants liked it. It was more familiar to them, even though they were completely unaware of having seen it before.

The flip side of liking the familiar, of course, is that the human mind has a very hard time with any sort of unknown. My four-year-old grandson Evan asked me the other day, "What's the biggest number?" I fumbled a bit trying to explain that we don't really know. He looked pretty unsatisfied until I said, "Infinity." He happily remarked, "Oh, okay, infinity," with a look that said, "Why were you holding out on me?" He had craved a concrete answer, but it didn't really matter what the answer was.

Similarly, when it comes to planning out the life span, we stick to the concrete answers we know, even if they're somewhat arbitrary. We have difficulty imagining ways of life that we have never experienced. Just a few hundred years ago, during the Middle Ages in Europe, it would have been hard for people to imagine anyone being healthy and active far past their mid-thirties. Nowadays, we consider people in their thirties to just be settling into adulthood! As a species, we're responders—we react to changes in our social environments, rather than anticipate them. Changes in thinking tend to follow behavior change, not precede it.

The danger that lies ahead for our society is that by failing to creatively and proactively adjust to life span changes, we will condemn the old people of the future to live like the old people of the past, even though they will be healthier, more mentally agile, and capable of doing much more. Can you imagine anything worse than a twenty-year twilight, because nobody has figured out what to do with an eighty-year-old who still has the body and brains of a sixty-year-old? If we settle for the status quo, not only are we going to doom the boomers to an outmoded way of experiencing old age, but we won't come up with plans that will help the next generations do better.

For enduring change, we must imagine new ways of living and break through all of the thinking habits that chain us to the present. We must try to generate realistic, humane visions of our future selves, and to imagine what we will truly want to do and what will make us happy when we are old. Once we do that, we can begin to set goals that will help us become those people— to do the work and make the changes and sacrifices necessary in the present to move us toward those goals. If we can't picture ourselves teaching, laughing, loving, and contributing to society when we're ninety and one hundred, then good luck is about the only thing that will get us there. Simone de Beauvoir once wrote, "If we do not know who we are going to be, we cannot know who we are: Let us recognize ourselves in this old man or in that old woman. It must be done if we are to take upon ourselves the entirety of our human state."

Scenario #2: We Spend Like There's No Tomorrow

There is one particular failure of the imagination that cognitive psychologists and behavioral economists have studied quite a bit: people's inability to predict how much money they'll need in the future. For the first time in human history, planning for decades of life in old age—decades that come with all sorts of uncertainties about health and financial needs—has become a necessity. Yet saving for our own for retirement is also new. Fifty years ago, workers' companies did the retirement planning for them, giving them a pension and a gold watch. Before that, your family took care of you from the short time between when you stopped working and the time that you died. It's as if no one has told people, "Times have changed. You are on your own." The moribund retirement savings rate reflects how slow people have been to adjust to this new reality. Americans' savings rates have decreased as life expectancy has risen. Meanwhile, the overall amount of debt that people carry has increased.

Yet if you are in debt, or seem unable to save a dime and are worried about your financial future, you're not alone. Again, you can blame your brain. Cognitive science is pretty clear: we're bad at saving for the future because we have such a hard time imagining ourselves there. When we do put aside money, we tend to undersave, because we generally see our future selves as more ascetic than our current selves, able to live on less money. Spouses tend to think that they will need considerably less income after one of them dies because the survivor won't want much. (They figure they'll be too depressed without their partner.) They think that they'll need only half as much money even though the car payments or the mortgage don't drop off by half when only one person lives in the home, or only one person drives the car.

Even people who feel financially stretched when they are young think that they'll be able to live comfortably enough after retirement, although by then their income will be even lower. After all, they reason, how much can an old person *need*? If you ask people to calculate the subsistence-level income they'll need for retirement, they'll suggest radically modest amounts. When you ask them if they truly could live on that amount at age eighty, they'll say they could manage. Yet if you ask them if they could live on it *today,* they'll say there's no way. Logically, it doesn't make sense. But cognitively, we do it all the time.

People generally overvalue the present and undervalue the future. Social scientists call this particular failure of the imagination temporal discounting, and it's very clearly a phenomenon that applies to decision making about money. If you ask people if they would like ten dollars today or twelve dollars next week, lots of people will take ten dollars right away even though, financially, it's a poorer choice. It may remind you of the saying "A bird in the hand is worth two in the bush." While it's a nice aphorism, from an investment perspective, it's a very bad deal. This sort of bias toward present income, rather than future income, is often at the root of people's failure to save enough for retirement. They'd rather have their full wages now to spend on immediate needs instead of putting some fraction of it away for future needs, even though allowing that money to generate interest would ultimately yield a larger sum.

Why do we let ourselves get sucked into such obviously bad deals? In deciding just about any course of action, we tend to reward our present selves and defer pain to our future selves. So just as we'll trade the slice of cake now for the diet next year, or smoke a cigarette now and put off quitting for another time, we'll spend now and pay later. We'll let our future selves deal with living on less so we can live on more now.

If this split between our current and future selves is so deeply ingrained psychologically, is there anything we can do to bridge the gap? Hal Ersner-Hershfield, a Stanford graduate student who works with me in psychology, thinks there might be. Along with Jeremy Bailenson, a Stanford professor of communications, he recently began to investigate whether virtual reality could help people better relate to their future selves. The researchers work with young volunteers who agree to be photographed so that an avatar—that is, a three-dimensional computer-animated image—of themselves can be created. Wearing virtual-reality helmets, participants are then asked to peer into a computer-generated "mirror," where they see their own avatar looking back at them. When they move, their doppelgänger in the mirror mimics their actions perfectly. But here's the twist: while those in the control group see an avatar that looks like themselves at their current age, the rest of the participants look into the mirror and see themselves forty-five years in the future.

Actual photo   Digital avatar   Age-morphed
                                              digital avatar

Their avatars have been electronically aged: their hair is gray, their jowls sag, and it's best not to speak of what is going on underneath their eyes, but they still look recognizably like themselves. Ersner-Hershfield then leads the participants through a series of tasks in which each person engages with his or her own virtual mirror image. By seeing their future selves not just as hazy images but up close, the participants begin to emotionally connect with this new self-image. The experience is truly surreal, but it suggests that being able to—quite literally—visualize and relate to your older self changes how you prepare for the future. At the study's conclusion, participants are asked to decide how to allocate a $1,000 windfall. Interestingly, participants who see their older selves in the mirror allocate significantly more money to retirement. Ersner-Hershfield believes that when we begin making emotional connections with our future selves, no longer seeing them as strangers, people will begin to save.

Our group preference for following the crowd isn't encouraging us to save, however. Every time I hear a story on the news about how little Americans are putting away for retirement, I fear that it will make the situation worse. I'm afraid that the lemming quality we humans have will kick in. Worse, the federal government isn't setting much of an example. Conservatives have long argued that governments should model their budgets after those of families by spending only the money they have. Instead, families have started modeling their budgets on government. We've become a nation of borrowers and we've accrued enormous debt. Can't afford something? Put it on a credit card! Reached the limit on your credit card? Order another card! We seem oblivious to the idea that one day debts come due, and continue to use plastic to buy things we couldn't afford to buy outright. (A "smart" friend of mine told me recently that his family finally had gotten their credit card use under control: now they only use it when they can't afford something!)

The usurious interest rates charged by most credit cards guarantee that in the long term we will have less money, just like the person who takes ten dollars now instead of twelve dollars next week. The truly frightening part of the problem is that we're creating a culture that says it's okay to be in debt for life, even though debt can be especially problematic in old age. Once people are on fixed incomes, as they typically are in retirement, they will find it virtually impossible to pay their debt down. For many, their biggest monthly expenses will be finance charges on purchases hardly remembered. The 2008 economic collapse led some people to make early withdrawals from their retirement accounts to refinance their mortgages, which left them with less available for retirement. Once on fixed incomes, they will have a smaller margin of safety to cover unexpected expenses or to hire the sort of help that older people often need, like someone to clean the leaves out of the gutters or shovel the driveway in the winter. They'll more likely have to limit those discretionary expenses that bring pleasure, like celebrating special occasions or traveling.

Yet most Americans do have opportunities to save. Many employers offer very generous programs to full-time employees: not only will they deduct a specified amount from employees' paychecks to be put in a tax-deferred 401(k) retirement fund—making saving easy and routine—but they often match a portion of the employees' contribution. Although this is a sweet deal, only about a third of eligible workers sign up for 401(k) programs. The rest lose both the tax break and the free matching contribution from the employer.

Economists scratch their heads about this apparently irrational behavior, but it's just another example of the human bias toward the status quo. As Richard Thaler and Cass Sunstein, the authors of *Nudge: Improving Decisions About Health, Wealth, and Happiness,* point out, the problem is that workers have to voluntarily sign up for 401(k) programs, making their way through the somewhat onerous process of deciding what percentage of their paycheck to contribute and which investment funds to choose. In other words, by signing up they have to choose an action outside of the status quo. However, Thaler and Sunstein write, when companies automatically enroll their employees and people have to opt *out* of the system, rather than *in,* participation skyrockets. Psychologists like to say that defaults contain messages about norms. In other words, if your employer essentially says, "We're going to enroll you in this program unless you tell us otherwise," it communicates the idea that saving for retirement is what most people do and the right choice. By putting the onus on workers to opt in, workplaces are instead conveying the norm that saving is something optional or special.

Furthermore, routinizing the process so that workers don't have to keep choosing to put money away takes some of the sting out of the perception that they're "losing" money to savings. Some workplaces offer a Save More Tomorrow program, in which employees agree to have their retirement contribution levels increase every time they get a raise, so that the numbers on their paycheck stay relatively flat. Not only do they save at a higher rate than their coworkers, they don't feel that they've "lost" that extra money.

Ultimately, the problem we face now as a culture is that we have deprioritized saving and taught people to spend like there is no tomorrow when, in fact, they will face more tomorrows than any generation ever has. Our culture has promised its citizens that retirement will be a carefree time of relaxation and financial stability thanks to Social Security, but in truth Social Security alone offers only a base level of support. Retiring boomers may be more financially strapped than previous generations not only because they have failed to save, and because companies today rarely provide pensions, but because they may have ongoing consumer debt or still be paying down mortgages as a result of borrowing against their homes during the housing bubble. The 2008 economic crisis has prompted financial problems even for savers, because so many people's retirement assets declined in value.

We risk a generation of retirees who feel anxious and strapped for cash, especially now that our government is going into debt with the same zeal as its citizens. I've consistently advocated that people in good physical health can—and should—work longer, in the hope that they will do so because they find work stimulating and personally fulfilling. But a future in which people *must* work longer, and into more advanced ages, because they are compelled to do so for their economic survival is a very grim one indeed.

Scenario #3: We Fail to Address Current Health Threats

It's important to realize that the technological and medical advances of the twentieth century merely gave us the *potential* for very long life, not a guarantee. Nothing is a given. There is a very real risk that global life expectancy, having hit its peak at the beginning of the twenty-first century, will now dwindle downward. Alternatively, people in the developed world could continue to live long lives, but in worse health.

Two very different types of health threats are appearing at the dawn of the twenty-first century, each of which threatens to become more common and more potent in the future if left unchecked. One threat is from the kinds of chronic diseases that afflict primarily affluent populations; the second is from contagious diseases that primarily afflict very poor countries. If you sighed in relief just now because the second problem isn't necessarily *your* problem, think again. In today's world where international travel and trade are commonplace, there are no barricades against contagious diseases. Global pandemics are real possibilities.

But first, let's consider chronic diseases. In the second half of the twentieth century, medical science made fabulous progress in limiting the spread of communicable diseases and treating acute illnesses such as bacterial infections. As a result, the major causes of disability and death in developed nations are now shifting to chronic, noncommunicable diseases like Alzheimer's disease, diabetes, and cancer. Today, coronary heart disease is the number one killer in the world, followed by stroke and other cerebrovascular diseases. You could think of these kinds of conditions as the "leftovers" that remain when most of the causes of premature death, like diarrhea and pneumonia, are reduced or eliminated due to a better health care and sanitation infrastructure.

Chronic diseases like arthritis and hearing impairments, which are not fatal but can lead to lifelong disabilities, are increasingly common. Speaking before a Senate subcommittee in 2007, Richard Hodes, director of the National Institute on Aging, said that despite significant improvements in health in recent decades, "More than half of all Americans over age 65 show evidence of osteoarthritis in at least one joint. Over half of Americans older than 50 have osteoporosis or low bone mass, and cardiovascular disease, cancer, and diabetes remain common among older Americans." These diseases that strike long-lived people are often more prolonged and sometimes more painful than the acute killers of the past. They progress slowly, limit functioning, and often are accompanied by secondary conditions, like the blindness associated with diabetes. For these reasons, chronic diseases are very costly to societies both in terms of medical care and lost productivity.

Chronic illnesses are more common in affluent countries than developing countries, but they are already top killers in China and India, too. Their causes lie mostly in behavior and lifestyle— in risks that people take freely, like eating foods high in fat and sugar, and sitting around instead of moving. In a terribly ironic evolutionary twist, these things that are now bad for us used to be good for us. It's a natural human tendency to like to eat, the more the better, and of course we like to rest. Back in times when food was scarce, labor was physically demanding, and people walked everywhere they went, it made sense to gobble up calories and rest whenever one could. Throughout most of our evolutionary history, humans struggled to get enough to eat. Until the end of the nineteenth century, even in developed nations, people couldn't count on enough food to go around. The nownotorious school lunch was by design high in fat and calories because public schools wanted to pack as much energy as possible into the one meal most school-age children could count on for complete nutrition. But today, when most middle-class Americans have more than enough to eat, we nevertheless remain biologically predisposed to the very eating habits that are now making us sick.

The problem has (literally) grown. By 2000 we reached an important turning point: more American adults were overweight than underweight. Today giant industries have begun to rake in enormous profits by turning out products that will only make us less healthy. For children in particular, this is problematic. Corporations are treating our schools as captive markets for soda pop and pizza sales. Television watching keeps children on couches for an average of thirty hours a week, and computers keep them in their chairs longer still. Inexpensive fast food has replaced fresh vegetables and fruits in many busy families' diets, far more for poor people because that's what's available in low-income neighborhoods. Sweetened beverages now make up a quarter of the daily calories that young adults consume. Schoolchildren are far less likely today than fifty years ago to walk or bike to school. Some schools don't have recess anymore for fear of lawsuits if a child should be injured. Instead, kids' time at school is mostly spent sitting.

Many experts believe that in a single generation obesity may erase all of the health gains made in the last fifty years. Extrapolating from current trends, epidemiologist Youfa Wang and his colleagues at the Johns Hopkins Bloomberg School of Public Health estimate that by the year 2030, 86 percent of American adults and 30 percent of children and teens will be overweight. By the year 2048, their study concludes, *all* adult Americans will be overweight. This trend toward 100 percent prevalence for obesity is particularly pernicious for female African Americans. Black women are expected to reach this point eighteen years before the rest of the adult population does, in the year 2030. Although half of all American children and teens are projected to be overweight by the year 2070, black girls are expected to reach that point twenty years ahead of them, by the year 2050.

Wang understands that we will never actually reach that 100 percent point because some people are genetically resistant to obesity and no doubt an exceptional few will resist with good health habits. However, the point is that the statistical trends are moving upward incredibly fast. This rising obesity rate bodes ill for the long-term health of future generations. Although an obese seventy-year-old has the same life expectancy as anyone else, he or she is likely to spend 40 percent more time disabled, and to incur $39,000 more in health care costs. Wang's study estimates that total health care costs related to obesity will double every decade, until by the year 2030 they absorb up to 18 percent of all health care dollars.

Obesity will also worsen young people's overall health outlook. For example, Amy Lerner, a biomechanical engineer at the University of Rochester, has documented alterations in gait among obese children that put them at risk for early osteoarthritis. Obesity is a risk factor for many chronic diseases, including heart disease, stroke, and diabetes. Most experts agree that obesity is the primary reason for the staggering increase in type 2 diabetes among Americans, particularly among our nation's children, even though just a couple of decades ago type 2 diabetes was also called "adult-onset diabetes" because it was restricted mostly to adults. Because its symptoms worsen over time, it's frightening to think of what may happen to a generation that does not merely grow old with the disease but grows *up* with it. Some health economists believe that the rise of diabetes in childhood, and its long-term attendant risks for heart disease and stroke, could potentially undo the improvements to health in old age made over the last half century, and ultimately shorten life expectancy.

Even worse, these conditions are likely to be perpetuated across generations. Overweight moms are more likely to be diabetic, diabetic moms are more likely to have premature babies, and those babies are more likely to become obese themselves as they reach adolescence. This particular combination—notably prevalent among the poor—of low birth weight followed by obesity in adolescence further exacerbates the risk of developing diabetes.

Chronic diseases pose new and troublesome conundrums. A century ago, the medical problems that beset us were solved by bench scientists looking through microscopes. Today, the treatment and prevention of chronic diseases will require significant lifestyle changes, based on the research and insights of social scientists studying human behavior. Today many financial stakeholders in the health care system—whether they are employers, heads of state, or international health agencies—feel stymied by long-standing cultural proscriptions that support the right of individuals to make lifestyle choices, even when those choices make them sick. Though there is the occasional provocative news story about a company that taxes employees who smoke or weighs them when they arrive at work, these stories are mostly reported as "Big Brother" interference.

I share the discomfort many Americans feel about these kinds of invasive interventions. Like them, I place a very high premium on freedom of choice. If people want to smoke and drink, I see that as their right, unless they smoke right next to me or drink and drive—in other words, unless they impose on *my* freedoms.

But mostly what I see as problematic is that employers are intervening at the wrong point in the cycle. Instead of punishing workers who are fat, why not change the work environment so that people eat better and move around more, by serving healthy food in the cafeteria and designing grounds that encourage walking? Similarly, instead of presuming that obese children are slackers with no self-control, why don't we stop selling them soda pop at school? We need to design environments that encourage good choices. Thaler and Sunstein call this "libertarian paternalism"— that is, allowing a free choice but setting up incentives so that people freely make the "right" choice. Some people don't like the idea of influencing others' behavior, but when you think about it, all cultures encourage *something*. Right now our culture encourages very unhealthy behavior, and it is literally killing us.

While chronic disease continues to emerge as a threat in the developed world, an older threat has reemerged in other parts of the globe. By the close of World War II there had been great hope that the most sinister of infectious diseases were close to becoming problems of the past. Malaria, smallpox, tuberculosis, and cholera had seemingly been eradicated in the developed world. Confident that progress would continue, in 1978 the United Nations issued a "Health for All 2000" accord which proclaimed that by the end of the millennium infectious diseases would no longer pose a significant problem to health in even the poorest nations. Progress had been so triumphant and so swift that confidence was high.

But in subsequent years, disparities in health conditions around the globe have widened, not diminished. In the poorest parts of the world, infectious diseases still take a heavy toll on public health. According to the World Health Organization, respiratory illnesses like pneumonia are the biggest killers in low-income countries, and instead of having been stamped out long ago, infections like diarrheal diseases, tuberculosis, and malaria are still killing millions each year. Along with measles and HIV/AIDS, these diseases are largely responsible for the 10 million annual deaths worldwide of children under the age of five.

New infectious killers have also emerged since those hopeful postwar days. By the end of 2007, more than 33 million people worldwide had contracted HIV/AIDS; that year it killed 2 million people, including 330,000 children. It is now the top cause of death in sub-Saharan Africa, where 60 percent of those infected are female. The toll it has taken on working-age adults is so profound that an entirely new population profile, shaped like an hourglass, can be used to describe the region. With so many parents dying from the disease, the only people who remain are their young orphans and the elderly. This devastating demographic pattern leaves dependents at both ends of the life span with few healthy adults in the middle to support them.

The continuing spread of these kinds of infectious diseases is not only a powerful factor in suppressing longevity in very poor regions of the world, but it has serious ramifications for the deepening of global poverty. When illness is widespread, people cannot work, hopes and dreams of parents are shattered as they watch their children die, economies are strained, and political unrest ensues.

As bad as the situation is today, it may grow worse in coming decades because virtually all of the projected population growth in the world will occur in economically disadvantaged regions, primarily in Africa and the Middle East, where living conditions are already poor and societal infrastructure is often inadequate. This growth will be primarily in cities, where overcrowding will contribute further to the spread of disease. Adele Hayutin, Director of Global Aging for the Stanford Center on Longevity, expects that the urban population in the fifty poorest countries worldwide will more than double to a collective 520 million residents by the year 2030. These patterns reflect both a movement from rural areas to cities and the appearance of new cities. Megacities—those with populations greater than 10 million—will increase the pressure on already weak urban infrastructures, creating fertile grounds for the spread of contagious disease. Megacities in very impoverished areas are at special risk, because diseases spread more rapidly in places where populations are physically fragile and living conditions are poor. Contagious diseases usually take their worst tolls on the people living in the least affluent regions of the world.

Yet a virus, of course, is oblivious to race, social class, religion, and nationality, and will not hesitate to cross borders. The flu pandemic of 1918 started in the United States and spread around the globe partly thanks to troops deployed to fight World War I. Today, contagious diseases like the West Nile virus, SARS, and bird flu could spread just as quickly thanks to international commerce and travel. A major outbreak in any part of the world could become a global pandemic and shorten life expectancy around the world.

It's important to remember that we have not been living longer because the human body has inherently changed; we have not evolved into a superresilient species. We are living longer because our environments have changed, and they could change again, for the worse. Viral infections that can sweep the globe remain a threat, and so are the eating and lifestyle habits that encourage chronic disease. Think of them as another kind of infection, one that, sadly, the United States has begun to spread to the rest of the world.

Scenario #4: We Let the Poor Stay Poor

You could say that longevity is a case of "good news, bad news." The good news is that we know it's possible to live into one's nineties and even reach one hundred in remarkably good shape. A significant minority of people are doing just that today. But the bad news is that most Americans aren't flourishing in old age. This isn't because of luck or fate. Aging in America follows a distinct class divide.

Affluent, educated Americans are aging really well. This group doesn't show much functional decline even into their eighties. They appear to have achieved what my colleague Jim Fries, a Stanford professor emeritus of medicine, calls a "compression of morbidity"—in other words, although their bodies ultimately fail, as all bodies must, the period of disability at the end of their lives is short, "compressed" to a year or so. Up until that time they are healthy, active, and contributing members of families, neighborhoods, and societies. This may be the best news yet, because we know that this outcome is possible.

What is it about being financially stable that lends itself to long life in America? You might guess that it's health care access, but although this is certainly an advantage, the same class-based patterns show up in countries like England that have high-quality universal health care. Although income level and occupational status are also influential, when push comes to shove, I think most social scientists would put their money on education as the most important factor in ensuring longer lives. Education predicts aging outcomes in study after study. Highly educated people get better jobs, they make more money, and they tend to have higher-status jobs than people with little education. They live in safer neighborhoods, practice healthier lifestyles, and experience less stress in day-to-day life. They are more likely to be the boss at work than to have to deal with a difficult boss. While income level best predicts how quickly people decline after they get sick, education predicts whether or not people get sick in the first place. When educated people get sick, they manage their health better. They have access to health care and consider more treatment options. They tend to participate with their physicians in health-related decisions, and tend to be more consistent in following a treatment regimen.

For example, there are substantial differences in health outcomes for people with different levels of education who have either insulin-dependent diabetes or HIV. Both of these diseases respond well to treatment, but the treatments themselves are complicated, and the onus is on the patient to adhere to the regimen every day. In the case of insulin-dependent diabetes, patients have to pay close attention to their body's responses to a variety of situations and medicate themselves accordingly. In the case of HIV, medications have to be taken on a strict timetable and with certain types of food. Dana Goldman and James Smith, economists at the Rand Corporation, studied differences in how well college-educated people and high school dropouts managed their treatments. For both diseases, educated people understood the instructions better and complied with treatment regimens more effectively, adjusting their schedules and modifying their environments. The researchers found that the correlation between education and health outcomes was fully explained by adherence to the treatment. Better compliance was related to reports of better general health, and better results on laboratory tests, such as higher CD4 cell counts in HIV patients.

On the other hand, people who have little education decline steadily in functional health throughout adulthood. Just as life expectancy increases have not been shared equally around the globe, the benefits of long life are distributed inequitably in the United States, where wealth and education are very unevenly divided among the country's citizens. Some had hoped that in America even the poor would eventually benefit from society's advances as the wealthy become ever wealthier, but recent studies provide a sober reminder that we cannot count on a trickle-down approach to raise the quality of life for everyone. Differences between the rich and poor, and between the more and less educated, are in fact increasing in the United States. As noted in chapter 1, affluent white women now live, on average, fourteen years longer than poor black men do. Gopal Singh, an epidemiologist at the Health Resources and Services Administration, and Mohammad Siahpush, a professor of sociology at the University of Nebraska Medical Center's College of Public Health, have studied the relationship between life expectancy and social class. They've found that disparities are widening.

Singh and Siahpush found that the difference in life expectancy between the most and least advantaged groups in the United States was 2.8 years in 1980. By 2000, that difference had increased to 4.5 years. Harvard economist David Cutler and his colleagues found a similar pattern when it came to education. Life expectancy past the age of twenty-five increased between 1990 and 2000 in the United States, but only among those with college educations. Compared to people with a high school education or less, the life expectancy of college-educated Americans had gained a 30 percent advantage. It's a shocking reminder that the toll of being poor and uneducated can be measured not just in life's quality, but in actual years of life.

To a large extent, these health differences can be explained by the fact that affluent people eat healthier meals, are less likely to smoke or be obese, and are more likely to seek medical care when problems arise. But these factors don't fully explain the linear relationship between affluence and disease. Increasingly, researchers are becoming convinced that poverty is associated with chronic activation of the sympathetic nervous system, the communication system between the brain and the periphery that regulates stress. Acute activation of the system is essential for survival. It's responsible for fight-or-flight responses; it's what helps you react instantly if someone is about to clobber you or if your car suddenly begins to career off the road. But when levels of chemical compounds that act as neurotransmitters and hormones, like cortisol, remain steadily high, the brain is essentially kept in overdrive. Arterial walls begin to stiffen, glucose is poorly regulated, fatty deposits build around the waist. In other words, there is a direct association between socioeconomic disadvantage and physiological indicators of stress.

What is perhaps most sobering is that researchers are observing these profiles associated with chronic stress in children under age five. Teresa Seeman, an epidemiologist at the University of California at Los Angeles and a lead researcher in understanding the pathways through which social class has biological effects, is seeing frighteningly high elevations of glucose in three- and four-year-olds. Seeman tells me, "We are seeing the same socioeconomic class gradients in biological parameters previously observed in adults in very young children. Children on the low end of the socioeconomic spectrum already have relatively poor glucose regulation, higher body mass, and higher levels of major stress hormones."

Here's one last, but really big, sign of trouble: findings from a recent report showed that life expectancy is actually *declining* in parts of Appalachia and the Deep South. Arguably, poverty takes its most profound toll in rural America, and that affects how well people fare in old age. Most of what we know about poor people is based on studies of the urban poor, but despite the harsh images we often have of city life, in some ways cities are easier places for people to get the services they need. Given the fast pace of New York City, many are surprised to learn that Manhattan is touted as one of the best locations in the country for older adults. Medical and social services, grocery stores and pharmacies, and people who can provide companionship are all available nearby, many within walking distance. "Poverty in rural communities is qualitatively different than urban areas," says Martha Crowther, a clinical psychologist at the University of Alabama who studies elderly poor people in the rural South. "Poverty is terrible anywhere, but at least in cities there are centers and agencies that provide assistance."

Rural areas, however, often lack the kinds of services that make it possible for older people to live independently. Even when they obtain medical coverage under Medicare, it sometimes doesn't make much difference if they can't find the doctors they need locally. Public transportation may be nonexistent. People may have to drive for many miles to find a Target or Costco. Instead, older people must rely on local friends and family for assistance, and these friends and relatives are probably poor themselves. High school dropout rates are higher among rural than urban youth, and unemployment is higher as well. Sometimes elderly people in rural areas do not have many younger relatives they can rely on. In areas where youth see no real options for their futures, the younger generation has often decamped for the city; those who remain are often struggling themselves.

Because of these differences—between urban and rural, rich and poor, those who do and do not receive a college education—not everyone in our country has an equal chance of aging well. We are dangerously close to becoming a nation whose fundamental principles are challenged by the stark inequalities that make the path to a better life elusive for so many. The philosophical and moral tenets underlying democracy are undermined when large segments of the population cannot benefit from the cultural and scientific changes that have led to long life. True, there will always be inequality in societies; some people will work harder than others, some will be smarter and more creative. But when some groups are so systematically disadvantaged that children under the age of five are on health trajectories that ultimately take a toll in years of life, we all have to question whether we live in a truly just society.

Scenario #5: We Forget to Plan for the Children

When we talk about aging, we usually think of ourselves, or of our parents. But we shouldn't just be thinking about adults. The youngest members of our society are aging too. Our myopia often makes us forget that today's little ones are tomorrow's old ones. Without concerted efforts to start designing their lives for old age right now, we face the real danger of a kind of *Groundhog Day* situation, in which each generation is taken aback by living as long as it does. Ours should be the last generation that arrives at old age unprepared.

I like to tell people that when I look at three-year-olds I see the first hundred-year-olds to live in the twenty-second century. They mostly laugh, but it's true—half of today's toddlers may live to be centenarians. Next time you look at children on a playground or in a shopping mall, squint a little and see them as older people. Consider what we can do for them right now to ensure their long-term futures are happy and healthy.

How today's children will fare depends a great deal on how we treat them now, and, frankly, we're off to a lousy start. We are the only nation on the planet that guarantees health care to old people while millions of children have no health insurance at all. Uninsured children are unlikely to get the primary preventive health care that really pays off, like vaccinations, even though we are learning more every day about the ways that early health status affects functioning in later life. Instead of making sure that they build strong bones by being physically active, we're putting kids in situations both at home and at school where they hardly move.

We're encouraging lifestyle habits that promote obesity, which could make kids sicker and frailer in old age than today's elderly.

A century ago, as fertility rates were falling, society's investment in public education was increasing. Today primary education is sorely lacking in many parts of the country. More high school students are going to college than ever before but the number of graduates has leveled. Only a little over 30 percent of high school graduates end up with college degrees. Our schools need a major investment if they are going to provide first-class educations for all of the nation's children. There is considerable controversy over whether more funding for primary education is the answer to its problems, but it's hard to believe that funding along with a considerable investment of time and smart advice from experts in education reform wouldn't help. At a point in history when we live in an "information society" and markets are increasingly global, today's children will need excellent educations—ones that continue throughout their lives—to prepare them for success.

Though I get uneasy when pundits pit the needs of the old against the needs of the young, it's true that government programs tilt heavily in favor of supporting older people. The AARP is the most powerful lobby in Washington. It's important to look out for older people's needs, but with so much attention being paid to prescription drugs and Social Security, we could forget to consider children's needs, too. We spend far more tax money subsidizing consumption of health services by the elderly than we invest in children's health care and education. Social Security and Medicare fulfill a social contract with yesterday's workers. Investments in our children today will pay enormous dividends in the future.

For hundreds of years, each generation has been more productive than the previous one. Technologies and health have improved steadily; each generation has been better educated than the previous one. It appears that this has recently leveled off. In an increasingly competitive global economy, we simply cannot allow a regression to happen. We have been so busy reacting aggressively to problems in the present that we're failing to address the foreseeable problems of the future, which will affect the well-being of our children and our grandchildren. It's a kind of myopia we can no longer afford.

8

Ensuring a Long Bright Future

You've been given a gift of time and can ensure that you use it well. Yet I can't think of a less creative or more misguided way to use those extra years than the way our society is using them today: adding years of leisure to the very end of life, while leaving young adulthood and middle age pressure packed and stressful. People now feel like they don't have enough time to do the important things in life when, in fact, they've got more time than ever before in the history of the species. You have the chance, starting now, to design for yourself an old age that is not only different, but better than any previous generation's in human history.

How should you plan for a very long and bright future? Much of the advice being offered today about optimal aging is specific tidbits about whether you should try to extend your healthy years by downing fish oil, or doing yoga, or playing endless rounds of Sudoku, but this kind of information can quickly become outdated. Instead, let me offer you a more enduring conceptual framework for how best to prepare for, and take advantage of, very long life. This framework rests on four basic principles: *envision, design, diversify,* and *invest.* I'll take a moment to explain what each of these principles represents, and then describe four areas of life in which I think they could be best applied.

ENVISION: We've been socially programmed to think about the ways we'll *cope* with old age. Instead, I challenge you to start thinking now about ways to thoroughly enjoy the years that lie ahead. Imagine what it might be like to live to a healthy, happy one hundred. Start daydreaming about the autumn of your life as much as you daydreamed about finding your perfect love when you were a teenager. Give it as much thought as you gave to your career aspirations when you were a kid. Instead of imagining all of the tedious work-related chores you won't have to do once you reach retirement, imagine in vivid detail what you'll *want* to do once your principal obligations in life to your family and employers are behind you, and your time is truly your own.

Giving is one of the most truly satisfying things that you can do, so as you imagine your future, think of what kind of bequest you could leave to the world. This doesn't necessarily have to be money left to family members or a valued institution. It can be a skill, a message, an artwork, a charitable organization, a cause that you have advanced. The boomer generation, in particular, could play the lead role in demonstrating to the world the power of the fifty-fifty model of life, in which you spend the first half of your life exploring the world and developing your skills, and the second half using that expertise to help others.

DESIGN: Your chances of enjoying good health, fiscal stability, and mental sharpness in old age will be determined largely by the choices you make in your daily life, starting today. But although we all have the best of intentions when it comes to our future well-being—we vow we'll stop smoking, we'll give up our fast-food habit, we'll save money in our 401(k) plans—willpower alone cannot keep us on the right path for eighty, ninety, or even one hundred years. The hard part isn't knowing the right path when you see it, it's staying on it. Knowledge alone isn't a very good taskmaster, and even the best motivation has a tendency to flag. It's easy to procrastinate or get distracted when slowly working toward very long-term goals, especially when the payback for good behavior seems so far off, the tasks seem insurmountable, and progress feels so incremental that we wonder if we are truly getting anywhere at all.

The key, instead, is to design your social and physical environments—your home, your bank accounts, your family's eating habits—so that your daily routine reinforces your goals. By taking actions to change your "default settings" you avoid having to make hard choices time and again. We'll talk more throughout this chapter about some areas in which this idea can be applied, but the main concept is to make doing the right thing for your health, your emotional well-being, and your money simple and routine.

DIVERSIFY: You know that diversifying is good for your stock portfolio, but it is in fact a good idea for most domains of life. Just as you shouldn't put all of your investments into a single fund or stock, don't put all of your social investments into only your children, your spouse, or your job. In an era of longevity, you'll likely experience a life that will move through many phases. You should diversify your expertise, because you may take on more than one career and fulfill many volunteer and civic roles. You should diversify your social network, because the nuclear family is no longer enough to provide, on its own, the social support you'll need over your lifetime. You should diversify your activities, because longer life presents the opportunity to break down those life course models that have mostly separated education, work and family, and retirement into rigid stages. Let's break away from the idea that life is so short that it allows you only one role, or only one social mileau. Plan for a life that is not only long, but broad.

INVEST: Because the baby boomers will pioneer extended life span in the developed world, the changes we make to the workplace, to the education system, and to our government network of social supports will all set the pace for the generations that come after us. The children in elementary school today are likely to live even longer than the boomers. So will the lessons we pass along about what it means to age, and what a healthy long life can be like. Let's make sure that today's children can look forward to an old age as promising as the one we can expect.

There may be no better financial or social investment we can make than investing in science. Investments in science not only will bring huge financial rewards, including high-quality jobs and new industries, but health and lifestyle improvements that cannot be valued in dollars. Of course, science and education go hand in hand. Investing in education may be the best way you can help put tomorrow's children on a trajectory that will help them achieve a healthy long life. Start with your own children or grandchildren, or with other younger relatives and friends, and then consider expanding your investments to the children in your neighborhood or perhaps around the world.

This conceptual framework—*envision, design, diversify,* and *invest*—is a good way to strategize for coming changes in any area of your life, but I've picked the following four because I think they are the most crucial in ensuring well-being in old age, and because we can begin to make changes in these areas of our lives today. As you read them, I hope you'll find ideas that will be applicable to your own life, and that you'll be inspired to reach out to others—friends, family, and coworkers as well as your local community organizations, religious groups, and even your congressional representatives—to talk with them about how we can all work together to achieve the cultural changes that will make long lives healthy and happy.

Nourish Your Social Relationships

Healthy humans need to be part of a group. That's how we survived throughout evolution, and that's how we survive today. Strong social relationships will affect not only your quality of life, but how long you live. Many of the social institutions that have supported humans throughout our history are rapidly changing, so we'll need to envision ways to successfully adapt.

The developed world is undergoing an incredible demographic shift, as life span increases and birthrates drop. In the near future, more generations of families will be alive at any one time than ever before, but nuclear families themselves will likely be smaller. More women than ever—some 20 percent—are not hav-ing children. Assuming current marriage patterns continue, the concept of family will become increasingly fluid, as members are added through remarriage or divorced couples go their sepa-rate ways.

For those of us in the boomer generation, the family that sur-rounds us when we reach old age may be both smaller than that of our grandparents, with fewer grandchildren and with more single heads of household, and more mixed. It may feature a greater proportion of people who are related to us by marriage rather than by blood, like step-grandchildren, and a wider array of exes and former in-laws. As families become more fluid and less defined by biological ties, they could become less stable, and offer fewer sources of social support than families once did. On the other hand, the presence of multiple living generations could offset that instability, at least from the point of view of young children, who will likely have a full complement of grandparents and great-grandparents alive at the same time and invested in looking after them. Having several generations of older relatives on hand could offer the family valuable resources.

With fewer family ties, it will be more important than ever to actively nurture them. Take especially good care of your brothers and sisters, because your relationships with them, as well as with cousins who are about your own age, will likely be the longest-lasting of your life. For some of you, they are people you will know for around one hundred years. Your siblings are the ones who share your oldest memories, and because you are close in age, they will go through life's milestones with you. In very old age, when time and ill health have transformed how the world sees you, they will be the ones who remember the way you were "back when." They are the ones you can count on for complete, and unflattering, honesty—they're the ones who will not hesitate to tell you when you have a hair growing out of your nose or when you have tucked the back of your skirt into your pantyhose. True, sibling relationships are often fractious, or may fade over the years, especially if you live far apart. But if you can still put aside your differences long enough to laugh together and have great conversations, these are relationships worth keeping.

Indeed, this is an important guideline for nourishing long-term family relationships: learn to let go of grudges. As families and friendships last for many decades, there will be inevitable conflicts. You'll be crossed, sometime double-crossed. But if we write off every person who offends us in some way, we'll be pretty lonely by old age. Sometimes there are truly good reasons to break away from unhealthy family dynamics, but in many cases family tensions stem from incidents so long ago that the original offense hardly matters anymore. If there are long-standing feuds in your family, do your best to move toward reconciliation. It sounds a little corny, but when you are angry at somebody over long periods of time, it hurts you much more than it hurts them. Experiencing anger at a persistent level is a form of stress—and we already know what stress does to your health and life span. Cultivate a spirit of forgiveness. It's good for your health. It's hard, and sometimes you have to give yourself time. A good strategy is to decide to behave as if you have forgiven the offender. Pretty soon, your emotions will follow.

Even families with strong ties need to nurture relationships beyond kin. Beloved family members die, children move far away.
So starting now, begin to diversify your "family" beyond your immediate biological ties and your relationship with your romantic
partner. Create meaningful, reciprocal bonds with people who
reflect different facets of your life—friends, neighbors, colleagues,
mentors. If you diversify you are better insulated against unexpected changes that affect your social support network, such as
illness, divorce, or relocation. The upside of creating "voluntary"
families is that you have the opportunity to create social networks
that include the people you like best. You don't have to lose the
sister-in-law you adore just because she and your brother divorced. You can include your best friend in family celebrations,
and get to know your best friend's family too.

Working to keep our families—whether related to us by blood
or by friendship—strong will take real effort. Many of us get so
wrapped up in work obligations in middle age that we cut off the
oxygen to our social lives. We don't even spend the time we'd like
to with our own children! It's a terrible idea to wait until retirement to savor your relationships—and a risk, too, since long life
is a general biological trend, but not a given for everybody. If
making time for family and friendship is your weak point, then
design your schedule so that time with loved ones is routinely included. Literally put family and social time in a regular rotation
on your calendar, and treat it with the same commitment you'd
give to any other meeting.

A colleague of mine points out that when her two girls were
young, she wanted to pick them up after school but couldn't because three o'clock faculty meetings often got in the way. Then

one day she realized that the reason the meetings weren't at one o'clock, which would have been more convenient for her, was because two of her colleagues had a regular squash match then. Their social commitment was written into their calendars, so they'd scheduled around it. Her children's pickup from school was not. From that day forward, she simply told people that she had a meeting at 3:00 p.m., and the faculty meeting was rescheduled for a time that worked better for everybody. She did have a meeting, of course. It was with her daughters.

If you're a workaholic and rarely take family vacations, try this—it's one of the best tips I've heard for busy people who struggle to disengage from work, and it comes from friends of mine, a married couple who once in a blue moon would take a long weekend to get away. Each time they realized how much it helped them relax and how good it was for their relationship, but once they got home they had a heck of a time scheduling another weekend getaway. Once they got back to the daily grind, years would go before they felt they could "afford" more time away. So finally they made a pact: they wouldn't return from one weekend getaway before making the reservations for the next one. Once they had a concrete date and had put down a deposit, they were sure to follow through. It's amazing what blocking a date on a calendar can do!

Finally, as you work to strengthen your social network, make sure you don't isolate yourself within a group of similarly aged people, no matter what your age is now. As we age, our social networks naturally narrow to those we care for most, so make sure you prune carefully. If everyone on your speed dial went to high school when you did, you've pruned too far. In old age you'll run the risk of being the last (and loneliest) man (or woman) standing.

We need to break down generational barriers, especially as core families become increasingly likely to span many generations. We need to stop acting in forced, unnatural ways as we reach across generations so that relationships can be strong and genuine. Older people need to make a real effort to know members of younger generations and treat them as fully functioning people. Especially when dealing with younger relatives they don't see frequently, older adults have a tendency to play Twenty Questions, asking them things like "How do you like school?" along with the traditional "My, haven't you grown." But kids can get overwhelmed by a barrage of questions, especially ones that can be met with one-word answers like "Fine" and "Yes." These exchanges don't build real intimacy the way simply sharing time and meaningful experiences does. Rent a movie to watch together and talk about it. Find out what music your young friends like best and ask to listen to their favorites.

Likewise, younger folks need to start building bonds with older people—not just their own grandparents—by inviting them into their lives. Younger people often have a standoffishness with older people. They don't want to offend them, so they treat them gingerly or patronizingly. Or alternatively, they just stay away. But ironically, unlike kids, most adults really like the Twenty Questions routine, especially when questions are asked with real interest and open-mindedness. For adults, when people ask questions about our personal lives it is a sign that they find us intriguing and desire our friendship. When younger folks ask meaningful questions, like "What was your life like during the

Vietnam War?" or even questions about growing older, they'll likely find that the older people in their lives will be happy to share their thoughts with them.

Because intergenerational ties will be important in an age of longevity, we should invest in them by helping the children in our lives have strong, comfortable relationships with relatives of different generations, even if they live far away, so that older people don't seem scary and strange. If you're the older adult who lives far away, reach out to the kids by doing more than just sending cards and gifts and visiting at holidays. You might be surprised how much more a teenager or preadolescent will open up in a long personal phone chat with an unconditionally positive grandparent than in a conversation with Mom or Dad, or how an invitation to spend part of the summer with a beloved aunt or uncle in a new city can be a real bonding opportunity and a chance to give parents and kids a break from each other. (In fact, it is a common practice in Germany and other parts of Europe for children to spend summers with their grandparents.) At home, help them get to know older adults in their own community who can be positive role models. Volunteering is often a good place to make contact with older generations.

We need to help future generations envision their own very long lives, just as we are beginning to do for ourselves. We should make it clear to children that long life is not something that's just for Grandma and Grandpa, but something that they should expect and prepare for as well. Ask the young people you know well what sort of old people they plan to be, and help them dream about long-term goals. Talk with them about your own aging, how it feels to grow old, what you wish you hadn't done, and those things you think you did right. Don't talk only about your aches and pains, but don't be afraid to talk about them, either. Your grandchild may become the scientist who finds a cure for arthritis because she knows it troubled you.

Young people, both children and adults, also need to know that you are enjoying life when you are. It will help them see older age as a time with ups and downs, just like the time they are experiencing now. Reassure them about what they can look forward to. One day when my mother was at the peak of menopause and having a hot flash, she remembers her mother-in-law whispering to her, "Know that it will get better as you get older, dear." I love to see the faces of my students when I get to tell them that as they get older they'll care less about what other people think of them.

You can also invest literally in your children and grandchildren. I like a model practiced widely among Chinese families in which older generations start saving for their grandchildren's education even before they are born! That's a great way to have compound interest work in your favor. You could also start retirement accounts for your children or grandchildren (or those of close friends, if there are none in your own family) when they are born. Even if you only have the means to contribute a few dollars at a time, over many decades compound interest will multiply these accounts' value many times over. Since financial assistance isn't within the reach of all grandparents, county and state governments could encourage this kind of investment in future generations by setting up programs that allow grandparents and great-grandparents the opportunity to earn tuition credits at local colleges for their family members in return for community service.

Although the prospect of changes in the family always sparks some concern, it's good to remember that family structure has consistently changed over history, always with trade-offs, for better and worse. No matter what changes family and social ties face as we adapt to our extra years, the most important message is to nourish important relationships, so they get stronger over time. You will need a strong convoy as you travel through life.

Work Longer, Save More

Starting with the boomer generation, let's get used to the idea of working longer. It's not just to ensure the solvency of the Social Security system—though it would help—or because many people will need time to bolster anemic personal savings accounts before embarking on multidecade retirements. It's because, for the most part, people enjoy their work—they are what they do. The great Sigmund Freud put work on the same plane as love when he wrote about the key ingredients of good mental health. Although not every moment on the job is a joy, over time work gives us many gifts: a sense of identity and purpose, the opportunity to use our skills and learn new ones, a network of familiar people who know us in ways that even our own family may not, and the chance to use our brains to solve problems. Longer lives should lead to longer working years. The trick is to make our longer passage through the working world both satisfying and stimulating.

Each of us should envision how we would like to allocate work throughout our lifetimes, and that will depend in part on how we see it interweaving with other commitments like family, community service, travel and education. Young people just entering the workforce are likely to have multiple jobs during their careers, so if you are in the earlier stages of planning your career think about the different jobs you will want to hold. Do you want to pursue flexible but perhaps lower-paying jobs early and late in your career but work like a dog in the middle? How will one type of job prepare you for a second and third? If you'd like to explore more than one kind of career in your lifetime, consider which abilities improve and worsen with age. If there is a lot of new learning involved, you may want to take on those jobs early in life. Conversely, if the position draws on long-honed skills or life experience, it's best to tackle it during midlife. From a cognitive perspective, becoming a pilot after you retire is not a particularly good idea, but becoming a teacher, politician, or a community organizer is a great one. (Always think twice before becoming a boxer.)

For people who see retirement on the horizon, think about ways to make the transition from work to retirement without abruptly jumping ship the day you turn sixty-five. Talk to your employer about what your plans are and what options might be available to you, such as reducing your hours, focusing on special projects dear to your heart, or mentoring younger workers. I often think that elementary school teachers, who may grow physically weary of a classroom of six-year-olds by the time they are approaching retirement, would make wonderful classroom assistants to new teachers, providing advice to the teacher and special attention to that troublesome student who disrupts the class.

Encore Careers, the movement Marc Freedman is heading at Civic Ventures, is offering satisfying new opportunities to people in midlife. With slogans like "Don't retire, rewire," people close to retirement age are being urged to turn to new careers instead, like litigators turning to public interest law, or corporate managers becoming high school principals. Bringing their expertise to new careers in socially significant fields like education, environmental protection, or divinity may be especially appealing to boomers who need to work longer and want to work on something different and meaningful.

No matter where you are in your life in terms of work, attempt to diversify your expertise. You may not think of your job as "educational," but in fact it is very likely one of the biggest sources of intellectual stimulation in your life. It provides you with daily challenges to meet, people with whom to exercise your conversational and social skills, and environments outside of your home to experience. It is probably the place in your life where you are most likely to encounter new technologies and to meet new people, including people from other age groups. With the employment phase of life stretching out longer than ever, it's important that work be engaging, rather than stultifying. For anyone embarking on a career, or considering a career change, think carefully about whether or not your prospective field will sustain your continued interest over a long period of time. I always advise my students to find careers that they love because, if they do, work will not seem like work.

Some professions, including jobs in the physical and social sciences, the arts, medicine, law, and engineering naturally lend themselves to continued growth and exploration, because the fields themselves are constantly changing as new technologies arise and new ideas gain prevalence. But many jobs are highly repetitive, and that's not good for mental agility. Some of the ubiquitous cognitive slowing observed as people age is due to the lack of new learning. If your job has become so automatic you don't have to think about it, it's time to move on. If you don't have the training or education to land a stimulating job, I recommend that you change what you do frequently enough that the change itself keeps you on your toes. If you work the checkout line at a grocery store, you may want move to the bakery department or ask for a transfer to a different store in the chain.

For most people, working longer will make good financial sense. Maybe you're one of those middle-aged people who haven't saved enough and are growing increasingly nervous as you approach sixty-five. Or maybe you did save responsibly only to watch the stock market collapse of 2008 take a hefty chunk. In either case, it's a good reason not to opt for early retirement and reduced Social Security payments. Yet many Americans are doing just that. As economists Alicia Munnell and Steven Sass at the Center for Retirement Research at Boston College point out in *Working Longer: The Solution to the Retirement Income Challenge,* the average American is now retiring at sixty-two or sixty-three and taking a smaller benefit. Don't even think about it! Not only will you get a smaller check each month for the rest of your life, but longer life means that you'll have more years to live on less. Yet the opposite is true as well—if you can hold off retirement until age seventy, you can receive one-third more in your monthly checks for the rest of your life. Munnell and Sass particularly advise married women to encourage their husbands not to retire early, because women are likely to outlive their husbands. Once the men die their spouses' benefits will be reduced, so it's best for those benefits to start at the highest level possible.

The federal government could do much to help us design extended work years into long life by boosting Social Security benefits for those who work past age sixty-five and not truncating those benefit increases at age seventy, as the system does now. As George Shultz and John Shoven recommend, we should drop the Social Security tax for those who have been in the workforce for a long time, perhaps forty years, which would give them an automatic "raise" and provide an incentive for employers to keep older workers on. Instead of starting abruptly at a fixed level that remains constant throughout a person's retirement, Social Security benefits should be more flexible, phased in gradually over a number of years for employees who wish to cut back working hours before ultimately reaching full retirement. This would encourage people to stay at least semi-employed longer. Likewise, employers should find ways to help older workers stay engaged part-time by offering them flexible hours, the opportunity to work from home, or other arrangements that make working feasible for them.

In this case, investing in your future actually does mean *investing*. Saving money is both practically and psychologically difficult for so many people. Everyone hates to lose money, and, for a lot of people, saving feels like giving their money away. It can be painful to feel that you are "losing" money you would prefer to be able to spend now. (Remember, your brain evolved to prioritize immediate needs over future ones.) With this in mind, we should design mechanisms into our own lives that make saving effortless. If you struggle to put money aside for retirement, or to overcome spending urges that soak up the funds you meant to sock away for old age, make the decision to save a done deal, rather than something you must convince yourself to do with every paycheck. Your employer, bank, or retirement fund manager can help you set up regular transfers that electronically route a portion of your paycheck *before taxes* toward a savings account so you won't have to think about it, or even stand in a line at the bank. Chances are, if you never see the money in your paycheck, you won't even notice it's "missing."

Employers can help make retirement savings the norm by enrolling workers in 401(k) plans from which they must opt out, rather than making them sign up voluntarily. They can make sure to offer Save More Tomorrow plans that boost workers' savings rates with each raise so that they can increase their retirement contributions without feeling like they are losing more money. They can offer workshops that help people evaluate their long-term needs.

How will you know when you've saved enough? Before you retire, take a test run. Calculate what your retirement income, including Social Security, will be, then live on it for six months while you're still working. If you are perfectly comfortable during those six months, and you can count on that level of income for twenty to thirty—or maybe forty!—years, then retire. If not, you will get a sense of how much more you need to save before you can retire comfortably.

Work changed dramatically in the twentieth century and it is likely to change just as dramatically in the twenty-first. For many, work will become even less physically demanding and will, hopefully, become more flexible as it becomes less important to be in a specific place in order to do a job. As people recognize that they have more years to work, and employers recognize that they need to accommodate the smaller pool of workers available to them, we will see new work patterns and options emerge. But the overarching theme will most likely be that people will need to work longer. The trick will be to change working conditions for jobs that are tedious, unpleasant, or physically dangerous or demanding and give people opportunities to retrain so that no one is stuck for decades in job he or she dislikes. The path to a good long working life, ultimately, starts with education.

Learn Throughout Your Life

Many scientists believe that the cognitive declines we see with aging come about, in part, because people don't do much new learning once they establish routines in a particular job or lifestyle, whether that's running a household or managing a company. Though the expertise you gain over a lifetime is enormously satisfying—and obviously useful—you'll need to make sure that you don't rest too comfortably on existing talents. You must challenge yourself in order to remain mentally sharp in old age. When you perform well-ingrained tasks you don't form new neural connections. It takes new learning to stimulate your brain in the way it needs to maintain optimal functioning.

Having watched our parents' generation struggle with Alzheimer's disease and other forms of dementia, we boomers are painfully aware of the toll that cognitive degeneration takes on families and quality of life, and we are eager to ward it off. As a result, a lot of folks are investing big bucks in computer-based brain games. Americans love the idea of buying a *game* that promises to solve our problems. There's nothing wrong with these games, and if you enjoy them, go for it. But don't expect miraculous improvements in your day-to-day cognitive functioning. If you play brain games long enough you'll certainly get better at the game, but currently there is very little evidence that these skills transfer to anything in the real world. Education via an indirect route is not nearly as good as taking the direct route. So if you're worried about no longer being able to remember your grocery list, well, practice memorizing your grocery lists. If you want to be more fluid in conversation, find more people with whom you enjoy chatting.

I worry about those boomers who plan to take traditional retirements and then sit by their swimming pool playing brain games on their iPods instead of doing something more mentally stimulating and socially useful, like teaching kids how to read. My favorite volunteer program is Experience Corps, which trains teams of older people to tutor children in inner-city schools. They work one on one and with small groups of students, teaching them to read as well as working on special projects principals identify. Their efforts are carefully structured to "raise all boats," at the same time they help students who are struggling the most. Changes in both the volunteers and the children are being studied by a group of researchers led by Linda Fried, an epidemiologist and dean of the Mailman School of Public Health at Columbia University. Their initial results are inspirational. Not only are the children doing better in school, but older volunteers are benefiting too. They are beginning to develop new friendships and getting physically stronger from getting out and about, and their brains are beginning to process information more efficiently!

More and more, we live in a culture in which knowledge is a currency. Being able to continually engage in the life of the mind, and to transmit knowledge to others, is the kind of gift that enriches you whether you receive it or give it away. We should re-envision a way to make education continue throughout life. Yet currently, education is a one-time-only proposition for most people, a long hard slog through the first two decades of life that abruptly ends at age eighteen or twenty-two and is not returned to again. As a result, schools are also one of the most age-segregated institutions in our nation. Lifelong education doesn't necessarily mean that you have to physically go back to school, taking time away from a job, paying expensive tuition, or commuting to a campus. (Although, yes, I certainly do think that universities should make the path back to class easy for older students who do want to return to campus; we should dramatically reform the concept that universities are for young people, building campuses and syllabi that reflect changed enrollments.) But there's no reason to think that formal education is the only ticket in town. We often conceive of education as something that can happen only in a classroom, but of course that's silly. Your brain learns just as well in a park or on a boat or in a hot-air balloon as in front of a blackboard.

Regardless of where you do it, you do need to stimulate your brain with continued learning. Two excellent ways, cognitive scientists say, are learning to speak a new language or play an instrument—unless, of course, you're a United Nations translator or a professional musician, in which case these abilities are old hat and you should try something else. Assuming these are novel skills for you, you can pick them up with private lessons, at a community center, by teaching yourself, or—in the case of language acquisition—through immersion. Travel is a great way to practice new language skills, as well as a way to meet people, sample different cuisines, and learn about the history and culture of faraway places.

There's no reason to think that education has to be done a certain way. If you're not the kind of person who learns best while sitting still, try something you always wanted to do that involves active, hands-on education. Start a garden, try out for the local community theater's play, buy a field guide and hit the hiking trail, take on a big garage project like restoring a classic car, or gather your watercolors and decamp to the seaside. If you feel most comfortable learning at home, there are online classes and instructional videos and books. If you learn best in a friendly, informal group, try things like book clubs or nature walks, or sign up for the lecture series at the local college, library, museum, or art film house.

What's important is that you don't let yourself stagnate, doing only things, or reading only professional materials, that are deeply familiar to you. Try something outside of your strong suit. If you are an accountant, taking night classes in math is not going to stretch your cognitive development nearly as much as, say, learning to play the banjo. If you are already fluent in three languages, learning a fourth will not challenge you in the same way that a course in pottery would.

I mentioned before that it is important to begin imagining what you'll be like as a healthy, happy older person and what sorts of contributions you'll want to make to the world. Start thinking about the practical things you must start doing now to reach those goals. What sorts of skills or training are you going to need to prepare for your ideal encore career or retirement fantasy? If you want to get involved in the nonprofit world, you'll need to learn something about these organizations before retirement age, so volunteer to serve on boards now and get to know the social issues relating to the kinds of nonprofits you'd like to work with. If you want to spend your time painting on an island somewhere, you might want to take a few art lessons ahead of time to make sure that you actually like painting. If you want to travel the world, learning a foreign language or two now will deeply enhance the experience you'll have once you finally start globe-trotting. Ironically, a rewarding retirement requires some work. If you retire and park yourself on the couch with no plans for what to do next, it's going to get pretty boring pretty fast.

Volunteering is a great way to learn something new while giving back your own skills and knowledge to your community. The new longevity has created an unprecedented opportunity for civic engagement by giving us more time that we can devote to exploring meaningful activities outside of our primary careers. Don't wait until retirement to start. If we can make paid work more flexible, and make part-time work or shorter workweeks more common, we can incorporate volunteering into our routines throughout life. In addition to that immediate feeling of satisfaction you get when you do a good deed, donating your time allows you to explore new interests, enjoy a break from the ordinary, or revel in something you truly love that won't pay your bills. It's a way to live a sort of double life.

For younger people or those considering career changes, volunteering can provide a useful window into possible professions.

If you've always wondered about working in the medical field, volunteering at the hospital would help you figure out if you want to spend more time there. For older people, it's a chance to take skills you have acquired at work and learn how to apply them in other domains that you care about. Perhaps you are deeply impassioned about politics but never chose it as a career. There's no reason you couldn't work the voter registration drive in your town or sponsor events in your community around meaningful national holidays, like the Martin Luther King Jr. Day of Service each January. If you always wanted to be a sailor, join the coast guard auxiliary. Maybe the NBA never came calling, but there's no reason you can't stay involved with basketball by teaching kids to shoot hoops down at the community center. As business leaders retire, they may want to offer their services to nonprofit organizations, which typically have only thin management staff and can use advice on strategy and marketing.

In the end, the most important gift we can give future generations is a good education: it's the only hope that our children's futures will be as good as ours. Let's invest in giving them the basic knowledge and skills that will enable them to enjoy a lifetime of learning. We need to push for a 100 percent literacy and numeracy rate, and that is just the minimum. Our children need to understand civics, global politics, and world cultures and religions. In their lifetimes, global travel will be as common as road trips are today, so they'll need to understand and appreciate different ways of living.

Let's also make basic financial education a part of the package, so that they understand the mechanics of savings, debt, and compound interest and can avoid some of the mistakes made by previous generations in failing to plan for retirement. Instill the value of saving in young children so that it becomes a habit they carry over to their adult lives. Model the value and joys of public service, too, so that they can make giving to their communities a lifelong habit, and continue to explore and learn about the world long after they are done with school.

Take Care of Your Body

The old rueful saw goes: "If I'd known I was going to live this long, I would have taken better care of myself." Today we have no excuse. If you are reading this book, odds are that you will live to be old. It will be infinitely more pleasant, and you will have so much more to give, if you arrive at old age strong and healthy. No matter how old you are today, or whether you've treated your body like a temple or like the thing you drag around to parties, never stop striving to increase your chances of a healthy old age. It's never too late to start and it's always too early to stop.

Regardless of the DNA your family's lineage dealt you, you still have a say in how it behaves. As the growing field of epigenetics is increasingly showing, lifestyle factors including nutrition, exposure to toxins, and exercise can play a key role in determining how your genes are expressed. Even if you can't control your genetic inheritance, you can, to some extent, control these. Don't assume that whatever health problems have plagued your family tree will inevitably doom you. Remember those twin studies proving that people with identical genes don't have identical fates, even when it comes to the development of highly genetically linked diseases. Think of the genetic code you inherited from your parents as just a starting point, not a map to the finish line. Let's do away with the idea of living fast and dying young, which encourages us to live recklessly for the sake of the present because we feel we have no stake in the future.

Admittedly, changing health habits can be really difficult. We all promise we'll eat better and exercise more, but most of us rarely stick with it. Routinizing some positive habits, like saving for retirement, is relatively easy because you have to struggle with it only once—you sign a few papers, and then you're done. But making good health habits part of your everyday life can be the hardest of all, because you can't make the decision just once and then forget about it. You have to decide what to eat every time you sit down for a meal and regularly will yourself to go out and exercise when you'd rather just relax.

The secret to changing habits is to design your environment so that it encourages good behavior. You can give yourself the best chance for success by removing the things that tempt you into bad habits. If you want to eat healthier, the best thing to do is to ransack the cupboards, removing the junk food and replacing it with thoughtfully chosen alternatives so that you can't go wrong when reaching for a snack. If it's too hard to resist the cakes and cookies in the grocery store, stop going to the grocery store and use a delivery service. (Of course, if you do your own shopping, remember the trick about grocery shopping *after* you've eaten, never before!) Or, start shopping at the farmer's market instead of the grocery store so you get fresh options and support your local growers at the same time. Don't go overboard, depriving yourself of everything that tastes good. If you hate wheat germ, filling your cabinets with nothing but isn't going to make you suddenly find it delicious; it's going to drive you into the arms of the nearest Burger King.

Design your daily life so that it prompts you to do the right thing. If you need to walk more, buy a parking sticker for work that requires you to park in the lot farthest from your building. Wear a pedometer so you track how many steps you're walking each day. Schedule regular dates to take your grandchildren to the park, and then make sure you do more than sit on the bench. At the very least, put away your remote control so you have to get off the couch to change the channel.

In fact, use the magic of scheduling to prompt all kinds of good health habits. If you forget to make dental appointments, schedule them all at once for the full year. Same goes for medical checkups and massages. Join health clubs if that will motivate you to stay physically fit, and if that's too expensive or doesn't appeal to you, find a walking partner who will meet you at a regular time. The fact that you have an obligation will get you out of the house. One great advantage to hiring a personal trainer is that you've got a schedule you have to keep. If that doesn't work, buy a dog.

We should make physical activity something to love, not something to dread. If exercise is something you'll never love, at least it can be something you do willingly. You don't need to be a member of a competitive team, or even engage in vigorous exercise. Just walk, stretch, and stay strong. Regularly engaging in moderate physical activity like walking can pay big health dividends: it can strengthen your bones, improve your mood, help control your weight, and help prevent diseases like diabetes, stroke, and some forms of cancer. Exercise is good for your mind, too; if your goal is staying mentally sharp, there is better evidence for exercise than brain games.

For many people it helps to leverage a little peer pressure and social activity to help you stay on track. One great way to do this is to meet some favorite colleagues for a walk during your lunch break or during that afternoon lull. When you chat with friends while you walk, you hardly know you're exercising. And why should so many community sports and amusements be just for kids? Let's get adults moving again too. A few years ago I heard a geriatrician comment, "The problem with old people is they don't dance anymore." Saturday night dances used to be commonplace. They were great intergenerational gatherings. Dancing is terrific exercise that people eagerly do, and of course the old couples at dances are always the best because they've had so many years of practice. Let's bring back the community dance and other regular social gatherings that encourage ordinary adults, not just the most athletic among us, to enjoy movement and do it in a noncompetitive atmosphere.

The trick is to create a world where the path of least resistance is the path to good health. We need urban planners to design neighborhoods and city complexes so that the easiest thing to do is walk to the store, instead of driving there. In the late 1800s, when rural folks began to move to urban areas, a playground movement began. The idea was to provide a safe place for children to get together and play outside even though they now lived in cities. Today we may need a Parks Movement, where every neighborhood has a park—even if it begins with a dirt lot—that draws the full range of ages, from the youngest to the oldest, with music, dancing, and local produce for sale, bringing back the idea of safe community outdoor activity.

Obesity is such a widespread problem that we'll probably need a very innovative, national public health intervention that supports healthy eating and exercise. Minimally, states need to reinstate gym class in public schools and bring back recess. But that's probably not enough. I wonder if schoolchildren should get ten-minute exercise breaks every hour in school. Just as public schools once tried to cram as many calories into a school lunch as possible, we now need nationwide plans to reduce empty calories and increase calcium and fiber in school lunches. For adults, I can envision a "seal of approval" that restaurants could place in their windows indicating they serve reasonable portions of healthy (and not tasteless!) foods. Finally, let's invest in future generations by making sure they don't repeat our generation's own health mistakes. Give your kids and grandkids the gift of good nutrition, and a taste for foods that are healthy for them. Kids will gain a lifelong craving for the comfort foods of their childhood, so provide them with fond memories of family recipes that won't kill them. An eighty-year-old friend of mine who lives in Oakland believes that the more real flavor food has the less of it people eat, so, like Julia Child, she is staunchly opposed to low-calorie cooking. Instead, she is teaching her young neighbors and relatives how to make traditional southern dishes substituting olive oil for bacon fat and using molasses in recipes instead of refined sugar.

Although our culture has somehow cottoned to the idea that kids will eat only pizza and chicken nuggets, in fact, if you start them young enough, kids will eat whatever the adults around them do. (I was convinced of this one day when I visited an Asian friend whose baby was sitting in a high chair happily eating sushi.) Of course we can change our children's eating habits! After all, if the tobacco industry can figure out how to make kids want to try foul-tasting cigarettes, then certainly we can get them to try tofu. Help your children learn about where food comes from, and what's on their plate. Let them help you plan meals, shop, and cook. When children are involved in food's production they are more likely to eat it, and some very inspiring programs are tapping into this truth, like culinary icon Alice Waters's Edible Schoolyard program in a Berkeley, California, public school, in which kids learn to raise, and then prepare, their own fruits and vegetables.

Putting It All Together

These four areas of daily life—relationships, work, learning, and health—will all be transformed by prolonged life. If we use our gift of extra time wisely, we can better our education, spend more time with our children, enjoy deep friendships that span many decades, and develop unprecedented expertise and talents over the years. We can stop separating life into artificial stages that focus sequentially on education, work, family, and finally leisure, and instead enjoy them all throughout life. We can finally end the tensions between family and work; if we open our eyes, we'll see that we now have time for both. We can end age segregation and allow children to really get to know older people as role models, so that they begin to dream of goals they'll pursue in their own eighth and ninth decades.

True, there are significant obstacles. We need to improve education and health habits, reduce class inequalities, and learn how to plan for the long term. To make sure that the gift of long life is evenly distributed around the globe, we'll need to develop wide-ranging public programs that will reduce poverty in this country and worldwide. We'll need to improve education in the poorest regions of the world, and to work with governments and nonprofit organizations to help them deliver the basic nutrition, sanitation, and health care services that made long life possible in the developed world. It's a really big job. But we've solved seemingly insurmountable problems before. Can you imagine traveling back in time just one hundred years and telling people that nearly every infant born in the United States would survive childhood?

In this country, which is expected to have more than one million centenarians by the year 2050, the challenge of reinventing very old age will be the greatest social revolution the baby boom generation ever faced. We can make it not only a biological inevitability, but a new life stage that is productive, enjoyable, and inspiring to the generations that come after us. Let's embrace the challenge of the fifty-fifty plan, using the second half of life to give back to our communities the many gifts that have been given to us. We'll need the experience, the wisdom, and the leadership of the boomers to create a world that knows how to handle the many open questions posed by the new longevity, and to prepare the generations that come after us for long, healthy lives. It's an enormous task, but we've always been good at changing the world. If there's one idea you should take away from this book, it's that there's so much to look forward to. Let's get moving! Our revolution isn't over yet.

ENDNOTES

Introduction

2 **Nervous folks who direct:** Blake, D., & Pickles, J. (2008). Apocalyptic demography? Putting longevity risk in perspective. Executive report, Chartered Institute of Management Accountants. Retrieved from http://www1.cimaglobal.com/cps/rde/xchg/SID0AE7C4D1-2CA621B0/live/root.xsl/28033.htm

2 *one-half* **of the baby girls:** Vaupel, J. (2000). Vive la femme. *Science, 287*(5454).

Chapter 1: Five Myths About Aging You Can't Afford to Believe

13 **American society is so age segregated:** Hagestad, G. O., & Uhlenberg, P. (2005). The social separation of old and young: A root of ageism. *Journal of Social Issues, 61*(2), 343–360.

18 **children tend to produce tensions:** Cowan, P., & Cowan, C. (1992). *When partners become parents: The big life change for couples.* New York: Basic Books.

23 **a mere four factors:** Knoops, K. T. B., de Groot, L. C. P. G.,

Kromhout, D., Perrin, A., Moreiras-Varela, O., Menotti, A., et al. (2004). Mediterranean diet, lifestyle factors, and 10-year mortality in elderly European men and women. *Journal of the American Medical Association, 292*(12), 1433–1439.

23 **when one twin exercised:** Cherkas, L., Hunkin, J., Bernet, S. K., Richards, J. B., Gardner, J. P., Surdulescu, G., et al. (2008). The association between physical activity in leisure time and leukocyte telomere length. *Archives of Internal Medicine, 168*(2), 154–158.

24 **if one twin developed Alzheimer's:** Gatz, M., Reynolds, C. A., Fratiglioni, L., Johansson, B., Mortimer, J. A., Berg, S., et al. (2006). Role of genes and environments for explaining Alzheimer disease. *Archives of General Psychiatry, 63*(2), 168–174.

25 **the disease itself flourishes:** Hossain, P., Kawar, B., & El Nahas, M. (2007). Obesity and diabetes in the developing world: A growing challenge. *New England Journal of Medicine, 356*(3), 213–215.

29 **six in ten American workers:** Thayer, C. (2007). *Preparation for retirement: The haves and have-nots* [AARP report]. Washington, DC: AARP Knowledge Management.

30 **want to assist their parents:** Pillemer, K., Suitor, J. J., Mock, S. E., Sabir, M., Pardo, T. B., & Sechrist, J. (2007). Capturing the complexity of intergenerational relations: Exploring ambivalence within later-life families. *Journal of Social Issues, 63*, 775–791.

31 **the typical inheritance:** Hurd, M. D., & Smith, J. P. (2002). *Expected bequests and their distributions* [NBER Working Paper no. 9142]. Cambridge, MA: National Bureau of Economic Research. Cited in *Health and Retirement Study Newsletter, 1*, pp. 4–7.

33 **extracts its own toll:** Meadows, D., Meadows, D., & Randers, J. (2004). *Limits to growth: The 30-year update.* White River Jct., VT: Chelsea Green Publishing.

34 **all of the global population growth:** Hayutin, A. M. (2007). *How population aging differs across countries: A briefing on global demographics.* Stanford, CA: Stanford Center on Longevity.

36 **surveys of college students:** The majority of younger people tend to favor actions benefiting older people and older tend to favor actions benefiting youth. Personal communication, John Rother, AARP.

37 **When you look across countries:** Gruber, J., & Wise, D. A. (Eds.). (1999). *Social security and retirement around the world.* Chicago: University of Chicago Press.

41 **difference in life expectancy:** Singh, G. K., & Siahpush, M. (2006). Widening socioeconomic inequalities in US life expectancy, 1980-2000. *International Journal of Epidemiology, 35*(4), 969–979.

Chapter 2: What Is Aging?

44 **Maternal mortality dropped:** Centers for Disease Control and Prevention. (1999). Ten great public health achievements: United States, 1900–1999. *Morbidity and Mortality Weekly Report, 48*(12), 241–243.

44 **as more children survived:** Francis, D. R. (2002, March). Why do death rates decline? *NBER Digest*, p. 3.

45 **there was a downside:** Diamond, J. (1997). *Guns, germs, and steel: The fates of human societies.* New York: Norton.

45 **diets became less diverse:** Diamond, J. (1987, May). The worst mistake in the history of the human race. *Discover*, pp. 64–66.

47 **suffered from rickets:** Hess, A. F. (1921). Newer aspects of some nutritional disorders. *Journal of the American Medical Association, 76*, 693–700.

53 **people who died in Europe:** Agence France-Presse. (2003, August 27). Death toll from Europe's heat wave could exceed 15,000: estimates. Retrieved October 31, 2008, from http://www.terradaily .com/2003/030827165837.vbless3o.html

56 **Changes in working memory:** Park, D. C., Lauten-schlager, G., Hedden, T., Davidson, N. S., Smith A. D., & Smith P. K.

(2002). Models of visuospatial and verbal memory across the adult life span. *Psychology and Aging, 17*(2), 299–320.

57 **Vocabulary and cultural acumen:** Schaie, K. W. (1994). The course of adult intellectual development. *American Psychologist, 49*, 304–313.

57 **more informed about politics:** The Pew Research Center for the People and the Press. (2007). *What Americans Know, 1989–2007: Public knowledge of current affairs and information revolutions.* Washington, DC: Author.

57 **crossword puzzle experts:** Hambrick, D. Z., Salthouse, T. A., & Meinz, E. J. (1999). Predictors of crossword puzzle proficiency and moderators of age-cognition relations. *Journal of Experimental Psychology: General, 128*(2), 131–164.

59 **"It's simple: Don't die":** Schneider, J. (2002, June 3). 100 and counting [electronic version]. *U.S. News & World Report.* Retrieved October 31, 2008, from http://www.usnews.com/usnews/biztech/articles/020603/archive_021563.htm

59 **what we know about centenarians:** Rosellini, L. (1995, August 20). Our century. *U.S. News & World Report.* Retrieved October 31, 2008, from http://www.usnews.com/usnews/culture/articles/950828/archive_032746.htm

60 **make it through their eighties:** Perls, T. T. (1995). The oldest-old. *Scientific American, 272*, 70–75.

61 **mental capacity at the age of 118:** Ritchie, K. (1995). Mental status examination of an exceptional case of longevity: J.C., age 118 years. *British Journal of Psychiatry, 166*(2), 229–235.

62 **proposed paying Calment $400 a month:** Whitney, C. R. (1997, August 5). Jeanne Calment, world's elder, dies at 122 [electronic version]. *New York Times.* Retrieved October 31, 2008, from http://query.nytimes.com/gst/fullpage.html?res=9C01E7D7113DF936A3575BC0A961958260

62 **life expectancy could increase:** Carnes, B. A., Hayflick, L., & Olshansky, S. J. (2002). No truth to the fountain of youth. *Scientific American, 286*(6), 92–95.

62 **in the vicinity of ninety years:** Olshansky, S. J., Hayflick, L., & Carnes, B. A. (2002). Position statement on human aging. *Journal of Gerontology: Biological Sciences, 57A*(8), B1–B6.

63 **researchers believe that the obesity epidemic:** Lakdawalla, D. N., Bhattacharya, J., & Goldman, D. P. (2004). Are the young becoming more disabled? *Health Affairs, 23*(1), 168–176.

64 **world record for long life:** McCann, J. (2001). Wanna bet?: Two scientists wager on whether humans can live to 130 or 150 years. *Scientist, 15*(3), 8.

Chapter 3: Reenvisioning Long Life

65 **has inched up a year:** Burrelli, J. S. (2004). *Science and engineering doctorate awards: 2003* [NSF 05-300]. Arlington, VA: National Science Foundation, Division of Science Resources Statistics.

65 **age at first marriage:** U.S. Census Bureau. (2001). *America's families and living arrangements: Population characteristics 2000* [Current Population Reports, Series P20-537]. Washington, DC: U.S. Government Printing Office.

65 **marriage has been delayed:** Teachman, J. D., Tedrow, L. M., & Crowder, K. D. (2000). The changing demography of America's families. *Journal of Marriage and the Family, 62*, 1234–1246.

66 **three fixed stages:** Kohli, M. (2005). The world we forgot: A historical review of the life course. In R. Miller (Ed.), *Biographical research methods*. London: Sage, 5–34.

68 **shipping elderly people off:** Pilling, D. (2003, August 7). Japan could "export" surplus centenarians. *Financial Times*, p. 1.

72 **Child Trust Fund account:** Bennett, J., Quezada, E. C., Lawton, K., & Perun, P. (2008). *The UK Child Trust Fund: A successful launch.* London: Institute for Public Policy Research.

82 **cognition and emotion blend:** Labouvie-Vief, G. (2003). Dynamic integration: Affect, cognition, and the self in adulthood. *Current Directions in Psychological Science, 12*(6), 201–206.

83 **"selective optimization with compensation":** Baltes, P. B., & Baltes, M. M. (1990). Psychological perspectives on successful aging: The model of selective optimization with compensation. In P. B. Baltes & M. M. Baltes (Eds.), *Successful aging: Perspectives from the behavioral sciences* (pp. 1–34). New York: Cambridge University Press.

84 **world's only advanced economy:** Ray, R., & Schmitt, J. (2007). *No-vacation nation.* Washington, DC: Center for Economic and Policy Research.

84 **takes only eleven days:** Expedia. (2008). *International Vacation Deprivation Survey.* Retrieved from http://media.expedia.com/media/content/expus/graphics/promos/vacations/expedia_international _vacation_deprivation_survey_2008.pdf

85 **it matters very much:** Caruso, C. C., Hitchcock, E. M., Dick, R. B., Russo, J. M., & Schmitt, J. M. (2004). *Overtime and extended work shifts: Recent findings on illnesses, injuries and health behaviors* [DHHS (NIOSH) Publication No. 2004–143]. Cincinnati, OH: National Institute for Occupational Safety and Health, 1–38.

88 **expect to live another eighteen years:** Arias, E. (2007). United States life tables, 2004. In *National Vital Statistics Reports* (Vol. 56, no. 9, pp. 1–39). Hyattsville, MD: National Center for Health Statistics.

89 **until age seventy:** If you were born in 1960 or later your eligibility for full Social Security benefits will be increased to 67. Retrieved from Social Security Online, February 19, 2009, http://www .ssa.gov/retire2/retirechart.htm

90 **"encore careers":** Freedman, M. (2007). *Encore: Finding work that matters in the second half of life.* New York: Public Affairs.

90 **"National Guard" for child care:** Hagestad, G. O. (1996). On-time, off-time, out of time? Reflections on continuity and discontinuity from an illness process. In V. L. Bengston (Ed.), *Adulthood and aging: Research on continuities and discontinuities* (pp. 204–222). New York: Springer.

92 **nearly seven in ten:** Reynolds, S., Ridley, N., & Van Horn, C. E. (2005). A work-filled retirement: Workers' changing views on employment and leisure. *WorkTrends Survey, 8*(1), 1–39.

93 **"retired husband syndrome":** Faiola, A. (2005, October 17). Sick of their husbands in graying Japan. *Washington Post,* p. A01.

94 **helps people find creative solutions:** Kim, S., Hasher, L., & Zacks, R. T. (2007). Aging and a benefit of distractibility. *Psychonomic Bulletin & Review, 14*(2), 301–305.

94 **Being slower to anger:** Charles, S. T., & Carstensen, L. L. (2008). Unpleasant situations elicit different emotional responses in younger and older adults. *Psychology and Aging, 23*(3), 495–504.

94 **more likely to forgive:** Cheng, S.-T., & Yim, Y.-K. (2008). Age differences in forgiveness: The role of future time perspective. *Psychology and Aging, 23*(3), 676–680.

Chapter 4: The Social Side of Aging

98 **fewer than three people:** Lang, F. R., & Carstensen, L. L. (1994). Close emotional relationships in late life: Further support for proactive aging in the social domain. *Psychology and Aging, 9,* 315–324.

98 **as great a risk factor:** Berkman, L. F., & Syme, S. L. (1979). Social networks, host resistance, and mortality: A nine-year follow-up study of Alameda County residents. *American Journal of Epidemiology, 109,* 186–204.

99 **already have mental representations:** Johnson, S., Dweck, C., & Chen, F. (2007). Evidence for infants' internal working models of attachment. *Psychological Science, 18*(6), 501–502.

100 **brains process new information:** Martin, J. M., & Cole, D.A. (2000). Using the personal stroop to detect children's awareness of social rejection by peers. *Cognition and Emotion, 14*(2), 241–260.

101 **Adler's subjective measure:** Singh-Manoux, A., Marmot, M. G., & Adler, N. E. (2005). Does subjective social status predict health and change in health status better than objective status? *Psychosomatic Medicine, 67*, 855–861.

103 **who had been studying monkeys:** Capitanio, J. P., Mendoza, S. P., Lerche, N. W., & Mason, W. A. (1998). Social stress results in altered glucocorticoid regulation and shorter survival in simian acquired immune deficiency syndrome. *Proceedings of the National Academy of Sciences USA, 95*, 4714–4719.

103 **allowed the virus to replicate:** Cole, S. W., Korin, Y. D., Fahey, J. L., & Zack, J. A. (1998). Norepineprhine accelerates HIV replication via protein kinase A-dependent effects on cytokine production. *Journal of Immunology, 161*, 610–616.

104 **studied the differences between adults:** Cole, S. W., Hawkley, L. C., Arevalo, J. M., Sung, C.Y., Rose, R. M., & Cacioppo, J.T. (2007). Social regulation of gene expression in human leukocytes. *Genome Biology, 8*(9), R189. doi:10.1186/gb-2007-8-9-r189

105 **having a satisfying social network:** Fratiglioni, L., Wang, H. X., Ericsson, K., Maytan, M., & Winblad, B. (2000). Influence of social network on occurrence of dementia: A community-based longitudinal study. *Lancet, 355*, 1315–1319.

106 **number of relational words:** Pressman, S. D., & Cohen, S. (2007). The use of social words in autobiographies and longevity. *Psychosomatic Medicine, 69*, 262–269.

108 **"Being alone is what is risky":** Berkman, L. (2000). Which influences cognitive function: Living alone or being alone? *Lancet, 355*(9212), 1291–1292.

108 **"social convoys":** Kahn, R., & Antonucci, T. C. (1980). *Con-*

voys over the life course: Attachment, roles, and social support. In P. B. Baltes & O. Brim (Eds.), *Life-span development and behavior* (Vol. 3, pp. 81–102). New York Academic Press.

111 **resiliency would be particularly important:** Berkman, L., & Glass, T. (2000). Social integration, social networks, social support and health (pp. 137–173). In L. F. Berkman & I. Kawachi (Eds.), *Social epidemiology.* New York: Oxford University Press.

113 **"If you had thirty minutes":** Fredrickson, B. L., & Carstensen, L. L. (1990). Choosing social partners: How old age and anticipated endings make us more selective. *Psychology and Aging, 5,* 335–347.

114 **Following September 11:** Fung, H. H., & Carstensen, L. L. (2006). Goals change when life's fragility is primed: Lessons learned from older adults, the September 11th attacks and SARS. *Social Cognition, 24,* 248–278.

115 **significantly more emotionally engaged:** Fredrickson, B. (1995). Socioemotional behavior at the end of college life. *Journal of Social and Personal Relationships, 12*(2), 261–276.

115 **"When we lament":** Saller, R. (2001). Family values in ancient Rome. Fathom Archive, University of Chicago Library. Retrieved from http://fathom.lib.uchicago.edu/1/777777121908/

118 **embedded in every marriage:** Bernard, J., & Bernard, J. S. (1982). *The future of marriage.* New Haven: Yale University Press.

118 **married people live about three years longer:** Fuchs, V. R. (2004). Reflections on the socio-economic correlates of health. *Journal of Health Economics, 23*(4), 653–661. doi:10.1016/j.jhealeco.2004.04.004

119 **often lose their social networks:** Miller, E. D., & Wortman, C. B. (2002). Gender differences in mortality and morbidity following a major stressor: The case of conjugal bereavement. In G. Weidner, M. Kopp, & M. Kristenson (Eds.), *Heart disease: Environment, stress and gender* (pp. 251–266). Washington, DC: IOS Press.

119 **The majority showed steep declines:** Schleifer, S. (1989). Bereavement, depression and immunity: The role of age (pp. 61–79). In L. Carstensen & J. Neale (Eds.), *Mechanisms of psychological influence on physical health: With special attention to the elderly.* New York: Plenum Press.

120 **five years after a divorce:** Waite, L. J., Browning, D., Doherty, W. J., Gallagher, M., Luo, Y., & Stanley, S. M. (2002, June). *Does divorce make people happy? Findings from a study of unhappy marriages* [report]. Institute for American Values, Center for Marriage and Families. Retrieved from http://center.americanvalues.org

121 **divorce remains common:** Cherlin, A. J. (2005). American marriage in the early twenty-first century. *The Future of Children, 15*(2), 33–55.

123 **prospect of being widowed:** Miller, E. D., & Wortman, C. B. (2002). Gender differences in mortality and morbidity following a major stressor: The case of conjugal bereavement (pp. 251–266). In G. Weidner, M. Kopp, & M. Kristenson (Eds.), *Heart disease: Environment, stress and gender.* Washington, DC: IOS Press.

124 **one in ten women:** According to the Census Bureau, in 2002 about 18 percent of women ages 40 to 44 had never had a child, compared with 10 percent in 1976. U.S. Census Bureau. Percentage of childless women 40 to 44 years old increases since 1976, Census Bureau reports [news release]. (2003). Retrieved from http://www.census.gov/Press-Release/www/releases/archives/fertility/001491.html

124 **one adult and no children:** U.S. Census Bureau. Americans marrying older, living alone more, see households shrinking, Census Bureau reports [news release]. (2006). Retrieved from http://www.census.gov/Press-Release/www/releases/archives/families_households/006840.html

125 **American children on average:** Cherlin, A. J. (2005). American marriage in the early twenty-first century. *The Future of Children, 15*(2), 33–55.

126 **closeness among brothers and sisters:** Cicirelli, V. G. (1991). Sibling connections in adulthood. *Marriage and Family Review, 16*(3/4), 291–310.

128 **One in every fifteen:** Fuller-Thompson, E., & Minkler, M. (2001). American grandparents providing extensive childcare to their grandchildren. *Gerontologist, 41*(2), 201–209.

128 **their grandchildren's primary guardians:** Minkler, M., & Roe, K. M. (1996). Grandparents as surrogate parents. *Generations, 20,* 34–38.

129 **"grandmother hypothesis":** Hawkes, K., O'Connell, J. F., Blurton Jones, N. G., Alvarez, H., & Charnov, E. L. (1998). Grandmothering, menopause, and the evolution of human life histories. *Proceedings of the National Academy of Science, 95,* 1336–1339.

129 **hunting and gathering communities:** Blurton Jones, N. G., Hawkes, K., & O'Connell, J. F. (1997). Why do Hadza children forage? In N. Segal, G. E. Weisfeld, & C. C. Weisfeld (Eds.), *Uniting psychology and biology: Integrative perspectives on human development* (pp. 279–313). Washington, DC: American Psychological Association.

129 **peak in the amount of food:** Hawkes, K., O'Connell, J. F., & Blurton Jones, N. G. (2003). Human life histories: Primate tradeoffs, grandmothering socioecology, and the fossil record. In P. Kappeler & M. Pereira (Eds.), *Primate life histories and socioecology* (pp. 204–227). Chicago: University of Chicago Press.

130 **Hawkes prefers "grandmother":** Hawkes, K. (2003). Grandmothers and the evolution of human longevity. *American Journal of Human Biology, 15,* 380–400.

Chapter 5: Collective Supports: Social Security and Medicare

139 **average age of "retirement":** Kolata, G. (2006, July 30). So big and healthy even grandpa wouldn't know you. *New York Times.* Retrieved October 29, 2008, from http://www.nytimes.com/2006/07/30/health/30age.html

142 **as high as 10.8 percent:** Walker, D. M. (2005). Current and emerging fiscal and retirement security challenges [PowerPoint presentation]. U.S. Government Accountability Office. Retrieved October 29, 2008, from http://www.gao.gov/cghome/cefrsc/img24.html

142 **dipped into negative territory:** U. S. Bureau of Economic Analysis. (2008). *Personal saving rate.* Retrieved October 29, 2008, from http://www.bea.gov/briefrm/saving.htm on

149 **virtually no other income:** Federal Interagency Forum on Aging-Related Statistics. (2008). *Older Americans 2008: Key indicators of well-being.* Washington, DC: U.S. Government Printing Office.

149 **their Social Security checks:** The amount of Social Security people receive is based on an average of earnings across their working lives. U.S. Social Security Administration. (2008). *Understanding the benefits* [SSA Publication No. 05-10024]. Washington, DC: Author.

149 **closer to one in two:** Sherman, A., & Shapiro, I. (2005). Social Security lifts 13 million seniors above the poverty line: A state-by-state analysis. Center on Budget and Policy Priorities. Retrieved from http://www.cbpp.org/2-24-05socsec.htm

149 **the official poverty level:** U.S. Social Security Administration, Office of Policy. Monthly statistical snapshot, Table 2: Social Security Benefits. Retrieved October 28, 2008, from http://www.ssa.gov/policy/docs/quickfacts/stat_snapshot/

151 **costly and disabling chronic conditions:** Dalstra, J. A., Kunst, A. E., Borrell, C., Breeze, E., Cambois, E., Costa, G., et. al. (2005).

Socioeconomic differences in the prevalence of common chronic diseases: An overview of eight European countries. *International Journal of Epidemiology, 34*(2), 316–326. doi:10.1093/ije/dyh386

153 **a 6.2 percent "raise":** Schultz, G. P., & Shoven, J. B. (2008). *Putting our house in order: A guide to Social Security and health care reform.* New York: Norton.

153 **a 50 percent tax:** Some of this deduction is returned after the worker reaches full retirement. But coming at a decision point in one's career, it is a clear penalty for gainful activity.

154 **regularly revisit eligibility age:** Shoven, J., & Goda, G. S. (2008). *Adjusting government policies for age inflation* [NBER Working Paper no. 14231]. Cambridge, MA: National Bureau of Economic Research. Retrieved October 30, 2008, from http://www.nber.org/papers/w14231.pdf

158 **"the ravages of illness in his old age":** President Johnson's remarks with President Truman at the signing in Independence of the Medicare Bill, July 30, 1965. Retrieved February 23, 2009, from http:/www.lbjlib.utexas/Johnson/archives.hom/speeches.hom/650730/asp

158 **cheaper to insure the young:** Bundorf, M. K., & Pauly, M. V. (2006). Is health insurance affordable for the uninsured? *Journal of Health Economics, 25*(4), 650–673.

160 **one in seven Americans:** The Henry J. Kaiser Family Foundation. (2008). Retrieved February 19, 2009 from http://www.kff.org/medicare/h08_7821.cfm

161 **$13 trillion behind:** U.S. Department of the Treasury. *The 2008 annual report of the board of trustees of the Federal Old-Age and Survivors Insurance and Federal Disability Insurance trust funds.* Retrieved October 28, 2008, from http://www.ustreas.gov/offices/economic-policy/reports/social-security-report-2008.pdf

161 **around $30 trillion:** U.S. Government Accountability Office. *U.S. financial condition and fiscal future briefing.* Retrieved October 28, 2008, from http://www.gao.gov/cghome/d08446cg.pdf

162 **close to 90 percent:** The Henry J. Kaiser Family Foundation. (2007, January). *Health care spending in the United States and OECD countries.* Retrieved from http://www.kff.org/insurance/snapshot/ chcm010307oth.cfm; see also "United States continues to have highest level of health spending" (2007, September 12). *ScienceDaily.* Retrieved September 9, 2008, from http://www.sciencedaily.com/releases/2007/ 09/070911155457.htm

163 **thirty thousand Medicare patients:** Brownlee, S. (2007). *Overtreated: Why too much medicine is making us sicker and poorer.* New York: Bloomsbury.

163 **roughly $700 billion:** Orszag, P. (2008). *Congressional Budget Office testimony: Growth in health care costs.* Washington, DC: Congressional Budget Office.

165 **within the next thirty years:** Goldman, D. P., Shang, B., Bhattacharya, J., Garber, A. M., Hurd, M., Joyce, G. F., et al. (2005, September 26). Consequences of health trends and medical innovation for the future elderly. *Health Affairs, 24*(2), W5R5–17. doi:10.1377/hlthaff .W5.R5

166 **fewer than 20 percent:** Cohen, J. T. J., Neumann, P. J., & Weinstein, M. C. (2008). Does preventive care save money? Health economics and the presidential candidates. *New England Journal of Medicine, 358*(7), 661–663.

167 **no better outcomes:** Brox, J. I., Sorensen, R., Friis, A., Nygaard, O., Indahl, A., Keller, A., et al. (2004). Randomized clinical trial of lumbar instrumented fusion and cognitive intervention and exercises in patients with chronic low back pain and disc degeneration. *Spine, 28*(17), 1913–1921.

168 **effectiveness of procedures:** Garber, A. M. (2004). Cost-effectiveness and evidence evaluation as criteria for coverage policy. *Health Affairs,* Jan.-June; Supplement web exclusives, W4-284-96.

172 **proceed from a set of facts:** Fuchs, V. R. (2008). Three "in-

convenient truths" about health care. *New England Journal of Medicine, 359*(17), 1749–1751.

Chapter 6: Investing in Our Future: The Case for Science and Technology

179 **"technophysio evolution":** Fogel, R., & Costa, D. (1997). A theory of technophysio evolution, with some implications for forecasting population, health care costs and pension costs. *Demography, 34,* 49–66.

181 **if current trends continue:** Wang, Y., Beydoun, M. A., Liang, L., Caballero, B., & Kumanyika, S. K. (2008). Will all Americans become overweight or obese? Estimating the progression and cost of the US obesity epidemic. *Obesity, 16*(10), 2323–2330. doi:10.1038/oby .2008.351

181 **prospect of 106 million cases:** Alzheimer's disease to quadruple worldwide by 2050. (2007, June 11). *ScienceDaily.* Retrieved October 29, 2008, from http://www.sciencedaily.com/releases/2007/ 06/070610104441.htm

184 **after the 1918 influenza epidemic:** Almond, D. (2006). Is the 1918 influenza pandemic over? Long-term effects of in utero influenza exposure in the post-1940 U.S. population. *Journal of Political Economy, 114*(4), 672-712, doi:10.1086/507154

186 **less fearful and anxious:** Parent, C. I., & Meaney, M. J. (2008). The influence of natural variations in maternal care on play fighting in the rat. *Developmental Psychobiology, 50*(8), 767–776. doi:10 .1002/dev.20342

187 **rats treated with drugs:** Yau, J. L.-W., Noble, J., Hibberd, C., Rowe, W. B., Meaney, M. J., Richard G. M., et al. (2002). Chronic treatment with the antidepressant amitriptyline prevents impairments in water maze learning in aging rats. *Journal of Neuroscience, 22*(4), 1436–1442.

190 **learning a second language:** Bialystok, E., Craik, F. I. M., & Ryan, J. (2006). Executive control in a modified antisaccade task: Effects of aging and bilingualism. *Journal of Experimental Psychology: Learning, Memory, and Cognition, 32*(6), 1341–1354.

191 **education may partially explain:** Langa, K. M., Larson, E. B., Karlawish, J. H., Cutler, D. M., Kabeto, M. U., Kim, S. Y., et al. (2008). Trends in the prevalence and mortality of cognitive impairment in the United States: Is there evidence of a compression of cognitive morbidity? *Alzheimer's & Dementia, 4*(2), 134–144.

193 **stem cells were, in fact, not the problem:** Conboy, I. M., Conboy, M. J., Wagers, A. J., Girma, E., Weissman, I. L., & Rando, T. A. (2005). Rejuvenation of aged progenitor cells by exposure to a young systemic environment. *Nature, 433,* 760–764.

194 **substance in the blood suppresses stem cell function:** Brack, A. S., Conboy M. J., Lee, M., Roy, S., Kuo, C. J., Keller, C., et al. (2007). Increased Wnt signaling during aging alters myogenic stem cell fate and increases fibrosis. *Science, 317,* 807–810.

195 **activates a protein:** Vihang, A., Narkar, V. A., Downes, M., Yu, R. T., Embler, E., Wang, Y.-X., et al. (2008). AMPK and PPAR agonists are exercise mimetics. *Cell, 134*(3), 405–415. doi:10.1016/j.cell.2008 .06.051

198 **early detection alternative:** Carstensen, E. L., Parker, K. J., & Lerner, R. M. (2008). Elastography in the management of liver disease. *Ultrasound in Medicine & Biology, 34*(10), 1535–1546.

203 **bathroom mirrors that can detect:** Marsh, J. (2002). House calls. *Rochester Review, 64*(3). Retrieved from http://www.rochester .edu/pr/Review/V64N3/feature2.html

205 **using computer-based games:** Jimison, H. B., & Pavel, M. (2008). Integrating computer-based health coaching into elder home care (pp. 122–129). In A. Mihailidis, J. Boger, H. Kautz, & L. Normie (Eds.), *Technology and aging: Selected papers from the 2007 International Conference on Technology and Aging.* Amsterdam: IOS Press.

211 **beliefs about performance:** Bandura, A., Freeman, W. H., & Lightsey, R. (1999). Self efficacy: The exercise of control. *Journal of Cognitive Psychotherapy, 13*(2), 158–166.

212 **Today 90 percent of designers:** Knowlton, B. (2006, January 1). Letter from America: Turning out gadgets for a $2-a-day multitude. *International Herald Tribune.* Retrieved from http://www.iht.com/articles/2005/12/30/news/letter.php?page=2

214 **a staggering $3.2 trillion:** Murphy, K. M., & Topel, R. H. (2006). The value of health and longevity. *Journal of Political Economy, 114,* 871–904.

215 **good health is good:** Deaton, A. (2006). The great escape: A review of Robert Fogel's The Escape from Hunger and Premature Death, 1700–2100. *Journal of Economic Literature, 44*(1), 106–114. doi:10.1257/002205106776162672

216 **workers in their early sixties:** Kirkegaard, J. F. (2007). *The accelerating decline in America's high-skilled workforce: Implications for immigration policy.* Washington, DC: Peterson Institute for International Economics.

Chapter 7: What Might Go Wrong?

224 **things far away look fuzzier:** Gilbert, D. T. (2006). *Stumbling on happiness.* New York: Knopf.

224 **affective forecasting:** Gilbert, D. T., Pinel, E. C., Wilson, T. D., Blumberg, S. J., & Wheatley, T. (1998). Immune neglect: A source of durability bias in affective forecasting. *Journal of Personality and Social Psychology, 75,* 617–638.

225 **imagine the taste of marshmallow while chewing liver:** Gilbert, D. T. (2006). *Stumbling on happiness.* New York: Knopf, 124–125.

226 **drawings of Chinese characters:** Zajonc, R. B. (1968). Attitudinal effects of mere exposure. *Journal of Personality and Social Psychology, 9*(2), 1–27.

236 **"show evidence of osteoarthritis":** *Burden of chronic disease: Statement before the Senate Appropriations Subcommittee on Labor, Health and Human Services, and Education,* 110th Cong. (2007, April 20) (testimony of Richard J. Hodes and Richard J. Turman). Retrieved from http://www.nia.nih.gov/AboutNIA/BudgetRequests/Burden_of_Chronic _Disease_2007.htm-_ftn2

238 **more American adults were overweight:** Caballero, B. (2007). The global epidemic of obesity: An overview. *Epidemiologic Reviews, 29*(1), 1–5. doi:10.1093/epirev/mxm012

238 **Sweetened beverages now make up:** Rajeshwari, R., Yang, S., Nicklas, T., & Berenson, G. (2005). Secular trends in children's sweetened-beverage consumption (1973 to 1994): The Bogalusa Heart Study. *Journal of the American Dietetic Association, 105*(2), 208–214.

238 **Schoolchildren are far less likely:** Kids Walk-to-School [program Web page]. Centers for Disease Control and Prevention. Retrieved October 30, 2008, http://www.cdc.gov/nccdphp/dnpa/kidswalk/

238 **obesity may erase:** Lakdawalla, D. N., Bhattacharya, J., & Goldman, D. P. (2004). Are the young becoming more disabled? *Health Tracking, 23*(1), 168–176.

238 **by the year 2030:** Wang, Y., Beydoun, M., Liang, L., Caballero, B., & Kumanyika, S. (2008, October). Will all Americans become overweight or obese? Estimating the progression and cost of the US obesity epidemic. *Obesity, 16*(10), 2323–2330. [Accessed July 2008 via advance online publication]

239 **an obese seventy-year-old:** Lakdawalla, D., Goldman, D., & Shang, B. (2005). The health and cost consequences of obesity among the future elderly. *Health Affairs, 24*(Supp. 2), w5r30–41.

239 **documented alterations in gait:** Gushue, D. L., Houck, J., & Lerner, A. L. (2005). Effects of childhood obesity on three-dimensional knee joint biomechanics during walking. *Journal of Pediatric Orthopaedics, 25*(6), 763–768.

239 **the rise of diabetes:** Olshansky, S. J., Passaro, D. J., Hershow, R. C., Layden, J., Carnes, B. A., Brody, J., et al. (2005). A potential decline in life expectancy in the United States in the 21st century. *New England Journal of Medicine, 352*(11), 1138–1145.

240 **This particular combination:** Valdez, R., Athens, M. A., Thompson, G. H., Bradshaw, B. S., & Stern, M. P. (1994). Birthweight and adult health outcomes in a biethnic population in the USA. *Diabetologia, 37,* 624–631.

240 **long-standing cultural proscriptions:** Yach, D., Hawkes, C., Gould, C. L., & Hofman, K. J. (2004). The global burden of chronic diseases: Overcoming impediments to prevention and control. *Journal of the American Medical Association, 291*(21), 2616–2622.

241 **"libertarian paternalism":** Thaler, R., & Sunstein, C. (2003). Libertarian paternalism. *American Economic Review, 93*(2), 175–179.

241 **"Health for All 2000":** Gannon, J. C. (2000). National intelligence estimate: The global infectious disease threat and its implications for the United States [NIE 99-17D]. Washington, DC: National Intelligence Council.

243 **a collective 520 million:** Hayutin, A. (2007). Global demographic shifts create challenges. *PREA Quarterly* (Fall), 46–53.

244 **Affluent, educated Americans:** House, J. S., Lantz, P. M., & Herd, P. (2005). Continuity and change in the social stratification of aging and health over the life course: Evidence from a nationally representative longitudinal study from 1986 to 2001/2002 (Americans' changing lives study). *Journals of Gerontology Series B: Psychological and Social Sciences, 60B*(2), 15–26.

244 **"compression of morbidity":** Fries, J. (1980). Aging, natural death, and the compression of morbidity. *New England Journal of Medicine, 330,* 130–135.

244 **same class-based patterns:** Banks, J., Marmot, M., Oldfield, Z., & Smith, J. P. (2006). Disease and disadvantage in the United

States and in England. *Journal of the American Medical Association, 295,* 2037–2045.

245 **how quickly people decline:** Herd, P., Goesling, B., & House, J. S. (2007). Socioeconomic position and health: The differential effects of education versus income on the onset versus progression of health problems. *Journal of Health and Social Behavior, 48*(3), 223–238.

246 **correlation between education and health:** Goldman, D. P., & Smith, J. P. (2002). Can patient self-management help explain the SES health gradient? *Proceedings of the National Academy of Sciences, 99*(16), 10929–10934.

247 **that difference had increased:** Singh, G. K., & Siahpush, M. (2006). Widening socioeconomic inequalities in US life expectancy, 1980–2000. *International Journal of Epidemiology, 35*(4), 969–979.

247 **among those with college educations:** Meara, E. R., Richards, S., & Cutler, D. M. (2008). The gap gets bigger: Changes in mortality and life expectancy, by education, 1981–2000. *Health Affairs, 27,* 350–360.

247 **there is a direct association:** Janicki-Deverts, D., Cohen, S., Adler, N. E., Schwartz, J. E., Matthews, K. A., & Seeman, T. E. (2007). Socioeconomic status is related to urinary catecholamines in the coronary artery risk development in young adults (CARDIA) study. *Psychosomatic Medicine, 69,* 514–520.

248 **children under age five:** Evans, G. W., & English, K. (2002). The environment of poverty: Multiple stressor exposure, psychophysiological stress, and socioemotional adjustment. *Child Development, 73*(4), 1238–1248.

248 **life expectancy is actually *declining*:** Ezzati, M., Friedman, A. B., Kulkarni, S. C., & Murray, C. J. L. The reversal of fortunes: Trends in county mortality and cross-county mortality disparities in the United States. *PLoS Medicine, 5*(4), e66. doi:10.1371/journal.pmed.0050066

249 **High school dropout rates:** U.S. Department of Agriculture, Economic Research Service. (2003, November). *Rural education at a glance* [Rural Development Research Report no. 98]. Retrieved from http://www.ers.usda.gov/publications/rdrr98/rdrr98_lowres.pdf

251 **a little over 30 percent:** U.S. Census Bureau. (2006). Educational attainment [table]. Retrieved November 20, 2008, from http://factfinder.census.gov/servlet/STTable?_bm=y&-geo_id=01000US&-qr_name=ACS_2006_EST_G00_S1501&-ds_name=ACS_2006_EST_G00_&-_lang=en&-redoLog=false&-CONTEXT=st

Chapter 8: Ensuring a Long Bright Future

259 **Cultivate a spirit of forgiveness:** Witvliet, C. V., Ludwig, T. E., & Vander Laan, K. L. (2001). Granting forgiveness or harboring grudges: Implications for emotion, physiology, and health. *Psychological Science, 12*(2), 117–123. doi:10.1111/1467-9280.00320

INDEX